The Perfect LOVE

The Perfect LOVE

RUTH MYERS

WATERBROOK
PRESS

COLORADO SPRINGS

THE PERFECT LOVE
PUBLISHED BY WATERBROOK PRESS
5446 North Academy Boulevard, Suite 200
Colorado Springs, Colorado 80918
A division of Bantam Doubleday Dell Publishing Group, Inc.

Scriptures given in this book include direct quotations, as well as the author's adapted and combined quotations, from the following translations and paraphrases:

Amplified — *The Amplified Bible,* copyright 1965, Zondervan Publishing House.

Berkeley — *The Berkeley Version in Modern English,* copyright New Testament 1945, Old Testament 1959, Zondervan Publishing House.

KJV — *King James Version.*

Knox — *The New Testament in the Translation of Monsignor Ronald Knox,* copyright 1944 by Sheed and Ward, Inc., New York.

Laubach — *The Inspired Letters in Clearest English,* Frank C. Laubach, copyright 1956, Thomas Nelson & Sons.

Moffatt — *The Bible: A New Translation* by James Moffatt, copyright 1950, 1952, 1953, 1954, James Moffatt.

NASB — *New American Standard Bible,* copyright The Lockman Foundation, 1960, 1962, 1963, 1968, 1971, 1973, 1975, 1977.

NCV — *The New Century Version,* copyright 1987, 1988 by Word Publishing.

NEB — *The New English Bible,* copyright 1961, 1970, the Delegates of the Oxford University Press and the Syndics of the Cambridge University Press.

NIV — *The Holy Bible: New International Version,* copyright 1985 by the Zondervan Corporation.

NKJV — *New King James Version,* copyright 1979, 1980, 1982, Thomas Nelson, Inc., Publishers.

NLT — *The Holy Bible: New Living Translation,* copyright 1996, Tyndale House Publishers, Inc. All used by permission, all rights reserved.

Phillips — *The New Testament in Modern English,* J. B. Phillips, copyright J. B. Phillips, 1958, 1960, 1972, Macmillan Publishing Company.

Psalms for Today —by R. K. Harrison, copyright 1961, Zondervan Publishing House

RSV — *Revised Standard Version Bible,* copyright 1946, 1952, 1971, the Division of Christian Education of the National Council of the Churches of Christ in the USA.

TEV —*Good News Bible: Today's English Version,* copyright 1976, American Bible Society.

TLB — *The Living Bible,* copyright 1971, Tyndale House Publishers.

Weymouth — *Weymouth's New Testament in Modern Speech,* by Richard Francis Weymouth, Harper and Row Publishers, Inc., James Clark and Company, Ltd., London.

Williams — *The New Testament: A Translation in the Language of the People,* by Charles B. Williams, copyright 1937 by Bruce Humphries, Inc. copyright renewed 1965 by Edith S. Williams, Moody Bible Institute.

Wuest — *The New Testament: An Expanded Translation,* Kenneth S. Wuest, copyright 1961, Wm. B. Eerdmans Publishing Company.

All *italics* in Scripture quotations are the author's.

The author has attempted to identify sources for all quoted material. Where this has not been possible, any information from readers is appreciated concerning further identification that could be given in future editions.

ISBN 1-57856-002-0

Printed in the United States of America
June 1998—First Edition

10 9 8 7 6 5 4 3 2 1

To the King

PSALM 45:1

CONTENTS

'The Greatest Unkindness'

JUST OVER THREE centuries ago the great Puritan theologian John Owen wrote, "The greatest sorrow and burden you can lay on the Father, the greatest unkindness you can do to him, is not to believe that he loves you."

Unfortunately many Christians today have difficulty believing that God loves them. One reason is that they intuitively know that they do not deserve His love. They think, "How can a holy God love a sinner like me?" They see God more as a judge than as their Father.

A second reason why many believers doubt God's love is that they don't see God meeting their expectations and desires. They have a vague but real notion that God should always do for them what they want. When those expectations are not met, they tend to view God as unloving and uncaring, as One who always says no to their requests.

A third and perhaps the most prevalent reason why we do not experience more of God's love is that we do not take the time to cultivate the depth of relationship with God that love requires. We tend to view God as a divine resource to help us get through life, but we don't give priority to developing a love relationship with Him.

Ruth Myers addresses all three of these issues in a challenging but encouraging manner. Moreover, she is not an ivory-tower writer. She has dealt with each of these areas from within the cauldron of her own life's experiences, and shares honestly her failures as well as victories.

This book is not light reading to be skimmed over in an evening. You will want to read thoughtfully and, above all, prayerfully. As you do, I am confident you will grow more in your experience of God's perfect love.

A GLAD PURSUIT

I TRUST YOU will enjoy reading this book as much as I have enjoyed working on it. I've found great joy in reviewing many of the rich truths with which the Holy Spirit has gripped my heart down through the years—truths that have molded my life, sustained me, and motivated me to let the Lord enfold me in His love. They've been like waves of refreshment flowing over my soul.

Many old songs, quotations, and poems have once more recaptured my attention, often with even greater vitality than in earlier years. They've come with fresh meaning as I've drawn them into my current experience.

Take, for instance, the poem by Hudson Taylor,

> Lord Jesus, make Thyself to me
> a living bright reality...
> more dear, more intimately nigh
> than e'en the sweetest earthly tie.

When I found this years ago, I prayed it from a forward-looking point of view, asking that this would be a growing experience as the months and years would pass by. I've now been praying it more from a here-and-now point of view: "Lord, do this for me today, in my current needs and situation."

Just last night, as I lay awake for an hour or so, my heart was filled with the song, "Sweet will of God, still fold me closer 'til I am wholly lost in Thee." I found myself crying out anew that this would be more true than ever in the moments and hours of each passing day.

How all of this has touched my heart with a greater-than-ever desire to know Him better and experience His love in new ways!

One reason this book has been a joy to work on—and, in fact, possible—has been the gracious help of our friends at WaterBrook Press. I especially want to thank Thomas Womack. He worked his way through reams of my written material—letters, articles, handouts, Bible studies—along with scores of cassette-recordings of messages I've given over the years—gleaning material that relates to knowing God and experiencing His love. He also structured an initial arrangement of the material, a momentous task that I would have found daunting—even impossible—with my present schedule and responsibilities (and my abilities—it's harder than ever for me to do complex organizing). The result was a body of material ready for rewriting, updating, expanding, and polishing on my part to communicate the wonderful love of God in the best way I could.

Warren (my husband) has also made a tremendous contribution to the book through his editing skills; whatever either of us writes always turns out to be a joint venture. Both he and Thomas have encouraged me greatly by their enthusiastic response to the contents of the book. In a recent letter Thomas wrote, "What an uplifting and deepening message this project has communicated to me all the way through, and so I have confidence and pray again that this will be true for many others as well."

As usual, finishing the book has been somewhat of a marathon—but also immensely refreshing, with an undercurrent of thanks to the Lord for His perfect, overflowing, never ending love.

My prayer for you as you read this book is that the Lord will lead you into a rich experience of His love that will keep growing as the days and months and years go by.

I pray for you a passage that has inspired me for decades to pursue a deeper experience of God:

...If you accept my words
    and store up my commands within you,
turning your ear to wisdom
    and applying your heart to understanding,
and if you call out for insight
    and cry aloud for understanding,
and if you look for it as for silver
    and search for it as for hidden treasure
then you will understand the fear of the Lord
    and find the knowledge of God. (Proverbs 5:1-5, NIV)

Dear Lord,
I ask You to be the One speaking here.
Reveal Yourself,
minister to the reader's heart,
quicken his or her love for You—
and do anything else You want to do
through these pages.

In Jesus' name.

'I MUST HAVE LOVE'

WHEN I WAS A TEENAGER, God began to deepen my appreciation for His love through "The Love of God," a song made famous by George Beverly Shea. This song describes God's love as "greater far than tongue or pen can ever tell." If the skies were a scroll and the oceans filled with ink, the song goes on to say, and if every stalk on earth were a writing quill, we still could never write in full this love God has for us. The skies could not contain it. The oceans would run dry.

Singing those words I truly felt the love of God. I knew that He understands, that He cares, that He's compassionate. I needed this knowledge then and I still need it every day. But I had not yet learned to let my roots go down deep into His love so that it was a constant influence in my life. Through the years since then, the Lord has been weaving into my life a richer awareness of how lavishly He loves me (and all of us) and how deeply He longs for each of us to experience His love. My heart has been opened again and again to delightful discoveries that have made me feel more satisfied and at rest in Him, more alive in His love, more liberated, more secure.

This book is the story of many of those rich discoveries, all of them available to anyone who truly wants to know God better.

A. W. Tozer portrays the knowledge of God stretching out before us like a vast ocean, with you and me like children playing along the beach (and perhaps now and then, I like to add, dipping our toes into the water). There's so much more to know and experience of this wonderful, loving God, and we've only begun.

Amy Carmichael, Irish missionary to India, deeply experienced the love of God, and in one of her poems implored Him to reveal His love even more:

> Love of my heart, my stream runs dry;
>> O Fountain of the heavenly hills,
> Love, blessed Love, to Thee I cry,
>> Fill all my secret hidden rills.
> Waters of Love, O pour through me;
>> I must have Love; I must have Thee.

I'm trusting that you've begun to read this book because you have this same longing deep within, even as I do: We *must* have love. We must have *God's* love. We must have *God,* the only source of perfect, unfailing love. I believe God has sovereignly brought you and me together at this time and through these pages, wanting to bless us in the adventure of letting Him fulfill our heart cry.

The Lord has this same deep desire for us to know Him and experience His love. With boundless emotional longing, He wants us to know Him as He really is. He has already handed us an invitation to this in His Word. And there we find the fullest portrait of Him, the most complete unveiling of His love, ready for us to contemplate and experience. From beginning to end, and in surprising and heartwarming ways, the Bible reveals a love that can flood our hearts with ever-increasing power through the Holy Spirit within us. It's a love that entirely satisfies, a love that brings true happiness and inner growth. It's a love that expands and corrects our thinking, changing us inside and out.

All of us in some degree have false or incomplete notions about God and His love, and these wrong ideas about Him lie at the root of many of our problems. So we come to the Bible to cut through the tangle of our false notions and find out what God is really like. With increasing spiritual vision we take in the truths about Him that sparkle on its pages. There we get to know our wonderful God and learn to actually experience His love day by day in our mind, our emotions, and our character. As a result, we love and trust Him, for this is the outflow of knowing Him. To truly know Him is to love Him.

As beginners in this quest to experience God's love, with such a long way to go, you and I will profit from asking ourselves certain questions: Are my concepts of God's love accurate? How much do I truly experience His love? How is it affecting my responses to Him and to life? How is it influencing my emotions, my daily choices, my effectiveness in fulfilling my daily responsibilities? And especially my attitudes and actions toward others? Am I facing problems in human relationships—conflicts, disillusionments—because I'm not truly experiencing God's love?

At times we mistakenly liken God's love to human loves we've known. People have failed us, so we're afraid that in some way God will fail us too—we imagine His affection to be fickle, unpredictable. In our mind there's a trace (or more) of viewing His love as reserved or calculating or grudging, rather than warm and overflowing. Perhaps we expect Him to measure out His love only according to how much we deserve it. If we don't perform well enough, He may respond with rejection or take away the things we value most. We may be afraid of yielding to Him because we're convinced He'll deprive us of the best in life.

Or we may see His love as a soft, overindulgent affection having no moral requirements, no connection with authority, or no accountability on our part. We picture Him as a sentimental grandfather in His heavenly rocking chair, winking at our sins and saying, "Boys will be boys...girls will be girls." We ignore or minimize the fact that He's righteous as well as loving.

In one way or another, we so often assume that God is like us. We fashion Him after our own image or after the image of other imperfect people we know.

Sometimes our misconceptions rest on conclusions we reached years ago through our experience with human authority figures such as parents, older family members, teachers, and pastors. These faulty conclusions are now deeply embedded in our minds and hearts. If our authorities were too permissive (especially in our early, formative years), we may fail to grasp how important it is to obey God. If they were harsh, we may see God as too demanding and never feel comfortable with Him. If they were unreliable, we may find it difficult to view God as trustworthy.

To live realistically we must correct our false ideas by continually feeding on the truth so that more and more it grips our hearts. Mentally we may have right concepts of God that haven't yet sunk in to take hold of our emotions. So we're still vulnerable to the tempting refrains of our false ideas—recorded in our minds so long ago—as they keep replaying within us.

On the physical plane we live realistically most of the time. We go around a tree rather than trying to walk through it. We take the stairs down from the third floor rather than jumping out of a window. We respect natural laws and know the consequences if we break them. We may not always eat or exercise properly, but we're usually not surprised at the results. We know what happens and why.

But spiritually and psychologically we're often quite unrealistic. Then we suffer the consequences without understanding the reasons. We live with illusions, false beliefs, negative emotions, disrupted relationships—so many factors that make our lives unsatisfying. We live much of our life as paupers, as down-and-outers, because we haven't really learned to enjoy the love of God.

The most important part of living realistically is to hold a true view of God. God is ultimate reality. He's the greatest factor in all that's real. When we let the truth about Him nourish us and remold our minds, this revolutionizes our lives.

SATISFY US EARLY

Psalm 90 is a prayer of Moses as he led the people of Israel in the wilderness. They had known many sins, many failures. But Moses knew the Lord well, and in verse 14 he prays to Him, "Satisfy us early [or "in the morning"] with Your steadfast love, that we may rejoice and be glad all our days" (RSV). The Moffatt translation reads, "May Thy love dawn on us undimmed." Moses knew the true source of all satisfaction: the Lord's steadfast love, dawning in our darkness. He knew this was the basis for joy even in the hard times. And he asked to experience it early.

I've found this Scripture a helpful one to pray. *Lord, do this for me: Satisfy me early, soon, this morning, with Your steadfast love, so I can rejoice and be glad all day long.* Then I pray the same thing for my husband and for us as a couple: *Satisfy us early with Your love.* And I spread out from there, praying for others: *Satisfy them (or him or her) this morning with Your steadfast love. Let Your love dawn on them this morning, that today they may rejoice in You.*

God has given us in His Word a beautiful picture of what His steadfast love is like. He wants to speak His love to our hearts, individually, tenderly. He wants you to take time to hear His words of love, and to let them dawn on you undimmed, that you may very soon be satisfied…and be glad all your days.

Dear Lord, I thank You that I'm Yours, that You know me through and through, and that it's no accident You've led me here to this book.

Father, I've tasted Your love, and I long to experience more deeply how You really feel about me. I long to know in my daily life the intense reality and great wonder of Your boundless love, which You so freely bestow on those who seek You.

Help me turn away from my misconceptions of Your love, from being casual or indifferent toward You, and from hectic, frantic activity that often makes even my time with You so hurried. I ask that through Your Word You will speak to me of Your love. May Your Spirit flood my heart with how You feel about me and how deeply You are committed to me. In fresh, new ways assure me that Your love for me is intensely personal, overflowing, and never ending—the one and only perfect love.

I pray in Jesus' name...

TWO

THIS IS REAL LOVE

"THIS IS REAL LOVE," we read in 1 John 4:10. "It is not that we loved God, but that He loved us and sent His Son as a sacrifice to take away our sins" (NLT). This is real love. This is where we find the kind of love we most deeply need—not in human relationships, but in God. If we want real love, ideal love, perfect love, God's heart is where to find it. It's the only love big enough to meet the God-sized needs of your life and mine.

Indeed God can and will go beyond merely meeting those needs. "God is so vastly wonderful," wrote A. W. Tozer in *The Pursuit of God,* "so utterly and completely delightful, that He can without anything other than Himself meet and overflow the deepest demands of our total nature, mysterious and deep as that nature is." These are words I've returned to again and again, for I've found them true. Down through the years, in a countless variety of circumstances in every season of life, God has proven to me that He can more than satisfy my heart—*as I let Him.*

The Lord can meet our every need because He is a God of perfect, overflowing love that has no limits. It's hard to know where to start in describing God's love. From beginning to end the Bible tells us how He feels about us. Many verses state specifically what His love is like, while in countless other passages we discern this love through His actions or words, as we learn to look for clues—just as we do on the human level when we like someone and try to find out whether he or she likes us. In the Bible those clues are everywhere.

At age thirty-two my husband Dean died of cancer, leaving me as a widow with two young children. During the months and years that followed I became more diligent than ever in seeking to know God and experience His love in new ways. (Trials have a way of driving us onward like that, don't they?) I bought a red notebook that I used only for recording truths about God. In the top corner on the front side of each sheet I wrote down some word or fact about God, something He would impress upon me through my times with Him: Refuge, Hiding Place, Power, Love, Bridegroom, Bread of Life, and so forth. On the front page for each topic I wrote out verses the Holy Spirit had used to grip my heart. Then I could go back to them again and again for refreshment and praise and thanksgiving. Some of the entries were a full verse, others just a phrase. I wrote each one in whatever Bible version I liked best for that particular passage, and sometimes partly in one version, partly in another. I also memorized many of these rich verses.

Often a verse would impress me mentally but I wouldn't yet feel it was truly mine. It had not yet deeply touched my heart. So I would record the reference on the back side of the page. Then later I could dig deeper into it, letting the Spirit make it real to my heart. On the back of the page I also put poems or quotes or devotional thoughts relating to the topic.

It grew to be a thick notebook. In times when I really needed a dose of God's love (or His peace, or strength, or whatever), I could open those pages and run back to Scriptures already full of meaning, truths He had spoken personally to me. And in those times of need they became lifesavers.

It helped so much to seek God diligently this way. I wish I could say that I've sought Him just as diligently every day and in every quiet time. I've gone through many times of dissatisfaction and unmet longings because I wasn't letting Him satisfy me. But He has been faithful to answer prayer, bringing me back to His personal love again and again, and keeping it a major theme in my life.

One of the most helpful quotes I came across during those years as a widow was something written by Hudson Taylor, pioneer missionary in China. He was facing the death of his dearly loved wife, Maria, and his children were all in school in faraway England. In this lonely time he found great refreshment through John 7:37, where Jesus invites anyone who is thirsty to come to Him and drink. "Who does not thirst?" Taylor wrote. "Who has not mind-thirsts or heart-thirsts, soul-thirsts or body-thirsts? Well, no matter which, or whether I have them all, *Come unto Me and…* remain thirsty? Ah no! *Come unto Me and drink!*

"What?" Taylor continued. "Can Jesus meet my need? Yes, and more than meet it. No matter how intricate my path, how difficult my service; no matter how sad my bereavement, how far away my loved ones; no matter how helpless I am, how deep are my soul yearnings, Jesus can meet all—all, and more than meet."

ALL WE NEED

One of my favorite psalms for starting my quiet time in a fresh way has long been Psalm 63. David wrote this psalm when he was in the desert of Judah. There in the desert he prayed, "O God, You are my God, earnestly I seek You; my soul thirsts for You, my body longs for You, in a dry and weary land where there is no water" (NIV). Yet only a few lines later David wrote, "My soul is satisfied" (NASB). He was satisfied not because he had escaped from the desert, but because of God's love and presence: "Your love is better than life" (verse 3). He knew that nothing in his physical situation could meet his deep needs—heart-thirsts and soul-thirsts much like those Hudson Taylor experienced.

Over time we come to God with such an assortment of deficiencies and inadequacies and emergencies: time and work pressures, marriage difficulties, rebellious or straying children, bereavement, financial problems, emotional problems, problems with other people, lost jobs, lost friends, lost happiness. We're in a dry and weary land, and we're thirsty. Even in our best times you and I have vast inner needs—the deep demands of our mysterious and deep nature, as A. W. Tozer put it. But God knows all those mysteries within us and all their depths, and He meets each one with a love that is great beyond measure.

After all, *He* designed you and me, mysterious inner needs and all. His masterly design includes having our deepest needs met only by Him. Only He can fill the God-shaped vacuum within us, as the great scientist and philosopher Blaise Pascal described it. That vacuum includes, for example, a deep inner need to *adore*: to love and be devoted to someone we can admire totally, always and forever, without the slightest reservation—someone who will never change, who will never disappoint us or fail us.

We often try to fill this vacuum through our spouse, our children, our friends, or other people. They mean so much to us. But sooner or later they all let us down in one way or another. After all, they're as imperfect and limited as we are, with their own human needs to attend to. We end up disillusioned. But is it fair to expect anyone or anything else to give us what only our perfect, all-sufficient God is able to give?

I'm not discrediting human love. Earthly relationships can be beautiful, and God has used them continually in my life as an expression of His love toward me. But as one Christian counselor said, when two people try to find ideal and perfect love from each other, it's like two paupers trying to borrow from one another. Neither has much to give; both remain unsatisfied.

I like Psalm 16:2,5 in the *New Century Version*: "Every good thing I have comes from You.... the Lord is all I need." The more we let God be God, the more we find that He is the answer to what we're lacking, the answer to what we're longing for. Our needs and our trials give Him a chance to reveal Himself in new ways. For every need in our emotional or mental or spiritual life, for every problem in our relationships, for every trial we go through, there's something in God (such as His love, His power, His provision) that can bring us through triumphantly—if we know and believe and count on Him in the hour of need. God is our first Source, and ultimately the only Source, of all we need for a full and satisfied life.

And we have such a great advantage in this relationship with God because it's internal. Every other love is limited by some degree of distance and by the barriers imposed by our physical bodies. But God dwells within us, so that our relationship with Him has unlimited potential for constant closeness and joy and fulfillment.

Here indeed is love.

FIRST LOVE

When I was ten, God (and my mother) used a famous verse about His love to give me my first conscious experience of it.

Four years earlier I had gone forward in an evangelistic meeting. The pastor had talked with me about the gospel and I prayed. Soon I was baptized and became a church member. But later on, all I could remember was my baptism. I knew about the cross of Christ and about His resurrection, but I remembered no personal contact with God. And I didn't know where I would go if I died. This worried me. If our pastor began preaching on hell, I'd slip out of the service, pretending I needed to go to the restroom.

My mother, sensing that something was troubling me, asked me about it one night. I didn't really want to tell her, for she thought I was a real Christian. But I admitted my fear concerning my eternal destiny.

In reply Mother did something so simple. She quoted a verse I'd known for as long as I could remember. But as she spoke, the truth dawned in my heart and I believed: "God so *loved* the world that He gave His only begotten Son, that whosoever believeth in Him should not perish, but have everlasting life." That night I believed in Christ as *my* Savior, and my fear and guilt rolled away. That night, for the first time I remember, I felt His love. All this happened in an instant, as Mother quoted John 3:16. When she finished, I bowed my head and thanked the Lord that He had given me eternal life.

When I entered my teenage years I didn't know any Christian young people who, as far as I could tell, were really living the Christian life. I had one friend a few years older who loved the Lord, but she seemed rather old-maidish and I didn't want to be like her. So I decided I wouldn't follow the Lord closely.

Behind this decision were wrong ideas about God. I didn't believe He wanted what was best for me. I was afraid that if I gave Him the controls, He would make me do what I didn't want to and I'd miss the best in life. In this time of rebellion I tried everything I dared, though in some things the Holy Spirit blocked me. And I became more and more miserable.

Finally at age sixteen I agreed to attend a Christian conference. There I saw young people on fire for the Lord and I received a big inflow of God's Word. One night I went outside under the trees and prayed, "Lord, I'll do anything You want me to—even be a missionary," which was the very worst thing I could think of.

Then came the years when my friends and I were singing about the love of God that's greater far than tongue or pen can tell, and I began to sense how important God's love is. But I still felt His love primarily when I was singing about it with others, and not when I was alone or when things went wrong .

As the Lord worked within me, my desires for the future gradually made a U-turn. I found I wanted to become a missionary after all, and I began preparing for this. A favorite verse became Psalm 84:11— "No good thing will He withhold from those who walk uprightly" (NKJV). As I followed Him I was discovering He knew better than I did how to satisfy me. Life was getting better, though not necessarily easier.

After I was graduated from high school, I set out for Northwestern Bible School and College in Minneapolis. There the Lord did more new things in my heart. I'd been having daily devotions since I was sixteen. Often it was the last thing at night when I could hardly hold my eyes open, but I congratulated myself for being such a good Christian. Then the Lord began speaking: "Ruth, that's not the point at all. I want you to come to My Word because you want to know Me." The lesson was reinforced for me by the hymn "Break Thou the Bread of Life," in the lines that say, "Beyond the sacred page I seek *Thee,* Lord; my spirit pants *for Thee,* O living Word." I still wanted Him to teach me the principles I should know from the Bible, but I began coming more often with the prayer, "Lord, most of all I want to know You." Since this is a request that's according to His will, He answered it just as He promised in 1 John 5:14-15.

There was one fellow in school who more than anyone else seemed set upon knowing the Lord, and I greatly admired him. Stan had plenty of work and study responsibilities, and between these and pursuing the Lord he didn't have time for dating. Being a little beyond reach like that made him all the more desirable. One of Stan's favorite Scripture portions was from Philippians 3. I began to pray over it—and to cry over it, for I was learning I had to get my heart needs met in my relationship with Jesus Christ and not anywhere else. It soon became a favorite passage of mine as well. Verses 8 and 10 in the *Amplified Bible* (condensed a bit) read:

I count everything as loss compared to the priceless privilege—the surpassing worth and supreme advantage—of knowing Christ Jesus my Lord. For His sake I have lost everything and consider it all to be mere rubbish, in order that I may gain Christ. *For my determined purpose is that I may know Him—that I may progressively become more deeply and intimately acquainted with Him, perceiving and recognizing and understanding the wonders of His Person more strongly and more clearly.*

Nothing else meant anything to Paul compared with the priceless privilege of knowing this vastly wonderful Person he had met. Back then I didn't have the Amplified version but I did have Philippians 3:10 in the King James: "That I may know Him." I began to hear Him say, "Ruth, this must be your major pursuit." God used circumstances to drive me to my knees and to begin praying along this line. And I discovered as a young single woman that the Lord could and did meet my deepest longing, if I let Him be my first love.

My younger sister Mary eventually joined me at Northwestern, and we found a poem that we often reflected on and used in prayer:

Purge me, Lord, of my follies; an empty cup let me be,
Waiting only Thy blessing, hungry only for Thee.

Can even the Lord pour blessing into a cup that is full?
Put treasure into a locked hand, be He ever so bountiful?
Empty me, Lord, and make me hungry only for Thee.
Only Thy bread once tasted can ever satisfy me.

DESIRED AND DESIRING

Then came another crucial lesson from the Lord, a brand-new revelation for me: Not only was He compassionate and understanding, not only was He always there to tenderly care for me and love me, but He also desired me; He longed for my fellowship.

Some time later I realized how strongly this truth had impressed me as I talked with a friend in college, a tough young man just out of the navy. Doug told me one day that he'd been having trouble getting out of bed for his morning quiet time. But he had found a verse that helped him. It was in Proverbs (I soon forgot the reference because I didn't feel inclined to write it down): "How long wilt thou sleep, O sluggard? When wilt thou arise out of thy sleep?"

Well, I thought, *that's fine for Doug. But I don't want to wake up to that.* I preferred hearing the Lord speak to me through Song of Solomon 2:13-14— "Arise, my love, my fair one, and come away.... Let me see your face, let me hear your voice, for your voice is sweet, and your face is comely" (RSV). How could the Lord say that to *me?* Because I'm one with Christ, and in my innermost being I'm beautiful with His beauty. Amazing! To think that my appearance is pleasing to Him, that my voice is sweet, that He desires intimate fellowship with me! What a motivation to spend time with Him.

Later I was struck by these words from an unknown author:

My goal is God Himself;
Not peace or joy
Or even blessing,

14

But Himself, my God.
'Tis His to lead me there—
Not mine, but His.
At any cost, dear Lord,
By any road.

Another truth dawned on my heart during that time—a truth that revolutionized my life. I found this truth in capsule form in Colossians 3:4— "Christ... is your life." And I personalized it to say, "Christ is *my* life." As one man of God put it, "It's not only true that my life is *Christ's*, but my life is *Christ.*"

How delightful it was to learn that Christ my Savior, the Lord of love, triumphant over sin and death, is my life! His Spirit is united with mine in a permanent union. And as I live by faith in Him, His Spirit unveils truth to me, empowers me to do His will, and pours out His love in my heart (Galatians 2:20, Philippians 2:13, Romans 5:5). What a vast difference this makes in how I view myself: I am united in the most intimate way with the Lover of my soul. I am able to enjoy His divine, self-sacrificing love and to channel it to other people with growing depth and constancy.

Once a year an elderly Southern gentleman would speak for a week in our daily chapel services. His name was Dad Byus. He wasn't particularly impressive in appearance; what I remember most were three funny little pin-curls of white hair hanging down his forehead. But he radiated Christ. As he preached he would suddenly burst out singing, "My wonderful Lord, my wonderful Lord, by angels and seraphs in heaven adored," and we would all join in. He often quoted these words: "I have seen the face of Jesus; tell me not of ought beside. I have heard the voice of Jesus, and my soul is satisfied." The Lord used this man's teaching to make me more hungry for Himself.

The same year that Mary joined me at Northwestern, two identical twin brothers enrolled and were noticed by everyone. They were handsome, they were musical, they walked closely with the Lord, and they dressed attractively. And they were the same age I was. Lots of girls liked the Denler twins. Mary and

I did too, but we didn't think they'd ever like us. My sister was so dogmatic about this that I said, "Mary, you can't be *that* sure about anything."

They didn't date anyone that first year. But the next fall Dean Denler asked me to go with him to an upcoming stage play, the big production of the school year. On the same day Gene Denler asked Mary. I found out later that Dean told his brother, "Ruth said yes, but she sure didn't look very enthusiastic." The fact was, I was shocked.

Mary and I talked about this upcoming date as we left the campus that evening, heading for home. At first our conversation was along the lines of how lucky can a girl be? Then the Lord brought to mind Psalm 73:25-26, a passage we had memorized: "Whom have I in heaven but You, and there is none upon earth that I desire besides You" (NKJV). God was reminding us that He was to be our first love. I don't think this verse means we can't or shouldn't have any other desires; rather it's saying, Lord, in comparison to my desire for You, I desire no one else. If ever I must choose between You and any other, I'll choose You.

The passage goes on, "My flesh and my heart fail; but God is the strength of my heart and my portion forever." Our flesh and our heart were failing, because we both felt that going out with the Denlers would surely be a one-time event. But God would be our portion forever—all through life and all through eternity. Only one relationship is sure to be lifelong. Only one Person is for sure our permanent life partner. And our best life partner, worthy above all others of being our first love.

The Lord reminded me of this many times. I'm so grateful He did.

PLOWING TIME

It turned out to be more than one date. Within two years we were engaged: Mary to Gene, and I to Dean. The Lord (through the Navigators) sent the twins ahead of us to Taiwan to pursue ministry opportunities there. On our way to join them a year and a half later, Mary and I spent half a day with Lila

Trotman, the wife of Dawson Trotman, founder of the Navigators. Lila knew that our future husbands would often be traveling in their ministry responsibilities. "Just remember," she told us, "God will make up for every moment you're apart." Then she added, "And He won't wait to do it until you're back together again." In other words, God would make up for our loss *with Himself.* My inner response to Lila's gracious counsel was, "Yes, Lord, You are well able to do this, and You will—if I let You." This was great preparation not only for marriage but also for the time, seven years later, when God would call Dean home.

Then it was on across the Pacific on a comfortable American President Lines freighter. Mary and I were so excited. To be used by the Lord in Asia had become the dream of our hearts, and now in 1952 this dream was coming true—as well as our dream of becoming Mrs. Denler.

A week after we arrived in Taiwan we had a double wedding in Taipei and headed to Hong Kong for our honeymoons. Then Mary and Gene flew off to the Philippines to serve the Lord there, and I went with Dean to southern Taiwan. Mary and I had always been close, the twins had been even closer, and most of our dating had been as couples together. So we were facing some adjustments.

Lots of them, in fact. And we had received little prior help on how to handle them. Decades later, Warren and I conducted many two-to-three-month orientation programs helping western missionaries prepare for life in Asia. But back in 1952, we new missionaries received one word of counsel on how to respond to all the unfamiliar ways of the Chinese culture: "Not wrong, but different." This was sound advice from a veteran missionary and dear friend, Dick Hillis, founder of Overseas Crusades. It has helped often in many relationships as well as in adjusting to other cultures. But there is more to it than that.

In our new surroundings we did not yet know the language. And I began to miss greatly the rich fellowship I had long known. There were a few older missionaries in our city, and that helped a lot. But it just wasn't the same as relating to loved ones and people our own age. Back in America I had enjoyed helping other young women grow in their faith, and I missed that as well. Two big surprises made our adjustments more complex: Dean and I had our two children earlier than we had planned. From the first we were grateful for those precious gifts from our sovereign God. And later I was so glad that Brian was six and Doreen almost five when their father died—old enough to have memories of him, old enough for me to communicate with them, and easier to care for than if they were still babies or toddlers.

Those years in Taiwan were good in so many ways, but they were hard years. They were a time of plowing in my life, when the steel of the plow was cutting deep into my soul. I could no longer feel the love of God as easily as I had before. I would tell Him, "Lord, I don't know what's happening to me. I don't know why my emotions don't cooperate like they used to." Then I would remember Hebrews 13:8 where God says, "Jesus Christ is the same yesterday and today and forever." So I would choose to believe that His love for me and His life in me had not changed, but were still as warm and true and certain as before.

How I missed my sister! I remember going out under the sky at night to decisively tell the Lord, "I don't have to see Mary. You are enough." Again He would meet the longings of my heart, but it wasn't with the easy joy I'd so often known earlier.

I experienced also the reality that my husband couldn't meet all my needs. Dean loved me very much, but his love wasn't perfect. Sometimes he was occupied with his own needs. Sometimes he would be away for weeks at a time. Often the Spirit would bring to mind Psalm 73:25-26, reminding me again: Only one Person is your best, your perfect life partner. Only One can be with you all the time and meet your deepest needs. You may love others as much as you can, as deeply as you will, but I must be your first love.

The truth of His love and the solid footing of His Word kept me steady. I found that so many truths I'd known in my head were getting rooted deeper into my life. The plowing time was of great value, and in the long run it made me love the Lord more. Then after about three years, He took me back to the second chapter of the Song of Solomon: "For lo, the winter is past, the rain is over and gone. The flowers appear on the earth; the time of singing has come, and the voice of the turtledove is heard in our land.... Rise up, my love, my fair one, and come away!" (NKJV). I felt God was telling me that the plowing time was over, and the winter done with, and that I could now look forward to a new fresh springtime of love with Him.

On the basis of Romans 15:32 ("that I may come unto you with joy by the will of God, and may with you be refreshed," KJV), I began to pray also for increased refreshment in ministry. I trusted Him to fulfill in a new way John 7:38— that as His rivers of living water flowed through me, I too would experience their life-giving freshness as I served others.

In His all-wise love, God still had more plowing times planned for me. Through each one He has strengthened my experience of His love. He has caused me to seek Him more desperately and know Him more deeply.

TRUEST GAIN

I've often appreciated the quotation, "Each loss is truest gain if, day by day, He fills the place of all He takes away."

In our second missionary term we moved to Hong Kong, where Gene and Dean together directed the Navigator ministry. A year later, in 1959, we learned that Dean had cancer. He lived only nine more months.

It was a fast-growing form of cancer and quickly worsened, often causing severe pain. We prayed, and others prayed. Twice, in direct answer to prayer, Dean experienced a dramatic turn for the better. But then God began to speak to our hearts, leading us no longer to claim healing and letting us know He wanted to take Dean home. He confirmed this by giving several men and women of God the same message. This helped us hold Dean in open hands and prepare our hearts for his homegoing.

Even in his suffering Dean would say, "Remember, Ruth, God has our best interests at heart." And God comforted both of us with a quotation someone sent us: "God is too wise to ever make a mistake, and too loving to ever do anything unkind."

My friend Doug—the one who shared with me the sluggard verse from Proverbs—sent us Jeremiah 29:11. This time his verse really appealed to me: "For I know the plans I have for you, says the Lord, plans for welfare and not for evil, to give you a future and a hope" (RSV). I had never focused on this verse before. Now I explored the full context while reading through the prophets. I discovered that history had proved this promise true for the people of God to whom it first was spoken. They suffered a great tragedy. Yet through it all the Lord protected them and eventually restored their fortunes.

I came before God and said, "Lord, You say that You know the plans You have for us. I personally don't really know what You're doing. Dean is just starting his work in Asia. He's got two little children. He's got me. I don't understand what's happening or why You're allowing this. But You say Your plans are good, and You've never lied to me. So I choose to believe You." Again and again God used Jeremiah 29:11 to calm my heart and remove my fears.

More help came from Psalm 31:15, which says, "My times are in Thy hand" (or as one version says, "My destiny is under Your control"). I realized that Dean's life was not in the hand of this dread disease. His life was not even in the hands of his doctor, a godly and skilled physician. Dean's life was in the hands of God. The sovereign God was with us, and we could trust Him.

Gene and Mary took care of our children while I stayed in the hospital room with Dean, sleeping in a smaller bed near his. Dean was growing weaker and was hardly able to speak. One morning as I woke up, he said to me in his slow speech, "You know, honey, I almost died last night."

"You did? No, I didn't know that."

His frail voice continued, "Oh, what a wonder it was!"

I tenderly urged him on. "Honey, what was a wonder?"

"Well...you just can't describe it."

"What was it you can't describe?"

Dean answered, "The wonder of being with the Lord." Then he began singing, and I joined him: "It will be worth it all when we see Jesus. Life's trials will seem so small when we see Christ. One look at His dear face, all sorrow will erase. So bravely run the race, till we see Christ."

Soon afterward, Dean's brave race was over and he went to be with the Lord. I had lost my best and primary human love. But I wasn't alone. I still had my first love; I still had my Source of deepest satisfaction. So the bottom did not fall out of my life.

I cried often. In my quiet times, no matter what I did, I would weep. I'd worship and cry. I'd pray and cry. I'd read the Bible and cry. But I also received rays of warmth from God, shafts of sunlight shining in through His Word, through other people, through other ways. For example, on the evening of the day Dean died, our daughter Doreen came rushing to me in the kitchen and said, "Just think, Mommy: My daddy can see the angels now!"

How grateful I was that God had taught me not to dare fixate on any other relationship, but only on Him. Only His love was sure to be lifelong.

HOLDING MY RIGHT HAND

Soon after Dean was promoted to glory I received a letter ending with these words: "May you find in the Lord Jesus Christ your Boaz." God was leading me to the book of Ruth as He had often done before. And what did Boaz do for Ruth? He satisfied her hunger and quenched her thirst; he provided her a home and supplied her needs; and he gave her a fruitful place in the harvest. I found the Lord doing these same things for me.

Six months after Dean's death the children and I traveled back to the United States with Gene and Mary. After another six months we said goodbye to them as they returned to Asia, this time to the Philippines. Then the three of us started a new chapter of our family life, settling in Colorado Springs. The children, especially Brian, went through deep struggles, for they had lost their father and now their extended family, including their Uncle Gene who was so much like their daddy. But they adjusted quickly to their new surroundings, to school in America, and to life in general. How grateful I am for the many people who have prayed for them back then and throughout the years!

Besides providing prayer backers and friends, the Lord as my Boaz also supplied our needs for a home and clothing and more. And He gave me a part in His spiritual harvest at Glen Eyrie, headquarters of the Navigators. There I had abundant opportunities for ministry, including concentrated training for other women on their way to serve the Lord overseas. I counseled women and girls individually, and spoke to women's groups and conferences and retreats.

When we had said goodbye to Gene and Mary, we hoped to join them later in Manila. But I had a deepening impression that the Philippines was not to be our field of service. I prayed about going back to Hong Kong, but again found no freedom of heart regarding this. Through counsel and prayer it seemed the Lord was telling me to stay at Glen Eyrie, helping train others who in turn would go into many places throughout the world.

But to think of perhaps never returning to Asia! Of perhaps never again ministering among the Chinese or Indians or Filipinos! Then I came across Deuteronomy 3:26-28. God had told Moses he was not to enter the Promised Land. Moses pleaded with God to let him go. The Lord's reply was final: "Let it suffice thee; speak no more to me of this matter.... But charge Joshua, and encourage and strengthen him: for he shall go" (RSV). Somehow this reaffirmed my conviction that, at least for the foreseeable future, we were to remain where we were. "You're not to go," I felt the Lord was saying, "and you're not to beg Me to let you go; instead you're to charge others who will go, and encourage and strengthen them." He graciously removed from my heart any restlessness about the matter.

I continued to be amazed at how God's love meets our needs when we let Him, satisfying our hearts and giving us contentment and joy. Soon after Dean's death my mother had sent me a Scripture—Isaiah 41:13, which says, "For I, the Lord your God, will hold your right hand, saying to you, 'Fear not,

I will help you'" (NKJV). *That's nice*, I had thought, especially in one version which says, "whispering to you, Fear not...." Though it didn't touch my heart deeply at the time, I memorized it. Later I learned how much I needed it.

Brian and Doreen would often hold my hand, and that meant a lot to me. I adored having them with me, along with the sense this gave me of still being in a family. But I needed more than that. Especially in the second year after Dean passed away, the loneliness and longing for love would often sweep in upon me in a deeper way than before.

We were living in a lovely third-floor apartment in Glen Eyrie's huge old castle. How we reveled in the many opportunities for fun and rich fellowship with Navigator staff and trainees, especially at mealtimes. But overnight we would sometimes be the only people in the castle and its scores of rooms. I was not afraid of our being by ourselves. But at times in those still, silent hours after I tucked the kids into bed, and in my growing loneliness, a host of "what-if" fears about my life would rise up. "What if God asks me to do this or that?" "What if such-and-such happens?" I'd even ask myself—while thinking about a man who was a good friend but whose wife I couldn't imagine being—"What if God asks me to marry him?"

So many different fears! "Lord," I would pray, "please say something to encourage me."

He would bring to me His promise in Isaiah 41:13, speaking it to my heart in the present tense: "I, the Lord your God, hold your right hand, whispering to you, 'Fear not, I will help you.'" As He spoke His Word to my heart, I found it helpful not only to listen, but also to respond to Him in thankful prayer.

When the fears returned, I would say, "Tell me again."

I, the Lord your God, hold your right hand...

"Lord," I responded, "I really need someone to hold my hand. And I have Someone: I've got You! I've never had anyone better and I never will." This opened up my receptivity so His love could meet my need.

I also discovered how much I needed someone to tell me the words "I love you." The kids said this often, but I longed for someone big to say it. The

Lord often did so by reminding me of Isaiah 43:4— "You are precious in my eyes, and honored, and I love you" (RSV). I was to Him like a precious gem, which is loved not for its usefulness but for its great emotional value. I was honored in His eyes—amazing! And at any moment I could pause and let Him say, "I love you."

Summer was the big conference season at Glen Eyrie and there wasn't room for us in the castle. During those months we moved into a house in the city, where my lonely times were more frequent. Our neighbors included our Navigator friends Leroy and Virginia Eims. One beautiful summer evening I looked over, saw their home, and envisioned them inside happily together. I'd been warned that when I saw happy couples together I would be tempted with jealousy, so I had prayed about this and decided on a way to respond. "Virginia has Leroy," I now began thinking, and I was tempted to complete the thought with "but I don't have anybody." Instead I prayed, "Lord, give Leroy and Virginia a good evening. Bless them. Bless their relationship. And I thank You that I have You. Now tell me how You feel about me."

You are precious in My eyes and honored and I love you.

"Thank You, Lord, that I still have the best love I've ever had or ever will have."

These were the years when my red notebook was filling up with God's personal words to me about Himself. I had started a new page with the heading "My _____," and had begun to fill the page with verses that actually used the word "my": my Rock, my Shepherd, my Champion, my Beloved, and so forth. I had settled on Psalm 16:5 in the Moffatt translation as my favorite verse for this page: "Thou art what I obtain from life, O Thou eternal, Thou Thyself art my share." My joy that God was "my Share in life" increased as I added Psalm 142:5, also from Moffatt: "I have Thee as my very own in the land of the living."

That summer I found myself focusing on God as "my Father." I had a wonderful earthly father who loved me deeply, and I had always thought it was great to have God as my Father as well. But now, in this time of deeper loneliness, it meant so much more. I especially liked Romans 8:16 where J. B.

Phillips, in place of "Abba Father," says, "Father, my Father." I'd wake up in the morning thinking, "Father, my Father!" For the first time I was really taken with this thought. I imagined crawling onto His lap as a little girl and nestling in His arms as I spoke the words, "My Father!"

One summer morning, the day after we had moved from Glen Eyrie for the conference season, I woke up filled with low and lonely feelings. I started my quiet time, admitting to the Lord that I really didn't feel like having one. My Bible reading for that morning was Psalm 102. I came to these words: "I am like a pelican in the desert, like an owl moping in the ruins...like a lonely bird on the roof" (Moffatt). Already I felt better—the psalmist had been even bluer than I was! The passage goes on to say that God does not change. So I could say to Him, "Lord, You're the same as You were when I lived on the Glen. You're the same as You were when I lived with Dean. You are not the least bit different." I rejoiced as He comforted my heart with His unchanging love.

Four years after Dean died, we were surprised with the opportunity to finally return to Asia for the summer, including a month's stay with Gene and Mary in Manila. After the initial excitement, my heart was flooded with fears about going so far by ourselves, and with anxiety about the many things that could happen to the children. I remembered all the sickness they had experienced out there before. I also recognized that in a special way we would be in Satan's territory. Then Psalm 121:8 came forcibly to mind: "The Lord shall preserve thy going out and thy coming in from this time forth, and even for evermore" (KJV).

Meanwhile, before we left Colorado Springs, several things happened that made me feel no one there really needed me. Probably most of this was only in my imagination, though I think some of my impressions were accurate.

For Brian and Doreen, the month with their Uncle Gene and Aunt Mary in the Philippines was especially a delight. Since Gene was an identical twin to their father, for them this was almost like being with Daddy again. Gene did an incredible job of giving them a good time. And what a joy it was to have the whole clan together once more!

Later we stopped in Hong Kong, one of my favorite places. While there we visited a counselor, who was giving a special test free of charge to missionaries (and I still qualified). After Dr. Rodd had tested and talked with each of us, he told me Brian had some thoughts and feelings I might want to find out about.

As the children and I went out to dinner that night, Brian hesitantly mentioned that there was something he should probably let me know.

"What is it, Brian?"

"Well," he answered, "I don't think I should tell you. It might make it hard for you to be a good mother."

"Oh," I said, "honey, please tell me. Mommy will understand."

Finally he came out with it: "You know…sometimes I wish you would die so I could go live with Uncle Gene."

I handled it without tears as long as I was with the children. "Honey," I told him, "I can understand that. He's a wonderful uncle. He's so much like your daddy. I understand why you feel that way."

But in bed that night I let myself have a long, hard cry: Even my kids didn't need me!

I knew this was a lie. Brian didn't mean he didn't need me. But that's the feeling I had.

The Lord lifted me from that experience to thrill me in a new way with what I mean to Him. I recognized the truth that if God were to take me home any moment, He would lovingly meet the needs of those around me in other ways. The fact is, most of us are probably needed here much less than we like to think. But for all of time and all eternity, there's an exciting sense in which God does "need" you and me. In one sense He has no needs. But in another sense He has love needs. He has longings. And we as His loved ones can fulfill His deep desire through our love and worship, our fellowship, our obedience. This quotation captured that truth for me: "Every soul is a vast reservoir from which God can receive eternal pleasure." Each of us can bring Him joy in ways no one else can. And that will never change.

FROM IMPOSSIBLE TO WONDERFUL

Someone has said, "When God wants to do something wonderful, He begins with a difficulty. When He wants to do something very wonderful, He begins with an impossibility."

After another four years went by the Lord led me to marry again. Warren Myers—who served in Asia during the same years Dean and I did—became my husband and the head of our family, warmly welcomed by our teenagers (though, of course, adjustments followed). That's the "very wonderful" part. The "impossibility" is how Warren and I were brought together. For years I had a profound respect for his walk with God and valued his friendship. Yet when Warren told me he felt the Lord wanted us to begin a relationship, I thoroughly disagreed.

The years went by. I'm sure it took clever strategy on the Lord's part to keep Warren unmarried, especially with lovely, godly women available, and unrelenting encouragement from friends that he find a wife. I prayed God would lead Warren to someone else. How grateful I am the Lord disregarded those prayers. As Hannah More, a British author and playwright in the early 1800s, wrote, "Did not God sometimes withhold in mercy what we ask, we would be ruined at our own request."

Warren had been twenty-three when he yielded his life to Christ as Lord. At that time God assured him that if he left marriage in His hands, He would not let him miss the right girl or marry the wrong one. Now, twenty-three years later, God answered by working in my heart in a thorough way. He gradually transformed my respect for Warren into love, eradicated my objections, and gave me a deep desire to become his wife.

Once again I knew I dare not hold this earthly love with a clenched hand. After all, Warren was God's man, not mine. So, even before we finalized our engagement, I promised to give Warren back to the Lord all the days of his life. I included that promise in my wedding vows.

A year and a half after Warren and I were married, we returned to Asia, where we have lived and ministered for most of our married life. For three years we had Brian and Doreen with us in Singapore, for twenty-three years they were half a world away.

Then in 1995 Warren was diagnosed with cancer—fourth-stage lymphoma. In the months and years since we learned this, he has been prayed for by the elders of our church (James 5:14-16) and by many others around the world, and he has undergone careful and promising treatment. With confidence we ask for complete healing, believing this fits in with our much deeper desire and prayer: "Our Father who art in heaven, may Your name be honored, may Your kingdom come, may Your will be done." We have a quiet faith that the Lord is healing him. Yet we refuse to clench our fingers around physical healing, unwilling to let go.

I want Warren to be healed. I want him to live a long time, and I believe he will. But more than that I want God's will. He knows the good plans He has for us, plans for welfare and not for evil, to give us a future and a hope. I believe this, and thank the Lord for it, because He's never lied to me.

DEEP ROOTS IN THE SOIL OF HIS LOVE

In the decades of living I've outlined here, I've seen God beginning to answer for me Paul's beautiful prayer for believers in Ephesians 3:17-19 (expressed here in *The Living Bible*):

> May your roots go down deep into the soil of God's marvelous love;
> and may you be able to feel and understand, as all God's children
> should, how long, how wide, how deep, and how high His love
> really is, and to experience this love for yourselves, though it is so
> great that you will never see the end of it or fully know or under-
> stand it. And so at last you will be filled up with God Himself.

This may sound like an impossibly high goal—to be "filled up with God Himself" and to fully experience a love that's so far beyond fully knowing.

But it's not too hard for God. Immediately Paul goes on to say, "Now glory be to God who by His mighty power at work within us is able to do far more than we would ever dare to ask or even dream of—infinitely beyond our highest prayers, desires, thoughts, or hopes." If we truly want to know His love more, we can use this prayer of Paul's to pour out our hearts to Him, and He will more than answer.

God offers us a perfect and permanent love, a love relationship that can meet our deepest needs at every point of life and forever. And He wants us to respond to His love. In His heart He is intensely involved with us.

I wonder if we are intensely involved with Him?

Father, thank You for the lasting intensity of Your overflowing, never ending love. Thank You that Your love is so much better than anything I could imagine or hope for in life.

Show me clearly and continually how to respond to You. Let my roots go deep into the soil of Your love. Day by day, hour by hour, fill me with Yourself.

I worship You because of who You are—a God who understands me and faithfully takes care of me, and a God of intense, ardent affection for me that will last for all time and eternity.

In Jesus' name...

Your personal gleanings for meditation, prayer, and action:

What Scripture or truth in this chapter do you feel the Lord is especially speaking to you about? What will you do to profit the most from this?

THREE

HIS ETERNAL LONGINGS COMING TRUE

THERE WAS A TIME when I was troubled by the command that Jesus says is first and greatest—that we should love the Lord our God with all our heart and soul and mind and strength. It made me feel uncomfortable and guilty. I wanted to love God this much, and I liked to think I sometimes did. Yet I knew I didn't all the time, and perhaps I never achieved it. I loved Him more than I loved anyone else, but love Him with *all* my heart and soul and mind and strength? No, I was so often distracted or distrustful or drifting.

Some years ago I realized this is the most flattering and complimentary verse in the Bible. I am so important to God that He wants *me* to love Him totally. We don't approach strangers on the street and say, "Please love me with all your heart!" They would think we were crazy, and they'd probably be right. Only if someone means a great deal to us, only if we really love that person, do we ask that. And it's what God has asked from us. This wonderful Person—the supreme Ruler of the universe, Creator of all things, the One possessing all power and exalted far above all, the most desirable of all persons—*He* asks me to love Him with all my heart. He tells you and me, "This is what I want from you first of all, more than anything else."

INTENSELY PERSONAL

Why is this so important to God? Why does He care so much whether or not we love Him? I think it's because He has always been a relational God. He was never a lonely, solitary figure somewhere out in eternity, all alone in the empty reaches of space. He has always been a triune God in intimate relationship—the Father, Son, and Holy Spirit in loving communion. And before time began He decided He wanted to include many others in that circle of love.

God is always yearning for us and always has been. We read in Ephesians 1:4 that before the foundation of the world God chose us in Christ. Throughout Ephesians we find a heartwarming picture of His eternal longing, His innate Father's heart for us, tender and loving and full of gracious intentions. He longed for children, for a family. He longed to have a bride for His Son, a bride on whom He could lavish His love. He longed for a temple for His Holy Spirit to dwell in, for bodies upon earth in which He could express Himself with an intimacy far surpassing any human relationship. He longed for a people to be His very own. Looking ahead from eternity past He envisioned a relationship with us that would embody the many-faceted delights He would later build into human relationships—the tenderness of a father with his child, the comfort and stimulation of friendship, the supreme joys of bride and bridegroom. And as He planned His own family, God chose you and me to belong to Him. We are God's eternal longings coming true.

God is wrapped up in mankind. He has been reaching out for personal involvement with us from the beginning of Genesis, and He still continues to reach out. Through the centuries He has delighted in all those who would acknowledge Him. He referred to Abraham as His friend. He called David a man after His own heart. His eyes search the whole earth to demonstrate His love, to show it in practical ways to anyone who will be wholly His, to anyone who will *respond*.

His love is not simply for mankind as a mass—not some sentimental, vague, diffused feeling, as the comic strip character Charlie Brown expressed it: "I love mankind. It's people I can't stand." No, God really likes individual people. His love is intensely personal.

Jesus showed this on earth as He concentrated on individuals. He showed no partiality, no tinge of preference for any particular size or color or talent or educational level or social status. He loved individuals impartially, yet intensely, all the while showing us what God is like.

The Cross gives us the greatest sense of God's personal love. He did not send His Son to die for mankind as a mass. In Galatians 2:20 Paul speaks of how Christ the Son of God "loved *me* and gave Himself for *me.*" Out of His infinite capacity to center in on each individual person, He died for me personally and for you personally. His love is not just for the sum of humanity, or even just for the church as a whole. Toward each of us it's a personal love for His precious child.

You and I have only a limited number of people we can know, much less devote time to and love in an intensely personal way. God has no such limit to His ability to love or His availability. With infinite capacity He can and does love you as though you were the only person who ever lived on this earth. This is what won me to Him the night my mother turned my attention to John 3:16 after sensing my troubled spirit: God loved *me,* and gave His Son for *me.* His love and His gift are personal.

This relationship with us is already something He cherishes, and it will reach perfection in the eternal future. It will be an everlasting revel of delight for both Him and us. As I've imagined being before His throne with those vast millions of believers, I've sometimes had a wistful feeling that I'll just be part of a crowd. Then I remember that even now He can zero in on me and give me intimate, delightful, personal fellowship with Himself. How much more will this be true when I'm fully in His presence with all His loved ones. We won't be disappointed. As C. S. Lewis wrote, "The happiness God has designed for His higher creatures is an ecstasy of love and delight with Himself and one another, compared with which the most rapturous love between a man and a woman on this earth is mere milk and water."

By choosing to love us in this intense and personal way, God has made Himself vulnerable. "God has bound up His happiness with ours," Tozer wrote, "and He'll never know unmixed happiness again until His work in us is finished and we're all gathered home." His pleasure is linked with ours: We can grieve Him (hurting ourselves in the process), or we can bring Him delight as we enjoy satisfying His longings for our love.

Perhaps you easily remember that God has compassion for you and is willing to help you. Or you may think of God as taking care of our needs in a somewhat condescending way—after all, we're His creatures, so He does His duty toward us. But maybe you've overlooked how intense His feelings really are—how He desires you, how much He finds delight whenever you cultivate your love relationship with Him as one who belongs to Him. When we overlook this we rob God's love of the emotional content which the Scriptures portray. "For the Lord delights in you," God tells His people in Isaiah 62:4. He loves us so much He will even serenade us: "He will rejoice over you with joy, He will rest in His love, He will joy over you with singing," we read of Him in Zephaniah 3:17. And Psalm 149:4 says, "The Lord takes pleasure in His people."

I'm sure you're as astonished as I am that God can find such enjoyment from intimacy with us. An InterVarsity Press booklet, *The Quiet Time,* puts it this way:

> That God desires our fellowship is one of the most amazing facts
> revealed in Scripture. The fact is so staggering…that it's extremely diffi-
> cult for us to grasp its meaning for us. That God should allow His crea-
> tures to have fellowship with Himself is wonderful enough. But that
> He can desire it, that it gives Him satisfaction and joy and pleasure, is
> almost too much for our understanding.

This amazing love, so undeserved, is indeed hard to grasp with our minds: God is so intimately and personally involved with me that He longs for my fellowship. But as someone has said, it is "darkness to my intellect but sunshine to my heart." You and I can actually bring God pleasure! As C. S. Lewis wrote, we can be "a real ingredient in the divine happiness…delighted in as an artist delights in his work or a father in a son." What better motivation can there be for spending time with Him day by day? When I get lukewarm or sidetracked by lesser pursuits (even in my quiet time), nothing does more to rekindle my heart than remembering how much the Lord desires fellowship with me.

At times we may have to honestly confess, "Lord, I don't feel like having my quiet time this morning, but my purpose is still the same: I want to know You and bring You pleasure." Amy Carmichael prayed, "O Lord Jesus, my Beloved, may I be a joy to You." It's a prayer He answers continually, as much as we allow Him to.

So we can let those words from the second chapter in Song of Solomon draw us to Him. In *The Berkeley Version* they read, "Arise, my love, my beauty, and come along with me…. Let me hear your voice, let me see your face; for your voice is sweet, and your face is lovely."

What? Me, Lord? Are you sure you haven't got the wrong number? I mean, I remember what an awful attitude I had just last night. I can name a long list of things about me that I know are far from attractive. But You say my voice is sweet to Your ears? And my face is beautiful?

"Yes," He says, "for I've made you a new person in Christ. Deep in the inner core of your being you're a brand-new person, and you're beautiful to me, and I love to hear your voice."

Lord, I don't understand how this could be—but it feels good! It warms my heart. Say it again, I want to hear more….

"Rise up, my *love*, my *fair one*, and come away…."

We bring God joy just by responding to Him, just by taking time with Him as His loved one, His fair one, to sit at His feet and let Him speak to us His words of love.

How easily we forget what an honored privilege it is to offer our personal worship to God. When you come before Him and worship Him, you give Him what no one else in the universe can give: your own personal love, your own personal adoration, your own personal response to Him. It comes through your unique personality, which He created. And He is grieved when you don't respond.

He uniquely fashioned each one of us for Himself. He didn't follow some pattern or mass-production mold. No, He wanted a variety of people, because the love coming from each of us satisfies Him in a different way, helping to complete His joy in being our Father, our Beloved, our Friend. Each of us is individually precious to Him and will be for all eternity, giving Him the unique intimacy He longs for, the intense pleasure and satisfaction of our personal response. Each of us individually is that vast reservoir we spoke of, from which God can receive eternal pleasure. You are that, and I am that. As we love God and respond to Him, He receives pleasure from the waters of our love.

MAKING GOD RICH

We are God's treasure! This is one of the most exciting truths in the Bible, and it came alive for me one July in the cool, beautiful mountains of Malaysia. We traveled there from Singapore for a vacation and also to do some writing. Again and again in my quiet time I found myself distracted with thoughts about a book we were writing. The creative juices (or whatever they are) would flow, and new ideas or fresh ways of saying old ones would keep coming. How could I help but write them down? After all, each one seemed like a special treasure that could so easily be lost. Often the inspirations were thoughts about the Lord— but if I wrote too much, might they not actually end up being a rival to Him? It seemed so. Or even worse, an idol!

So I prayed, "Lord, more and more may I be taken up with You as my treasure. And may I see more clearly that I'm a treasure to You, created to bring You joy." I asked that He be central in my time with Him in a special way, that He would rein my thoughts in, and that I would write just enough to aid my praise for Him, my communion with Him, and my praying for others.

My meditation on those days focused on the amazing fact that God takes special delight in each of us as His own priceless possession, cherishing and guarding us and looking out for our best interests.

The Bible also tells us that God is *our* treasure, *our* inheritance—our portion, the best life can offer us now and forever (Psalm 73:25-26). As Tozer writes, "The man who has God as his treasure has all things in one, and he has it purely, legitimately, and forever." In view of God's power and majesty and tender love, this is easy to understand.

But that *we* are *His* inheritance, *His* treasure—isn't this incredible? *The Living Bible* puts it this way: "Because of what Christ has done we have become gifts to God that He delights in.… God has been made rich because we who are Christ's have been given to Him!" (Ephesians 1:11,18). Other Scriptures confirm the truth that we are God's special treasure, a source of delight to Him. God looks at us and thinks, *"He* belongs to Me…*she* belongs to Me— I am so rich!" We're gifts that Jesus has given Him, and very special gifts too— just what He always wanted! As Tozer says, we are more valuable to Him than galaxies of newly created worlds.

When we realize we're that important to God, it does something to how we think about ourselves. Not that it makes us proud. Pride means we take the credit for who we are. But God wants to see us hold our heads high in thankfulness because we know He loves us and has made us members of His royal family. He gets all the credit. It is He who made us; it is He who brought us to Christ and purified us; it is He who has given us new life in His presence, now and forever.

Throughout all eternity we'll bring Him joy. We'll be His jewels, "His prized possession…His special possession" (Malachi 3:16-17, RSV and Moffatt). We'll be "a crown of beauty…and a royal diadem in the hand of our God" (Isaiah 62:3, NASB)—a treasure He will hold close to His heart, a crown He'll lift high to show His magnificent handiwork. For eternity we'll be a glory to our Designer and Maker.

But God doesn't wait until eternity to treasure us. He treasures us now, in spite of our warts and wrinkles and blemishes. We're chosen ones, holy and beloved, honored in His eyes today, and bringing Him joy as we worship Him and walk with Him and talk of Him to each other.

Even now we're just as near to God as Jesus is. In the first chapter of Ephesians we read that He has made us welcome into the same everlasting love He bears toward His Beloved Son. And Jesus, in His high priestly prayer in John 17, said that the Father loves us in the same way He loves His Son. There's a wonderful old hymn that includes these stanzas,

> Near, so very near to God,
> Nearer I could not be,
> For in the Person of His Son
> *I'm just as near as He.*

> Dear, so very dear to God,
> I could not dearer be;
> The love wherewith He loved the Son,
> Such is His love for me.

God gives many illustrations to show our precious value to Him. As He delighted to be among His people of old, dwelling in the temple at Jerusalem, so we are now His temple, His dwelling place (Ephesians 2:21-22).

Think of how parents treasure each newborn child, marveling at the handiwork of God—at the tiny, perfect toes and fingers; how they envision the inner person ready to unfold; and later how they rejoice at each stage of growth. So our heavenly Father treasures us. We have been born into His family; we are really and truly His children, loved with a deep, unchanging love (1 John 3:1-2).

As an artist treasures each masterpiece he produces (imagine how Michaelangelo must have treasured his statues of Moses and David, and how Monet must have treasured his cathedral paintings, each with a different lighting, a different impression, and each so beautiful)—so God treasures each of us as His work of art, one of His masterpieces, both naturally and spiritually (Psalm 139:13-16, Ephesians 2:10).

And the illustration I like best: the bridegroom and bride. "As the bridegroom rejoices over the bride, so your God will rejoice over you" (Isaiah 62:5). In the Song of Solomon it's the bridegroom we hear calling, "Rise up, my love, my fair one, and come away...." As a couple in love treasure each other—as a bridegroom rejoices over his bride—so the Lord, as our inner and eternal Life Partner, treasures us.

The Lord takes special pleasure in us as we respond to Him with love, worship, faith, and obedience. As we let Him be our chief treasure we bring Him those unique joys that no one else can bring. And we bring Him unique griefs as we ignore Him and speed through our days, giving Him little thought. Day by day, moment by moment, you and I determine whether He loves us with a glad love or a grieved love.

Why does God so long to be our treasure and our first love? It's because we're *His* treasure, His eternal longings coming true, and therefore He wants only the best for us. He created us so that our lives operate best when (and only when) we let Him be our treasure.

Wonderful God, thank You that I'm so important to You, so valuable, that You ask me to love You with all my heart and soul and mind and strength. I praise You that You always have been and always will be intimately relational. I thank You for the honoring truth that I am Your eternal longing coming true.

How amazing it is that Your love for me is so intensely personal! I'm so glad that You like me as well as love me, and that You desire me and delight in me. Because Your pleasure is so linked with me, I ask that You help me learn how to please You and not grieve You, as I respond to You and let Your love satisfy me.

Thank You especially that You demonstrated Your love through the Cross of Your Son Jesus Christ—that He loved me and gave Himself for me.

> *O Lord, I cannot plead*
> *my love of Thee;*
> *I plead Thy love of me;*
> *The shallow conduit hails*
> *the unfathomed sea.*
> —Christina Rossetti

Your personal gleanings for meditation, prayer, and action:

What Scripture or truth in this chapter do you feel the Lord is especially speaking to you about? What will you do to profit the most from this?

FOUR

DRAWING US NEAR

BECAUSE YOU ARE a special treasure to God, He is working to draw you into a deeper love for Him—away from any idols in your life, away from rival interests, away from giving first place to His good gifts instead of to Him.

In Jeremiah 31:3 the Lord tells His people, "I have loved you with an everlasting love, therefore with lovingkindness I have drawn you" (NKJV). Every hour since you first met Him, He has been pursuing you, seeking to draw you closer as a mother draws her child, as a bridegroom his bride. He wants you near.

I've found through the years that He draws us in many ways. He wants us to understand the ways He does this, so that we can respond to them and enjoy a closer, richer relationship with Him. In the portrait of the Lord and His beloved in Song of Solomon 1:4, the bride entreats Him, "Draw me after You, and let us run together" (NASB). Isn't this a tender, meaningful prayer? *Draw me after You and let us run together—today! Every day! And always.*

Sometimes I change it to "Draw *us* after You" as I pray for Warren and me: "Draw us, Lord, and let us run together with You—and also with one another—with ever-expanding delight and harmony." I pray it for others one by one or couple by couple—for family members, for dear ones we've ministered to in Asia, for colaborers and friends. Slowly I enlarge the circle: "Draw them after You, and let them run together with You and with one another."

One morning in Singapore I was having my quiet time with the Lord, looking out over our lovely tropical garden. I felt deeply anxious about our grandchildren. My worry had been fueled by reading about New Age leaders and their designs for indoctrinating children. That morning it dawned on me in a new way that the answer rested in the Lord's gentle, persistent drawing power: "Lord, draw them after You, so that they'll run with You." Then and later I found deep joy simply asking the Lord to do this, and to give them three things as the months and years hurry by: a deep desire to know Him and walk with Him; a discerning spirit to detect evil, regardless of how appealing its mask might be; and the power to steer clear of evil and keep running through life with Him.

Draw us after You. He answers this prayer because He wants to have us near. And how does He draw us?

I believe He grants all of us certain love-gifts that help us come closer to Him and know Him better. Five of these stand out to me as foundational to our love relationship with Him: His Word, His indwelling Spirit, the body of Christ, the circumstances of our daily lives, and the path of obedience.

The first love-gift is His Word, where we find our most beautiful and comprehensive portrait of Him. As we take time to listen, He keeps telling us there—from cover to cover and in a multitude of ways—that He loves us, and how and why and how much. Everything in Scripture helps us know Him better if that's truly what we seek, and if we let His love-messages soak in. The narrative stories, for example, reveal so much about Him as they record His dealings with people (both individuals and groups), just as we get to know a fellow human being better by observing how he or she interacts with people. The laws and commands in the Bible also reveal who the Lord is. They show us what He stands for, the principles He delights in, and His concern to lead us in paths that keep us from harm and assure our well-being and that of others, especially our children.

Another of God's love-gifts—His basic provisions to help us know Him better—is His indwelling presence through the Holy Spirit. As we feed on

God's Word, the Spirit empowers us to see and understand the Lord and His love. He takes the truths about Jesus and makes them real to us in the core of our being, in the holy sanctuary deep within us. As a result, our knowledge of the Lord is more intimate than our knowledge of anyone else. He guides us into truth not just intellectually but in experience—in how we think and feel and choose. The Spirit Himself fills our hearts with God's love (Romans 5:5) so that it satisfies us and flows out to others.

The third love-gift that helps us know God and His love better is the body of Christ—other believers. In such special ways He reveals Himself to us through fellow Christ-followers—through pastors and teachers, counselors and mentors, and also those with less-obvious gifts. Whatever their spiritual gifts, we are enriched through them. Beyond this, we profit greatly from the way their lives reveal Christ. We see their faults; no one is a perfect channel of God's love. But we can also see the Lord in one another as we want to. We can choose to concentrate on Christ in them, making their strengths our major focus, rather than their flaws and failures. As we behold Christ in them, He draws us closer to Himself.

This love-gift includes members of our families who know the Lord, including our spouses. Warren loves me dearly and tells me so often. He's godly, a man of prayer, considerate, strong, loving—I could go on and on. I'm grateful for how the Lord portrays His character through Warren. As I accept my husband as one of God's many beautiful love-gifts to me and lift my heart in thanksgiving and praise, this draws me to love the Lord more—and to love Warren more too.

The fourth basic provision, or love-gift, is simply the circumstances of daily life. God so acutely wants to enrich us through knowing Him better and becoming more like Him; to this end He arranges our days with the proper mixture of joys and trials, gains and losses, pleasure and pain. He holds our lives in the hollow of His hand, and into that place of security He brings the blessings and troubles we need: "I'll let this trial through," He says, "because it will strengthen her. No, not that one; it's more than she could bear right now." And, "I'll bestow this joy because it will help heal him, but not that one, though he really wants it, because it would be harmful to his best interests."

Let's compare God to a skilled baker and ourselves to the cakes he is making. Our Maker doesn't make any of His cakes the same, but has a unique recipe for each. With a scrumptious end product in mind, He follows each recipe with great care.

"But, Lord," I may say, "You put chocolate in *his* life, and I'd like a little in mine"—not realizing that God intends me to become a beautiful angel food cake. Chocolate would spoil it.

"But, Lord, not a dozen egg whites! I've had six already and that's plenty." No, the cake wouldn't rise well.

"A little more sugar, Lord. And none of that cream of tartar or I'll choke!" But the cake wouldn't be as delicious.

"Lord! Fifty strokes is enough beating. I won't need a hundred." Do you want the cake to be lumpy?

Then into the oven. "Lord, please turn down this heat! It's not fair to have me at 400 degrees when many get by with 350. Or at least pull me out after thirty minutes; I simply can't take forty-five."

We grieve God and cheat ourselves when we resist His design. He wants us to cooperate so that His blend of joys and trials will more quickly, more fully result in the end product He envisions for us—our entire person conformed to the image of His Son. He's working to beautify us with the poise and strength of Christ's character, with His winsomeness, with His peace and gladness, which were so deep that even on His way to the cross He could tell His disciples, "My peace I give you…. I want you to have the same joy I have" (John 14:27, 15:11, NCV).

These love gifts—God's Word, His Spirit, other believers, and the circumstances He allows or sends—draw us closer to Him. They help us stay on the path of obedience, which I think of as the fifth love-gift that helps us know God better. (We'll consider this one more fully in Chapter 8.) We can run through life with the Lord only as we choose His paths—the paths where He manifests His presence. He won't run with us on paths of disobedience. It's not that He'll forsake us, even as the sun does not forsake the earth when night falls or when thick clouds roll in. But His presence won't be real to us; the warm, glad companionship won't be there.

So draw me after You, Lord, and let us run together. The image recalls the song, "My God and I go in the fields together; we walk and talk as good friends should and do. We clasp our hands, our voices ring with laughter. My God and I walk through the meadow's hue." Running with Him means pleasure and carefree enjoyment.

Running with Him also includes running with perseverance the race marked out for us (Hebrews 12:1). We're running with One whose earthly race ended in a cross, and our own path includes the fellowship of His sufferings. Only the way of the Cross leads home. I may fantasize that just around the corner life will become easy—as soon as this or that particular commitment is over, this deadline met, this change made, this problem solved, this job done, and on and on. But will the day come when I won't have to deny myself, take up my cross daily, and follow Him—when I'll have earned the right (Luke 9:23-24) to save my life rather than lose it for His sake?

Do I even want such a day to come? My heart has been stirred by Phillips Brooks's poem:

> Be strong.
> We are not here to play, to dream, to drift.
> We have hard work to do, and loads to lift.
> Shun not the struggle; face it. 'Tis God's gift.

So I pray, "Lord, enable me to say yes to running in carefree delight—and also to running with perseverance. Give me grace to say yes to paths of struggle and pain and disappointment whenever that's what You plan for me."

KISS THE JOYS

How glad I am that life is more than trials. Isn't it true that when the Lord brings a super-special gift or event into our lives, it's not one lone mountaintop upon a bleak plain? Rather it's a high summit among a range of other majestic peaks. It's a refreshing oasis in a land of oases, not (at least spiritually) in an otherwise barren desert. How often, in His gracious will, He lets us live in a well-watered land filled with opportunities, special surprises, rich relationships.

We're to receive these countless joys as love-gifts: "Lord, this shows what Your heart for me is like—You love to do things that delight me! Thank You!" The gifts, all of them, should draw us nearer to the Giver. We're to freely enjoy them, but not clutch them.

Our son, Brian, helped us appreciate these lines by William Blake:

> He who binds to himself a joy
> Does the winged life destroy;
> He who kisses the joy as it flies
> Lives in eternity's sunrise.

We're meant to kiss our joys, rather than clench them tightly and destroy them. Sometimes we turn our joys into trials by clinging to them too tightly. This often happens in our parenting, when we're not willing to release our children for the next stage in their growth.

Sometimes I find it hard to "kiss the joy" of my hopes and dreams that our children will enjoy relatively trouble-free lives. My natural response has always been wanting God to shield them from painful experiences. I believe it's good to pray that He'll prevent any trials that would not best serve His purposes for our loved ones, and especially that He'll keep them aligned with Him and His Word and thus prevent self-inflicted problems.

But years ago as I studied the sovereignty of God in the Scriptures, He reminded me that often He shelters us under His wings not so much *from* trials as *in* trials. Generally He allows us to experience the problems normally faced by mankind, for trials serve His high purposes in our lives. He uses them to make us more like Christ, to glorify Himself through us, and to store up for us an eternal weight of glory immeasurably greater than our troubles and losses and pain. (Imagine that *weight* of glory! Won't we be glad then that He didn't over-protect us now!)

This truth has helped me trust God for our family and for others, as well as for myself. As I focus on God's purposes, I'm able to choose against my over-protective responses. Then I pray that He will shield us from harm in the midst of our hard experiences—that He'll enable us to cooperate with Him so that He can work out His good purposes. And best of all I ask that we'll know Him better through all that comes our way, that we'll experience the truth: "Each loss is truest gain if, day by day, He fills the place of all He takes away."

Psalm 34—which tells us, "Many are the afflictions of the righteous" (verse 19, RSV)—also assures us that "those who seek the Lord lack no good thing" (verse 10). Rich supply in the midst of trials seems to be God's intention more than insulation from difficulties and dangers.

We're so grateful that we could have our children with us while they were passing through adolescence. The comfortable organization of childhood, with its dependence on parents, was replaced temporarily by *dis*organization of personality; this was preparing them for their *re*organization as independent adults. Like any reorganization or remodeling it involved struggles, inconveniences, even distress—but I knew the end product would be worth it. God had given us tremendous promises for our children, such as Isaiah 54:13— "All your children shall be taught by the Lord; and great shall be the peace of your children" (NKJV); and Isaiah 49:25— "I will contend with him who contends with you, and I will save your children"(NKJV). So when my focus was on the Lord I had a deep assurance that Brian and Doreen would "turn out" all right. But when my eyes were diverted to the multitude of subtle influences that could affect them in today's world, my faith easily gave way to anxiety and inner tension and tight shoulder muscles.

I discovered that I often looked on the children as an extension of myself, in the sense that I overemphasized the part I was to play in their lives. Repeatedly I found deep relief in telling the Lord, "Father, she's not an extension of me, but of You! So I picture You in touch with her, working in her life whatever she needs in this present struggle or situation." I prayed that God would inoculate Brian and Doreen against influences they would face later. By this I meant two things. First, that He would give them the right amount of exposure to worldly ideas and philosophies and pressures while they were still with us. Next, that He would give them (through His Word and us and others) increased insight and discernment that would protect them when they returned to America for college and the launching of their adulthood.

In the Christmas season of Brian's senior year I became aware of a specific fear for him lurking just beneath my level of consciousness. Now and then it surfaced slightly. But I had never faced it squarely and resolved it. I talked with Warren about the worst possibility I could think of, then held it up before the Lord. I prayed, "Father, I don't believe this type of experience would be Your will for Brian. But perhaps for some reason beyond my understanding, his life in the long run would magnify You more by his passing through this. So You have my permission to let it happen." (He never needs my permission; but at times, for my sake, I need to give it!) This type of praying helped me be willing for anything that might have to be part of God's unique plan for our teenagers. And this willingness made it easier to trust God to be at work in their lives.

The truth that God protects us *in* trials more than *from* them hit home for me even more deeply after the children had grown up and were an ocean's width away. The moment soon came when Warren and I, after a furlough in the States, boarded an Asia-bound DC-8 to return home to Singapore, leaving Brian and Doreen behind. Traveling through the night, while most passengers slept, I sat meditating amid tears. Psalm 31:19 vividly reminded me of the great goodness the Lord has stored up for us. Psalm 23:6 came to mind: Surely goodness and lovingkindness would follow us all the days of our lives, and we will dwell in His house forever. We all belonged to Him and to one another for eternity.

In my feeling of loss I was reminded of the importance of praise as the always-right response to God's love, whether He is displaying it through joy or trial. We're told to "continually offer the sacrifice of praise to God, that is, the fruit of our lips, giving thanks to His name" (Hebrews 13:15, NKJV). I was learning that praise is not to be a fringe activity in our lives, but a basic occupation. It is essential, not optional. It is to be constant, not occasional. As Bible teacher John Mitchell helped me understand, "To thank God when we don't feel like it is not hypocrisy, but obedience." He based this on 1 Thessalonians 5:18, which says, "In everything give thanks," not "In everything feel thankful."

Yet thanking God in every situation poses problems. We live in a fallen world that harbors ugliness and injustice. People suffer because of events over which they have no control, and it seems God so often meets us in His most special ways in far-from-ideal situations. Such distressing circumstances, taken in the right spirit, give Him the opportunity to reach down into the ugliness and produce beauty. "Problems are the raw material for God's miracles," Corrie ten Boom would often say. Hudson Taylor described our trials as the platform on which God reveals Himself, showing how loving and powerful and wise He is.

As we headed back to Asia, I was learning in a new way an old lesson: Praise helps me yield to God as the Director and Chief Actor in each scene of my life's drama. Then He uses my disappointments and distresses to bring inner growth and glory. He weaves all my trials—and even my failures—into His perfect design for the fabric of my character.

My failures. This was the hardest area to give thanks for, especially when they had affected loved ones. As Brian and Doreen stepped into the adult world it was a joy to see many beautiful things in their lives. But it hurt to see areas of need and struggle that stemmed in part from ways we as parents had failed them. A friend reminded me that even parental shortcomings are part of the "all things" that God will use to make a man and woman who will accomplish His unique purposes. Again and again, as remembrances of my failures would push their way into my consciousness, I would let God's total forgiveness dissolve my regrets. Then I would go on to praise Him who accepts us all just as we are and lovingly works to make us more than we are. I realized He didn't expect either me or my children to be finished products yet.

In those days the Holy Spirit was repeatedly challenging me through Philippians 3:14— "I leave the past behind and with hands outstretched to whatever lies ahead I go straight for the goal" (Phillips). This verse relaxed my heart's defenses and untied its emotional knots. It helped me recognize the self-protection I sometimes slipped into, the inner stance of having my hands held up to ward off danger and trials. I would pray, "Thank You, Lord. I don't know what lies ahead, but You do. Thank You that the future holds You, and You hold the future. Thank You that I can pray for myself and my loved ones with expectancy, praising You ahead of time for answers that right now are visible only to You. And thank You for that day when we'll praise You not in the midst of trial but in total joy and fulfillment, as finished products for Your glory."

Still, times of loneliness and anxiety would sometimes sweep over me while we all coped with constantly changing circumstances. In that first year apart from us, Doreen was facing major changes. The Lord was sustaining and blessing her in numerous ways, both in her own life and in helping other girls grow spiritually. In her first semester as a "missionary kid" returning to the United States, God had also provided her with an ideal roommate. Now her roommate was getting married.

So more than ever she missed our times of talking things over, sharing helpful Scriptures, and studying the Bible together. I missed those times too! Doreen's spiritual devotion and hunger for the Word had long been a joy to us.

At that time she confessed in one of her letters that she longed to be "personally preached at." I wrote back, quoting Romans 8:28, which in the Williams translation says, "All things *go on working* together for good." I commented, "That's one continuing thing, one thing that goes on though many things change!

"Another thing that never changes," I reminded her, "is God's loving involvement in our lives. It began before we existed and will continue forever." I quoted more of the passage in Romans 8—"For whom He foreknew, He also predestined to be conformed to the image of His Son"—then continued,

"Whom He foreknew..." This means more than factual knowledge. God always knows all things factually, including the future. But there's another kind of knowledge—that of personal experience and involvement. For example, Psalm 1 says that the Lord "knows" the way of the righteous, in contrast to the way of the wicked. Well, factually He also knows the way of the wicked. But He identifies with the way of the righteous in *a personally involved way.*

So He "foreknew" you and me—He was lovingly involved with us before we existed, before the world came into being. One version translates it, "whom He fore-approved," and another, "whom He set His heart on beforehand"! In His heart, from eternity, foreknowing each of us, He said, "I set My heart on her—I approve her to be Mine—and I shall make her like My Son, molding her into His image. I appoint her ahead of time for this destiny."

I concluded the letter this way:

Each one whom God foreordained for such a destiny He also called, and justified, *and* glorified. "To those whom He justified He has also given His splendour, raising them to a heavenly dignity and state of being" (NEB and Amplified). Ours is a place of highest privilege—enthroned with Christ, sharing His position which is infinitely superior to any conceivable earthly status. Status that will never change in a Kingdom that will never be shaken—in the one sphere where position matters....

So—roommates get married, people move away, situations, responsibilities, and opportunities vary from month to month. But nothing truly essential changes. Nor does my love for you!

INTO THE BATTLE

A couple of years earlier, Brian, then eighteen, had come to a terrifying realization: He had become trapped in existentialism, agnosticism, and nihilism—modern philosophies that relentlessly led so many young people to abandon their faith and eventually, for some, to commit suicide. This ushered Warren and me into years of spiritual warfare and (especially me) times of inner turmoil.

When Brian was still in high school he had gone on a spiritual leave of absence (or was it absence without leave?). One day he had assured me, "Mom, I know how to come back anytime I want to."

"How?" I asked.

"Through the Word." Not a bad idea. But now that he was caught in these philosophies, he couldn't break loose, even through coming to the Scriptures.

I was the one he confided in. I was hesitant about saying too much, but Warren told me, "You've got to get in there and listen and talk with him." So—both in Singapore and later in the U.S. when Warren and I were on furlough—Brian and I would sit and talk for hours. Then I'd go back and cry on Warren's shoulder. Once in a while, without my mind's permission, I would cry while Brian and I were together. Then I'd be so afraid that he wouldn't want to talk anymore. He's a sensitive, tenderhearted son and wouldn't want to hurt me. So I'd tell him, "I'm crying a little, but if you don't talk I'll cry even more."

As those tough months and years crept by, Brian now and then reported inner "rumblings" or shafts of light that we believed were the prelude to his spiritual breakthrough. Later he told me, "It's strange, Mom. I didn't even know if God existed, but somewhere inside, at least at times, I had a deep confidence in His sovereignty."

God used truths from His Word to rescue Warren and me from fear and unbelief—two ways Satan likes to cripple us. One spiritual battlefield, I knew, was within us, in our minds and hearts. To help me stay rooted in the victory that I knew Christ had already won, I used a plan that Dr. Bob Johnson, a friend and counselor, had shared. I arranged the steps into the form of an acrostic, ART:

Acknowledge what you're thinking that gives Satan an advantage and fits in with his purposes. (To cast something down we must first admit it's there.) Acknowledge also the feelings that come with these thoughts. If you've welcomed and fed these thoughts, confess this as sin. Pour out your heart to the Lord, letting Him in on what you feel (Psalm 62:8).

Renounce these false, negative, or impure thoughts. You've confessed them to the Lord; now choose against them. Choose not to drain your inner strength by nurturing the disruptive feelings that accompany these thoughts. Be decisive about this. Shout it if necessary: "This is not the way I'm going to think!"

Think the *truth* with *thanksgiving*. This brings your thoughts under Christ's authority. Prepare ahead of time for this. For each battle that's common in your life, ask the Lord to lead you to a specific truth, a specific Scripture, that will rescue you. Soak in these truths, letting the Holy Spirit touch your heart with their meaning. Store them in your heart. Then when the false or troubling thought plays over and over in your mind like a broken record, create a new pattern by thinking the truth over and over. Truth is a powerful sword that casts down false thoughts. It's a light that dispels darkness. And thanksgiving helps release truth's power within you, devastating the enemy's purposes.

ART helped me do what 2 Corinthians 10:5 says: to cast down every high thing that exalts itself against the knowledge of God, and bring every thought into captivity to Christ.

Dr. Johnson encouraged Brian to use the above three steps. Later Brian told us, "At first I felt that rejecting and replacing a mere thought would be futile and inadequate in overcoming my negative emotions. It seemed like trying to empty an ocean with a teacup. But after putting these principles of thought control into action, I began to see it differently. It was, instead, like opening a drain in the ocean's bottom, which became wider with each positive choice."

Brian finally made a definite choice to "admit my Christianity" as he put it. Much had prepared the way for this, including many who prayed and many

who repeatedly offered him a supportive arm. One was Bob Johnson, whom
I mentioned above. Another was Bobby, a friend who met him frequently to
talk over lunch. Brian's final decision wasn't easy, for it involved a major identity crisis. It meant letting himself go, dropping from the noble and touching
position of "lonely, unfilled searcher" to what seemed to him a vulnerable,
horrible position of sameness—just another Christian.

In making his decision, he simply asked God to save him from himself
and set him free. Brian wrote:

> Many times I had prayed virtually the same words and yet nothing
> "happened"—but the whole crux of the matter lies in that word, for
> I somehow never realized that belief isn't something that happens to
> me but something I *do*.... That made all the difference.... True
> knowing, from which understanding is derived, must spring from
> action, not contemplation....
>
> I can say without hesitation that I am a Christian and yet
> intellectually I don't "know" that God exists, and emotionally I
> have not experienced that blessed Relation which lies at the root
> of all knowing.

Brian knew he had taken the needed "leap of faith." "Take the leap into
what seems like an empty gulf," he had read, "and God will catch you." He was
also keeping a regular quiet time with God and doing other things he felt are
part of believing action. But he still didn't feel "caught." He wrote, "The
unfilled gulf seems too great to bear...but I believe without hesitation I will
be caught and uplifted."

I had been reading in Exodus how God led His people out of Egypt not
by the direct, seemingly easier route but by one that human planning would
never have settled on. God knew the dangers of the obvious route. He also
foresaw the greater experience of His power that would come along the Red
Sea path He chose. So Warren and I praised the Lord for the exact route of deliverance He had planned for Brian.

Brian's emotions were slow to cooperate with his actions, but the coming years saw steady growth and many victories. For his parents it was a living object lesson on how we can choose *against* the domination of our dark emotions—not by ignoring them but by acknowledging them, then choosing the thoughts and actions that tend toward a positive inner response.

One summer Brian and Doreen traveled through Europe by bicycle and tent for four months, then flew on to Singapore for a reunion with us. (Warren had seen them on ministry trips, but I hadn't seen them for two and a half years.) They were brimming over with stories of fun times, stresses, lessons learned, and impressive answers to prayer. And both quickly got involved in ministry to young people in Singapore—Doreen for only a short while before going back to her university in the Midwest, and Brian as he stayed with us for more than half a year.

Brian wrote to friends in the U.S.:

My time in Europe and Singapore has changed my life. For the first time I have experienced the reality of Him in me—not a charismatic sort of high, but rather an inner fullness that "comes out" when I'm around others—a love, compassion, caring, and joy, which I know is not me but Him. Of course there are still valleys—for what are mountains without them?—but they don't go half as deep, and I can take joy in them because I know I'm being worked on.

The Lord has given me a good ministry with the kids at the American High School here. I'm meeting with several every week.... If you think of it, pray that He will help me take their hand, that He would build them up through me, and that He would give us a friendship in which we are touched and fulfilled on the deepest levels.

After our children's university days came marriage to a godly man for Doreen, and seminary for Brian (with marriage and a pastorate coming later). Brian lived with my mother in Minnesota during his summer vacation in 1980. It was an emotional and eventful time. Mother, age eighty-four, was preparing to move out of her home—the house that had represented such an earthly anchoring place for our family for many years. The following letter from Brian was a great help to me, far away in Singapore and longing to be in on the family event. It both released needed tears and reminded me to use my memories creatively and move on into the future in a positive, forward-looking way.

Dear Mom and Dad,

What a week! "The move" has finally begun—Grandma's move, but in a way all of ours, as we are all being moved along with Grandma emotionally. The end of an era....

As we sort through the old paraphernalia of our family's past, stored over so many years in the basement, upstairs closets, and barn, the events and spirit of that era are called back with almost painful clarity. Smells alone can bring back whole worlds of experience. And when the smell accompanies its object—an old brown photograph, a yearbook, Uncle Jake's favorite marbles, Grandpa's long cloth scroll illustrating on a cross the themes of world history, Mom's tiny baby booties, old recordings of Uncle Gene and Daddy, their color movie of post-war Europe, and on and on—then the nostalgia becomes intense.

I was working on my Sunday school lesson an hour each day, and was often on the verge of tears. It was my last lesson on Psalm 119, in which I tried to give more concrete form to my "Theology of Action"—underlining the need for vigilant, concrete actions in our relationship with the Lord versus an overemphasis (usually addictive) on short-lived emotionalism. And that bracing mindset, that cutting-edge of forward-looking Action with respect to the Lord was somehow set in its full perspective as we looked back nostalgically over our shoulders. Each view reinforced the other.... They came together and produced in my heart one very distinct response of gratefulness—gratefulness to Him; I felt somehow completely wrapped up in His presence. The family gathered, the warmth and stability of old things in one place, the memories—I wanted to hold on to those moments forever. Timeless moments, dreamy, almost slow-motioned. Each word uttered by Uncle Jake, Grandma, Uncle Gene, Aunt Mary, seemed to have universal significance. It was all so familial, soothing, reassuring. The room seemed blanketed in a soft, personal, and very tender atmosphere....

The home is slowly being emptied. The one place that would never change is losing more and more of its character as each day passes. A hollowness is creeping in. The rooms and shelves seem shocked to be empty. A home is being turned into a house. And with each truckload a feeling becomes almost audible—the house seems to whisper (almost sigh) with a strange sense of urgency, "It's time to go."

Time to go. Yes—time to kiss our past joys gratefully, without grasping them; to press on in the present joy of Action directed toward the future. "Kiss your joys, don't grasp them," I keep telling myself. Kiss them, don't grasp. Kiss them gratefully and press on.

INTO THE WILDERNESS

Kiss the joys gratefully and press on—onward to more joys but also to promised trials, all these together disclosing more of the Lord's loving design. As the hymn says,

> Every joy or trial falleth from above,
> Traced upon our dial by the Sun of love.

God is love, and all He says and does affirms this. How we rejoice when, in love, He shields us from obviously harmful things or brings unmistakably good things our way. Yet whatever He allows to touch our lives—seemingly good or bad—is an expression of His love and His desire for us. Whatever He permits or sends is an invitation to draw closer to Him.

For years I've enjoyed Florence White Willett's poem that begins,

> I thank God for the bitter things;
> They've been a friend to grace.
> They've driven me from the paths of ease
> To storm the secret place.

The experience of trials—the taste or more of bitterness—often spurs us to let God love us. It makes us more aware of our needs and urges us to come to Him with them, seeking His presence and help.

In Hosea 2:14 the Lord says figuratively of His people, "I will allure her and bring her into the wilderness, and speak tenderly to her" (RSV). Sometimes God must place us in the wilderness, setting us apart in a dry and thirsty land. He does this to draw us, allure us, and speak gently, kindly to our hearts.

Without trials, how would we really know how loving God is? What if we never faced loneliness or heartbreak, praying with empty hearts, "Lord, I need Your love"? Would we ever truly hear His reassurance that we're precious in His eyes, honored and deeply loved?

Without the assault of trials, how often would we run to hide in the shadow of His wings? David's prayer in Psalm 36 shows that this shelter is not like a cramped, dark, damp, meagerly stocked air-raid shelter. The Lord's refuge offers protection, but it offers so much more. It lets us feast on the abundance of His house, drink from His "river of delights," and enjoy the light of His presence.

Without trials as God's platform for revealing Himself, how else would we know His power? Just by reading about it in the Bible? This is essential. It gets the concept into our mind. But when we're caught in an impossible circumstance and cry out to Him and He answers with deliverance, then we know on a deeper level: Our God truly is powerful!

Apart from difficult circumstances, how earnestly would we seek Him? How deeply would we know Him? I'm sorry to say this, but isn't it true that you and I would soon be distracted and often forget Him if everything always went smoothly?

RELEASE AND ENLARGEMENT

Trials also prepare the way for God in His love to do greater things in our lives. One night in Singapore I woke up and couldn't get back to sleep. After lying there a while, I did what I often do in such predicaments: I went into my office next to our bedroom and read a few pages from daily devotional books by A. W. Tozer and Oswald Chambers. Something I read brought to my mind the thought, "Discouragement often precedes enlargement." Several friends and loved ones who were facing discouragement and worse came to mind. So I prayed that God in His time would use these difficulties to bring enlargement.

In my quiet time the next morning, Psalm 66:10-12 (NASB) came to my attention:

> For Thou hast tried us, O God;
> Thou hast refined us as silver is refined.
> Thou didst bring us into the net;
> Thou didst lay an oppressive burden upon our loins.
> Thou didst make men ride over our heads;
> We went through fire and through water;
> Yet Thou didst bring us out into a place of abundance.

Through this passage the Lord reminded me of how He works: He uses not only discouragement but also desperate situations to bring new release and enlargement into our lives. The more desperate and impossible our situation, the more glory it can bring to God. Think of Abraham as Romans 4 describes him—his body as good as dead. And think of Daniel's three friends, thrown into the blazing furnace (Daniel 3). Tough times, testings of faith—but great results! I found myself encouraged to believe this principle and pray accordingly.

Isn't this release and enlargement exactly what we want? In dealing with trials I've found it helpful to have my true goals clearly set beforehand and to keep them in my consciousness: to love God and know Him better, to be conformed to Christ's image, to glorify Him and do His will. Then when I feel disappointed or distressed, the Lord can more quickly bring me back to this perspective: "This trial comes to fulfill my chosen goals even though it frustrates my surface desires. Therefore I welcome it."

Isn't it wonderful that we can count on One who is all-powerful and all-wise, and who loves us perfectly? Warren and I often go back to the full stanza by Frances Havergal:

> Every joy or trial falleth from above,
> Traced upon our dial by the Sun of love.
> We may trust Him fully, all for us to do.
> They who trust Him wholly, find Him wholly true.

So we can celebrate every trial because of its potential. Our celebration can take the form of exuberance or simply a quiet purpose of heart. Either way, how appropriate it is to celebrate, in view of who God is, who we are in Christ and what He is making us by His transforming touch! When I fail to celebrate—as when I struggle resistingly with "too much to do"—I lose both spiritual joy and physical vitality.

My favorite praise word is exult. What a heart-expanding word! It's what the team and its loyal fans do when they win the national championship or the World Series or the Super Bowl. If they have reason to be elated, how much more do we! I like to think of exulting as lifting my heart above the frustrating, the pressing, the frightening, the sordid—lifting it up to the Lord with a sense of glad triumph.

In Romans 5, Paul speaks of exulting not only in our God and our hope, but also in our trials. Why can we exult in trials? Because of our God and our hope—our loving, sovereign, caring God and the glorious destiny He's preparing us for. "Whatever we may have to go through now is less than nothing compared with the magnificent future God has planned for us" (Romans 8:18, Phillips). So it's altogether reasonable to exult in our troubles—to "welcome them as friends!" as Phillips puts it in James 1:2-4.

I like to think of responding rightly to each trial as an investment that will earn dividends far beyond the cost to us—inexhaustible dividends that will increase our glory forever in the truly golden years when we'll be with the Lord.

Other dividends we gain now. For me there was only one real sacrifice to living and serving in Asia most of my adult life: being separated from loved ones, especially from our grown children and, later, our grandchildren. We have six of them, with ages ranging from sixteen to four, each so unique and special— Kristen, Amy, and David Wirsig; Jordan, Rachael, and Cameron Myers. Often longings to see and hold and talk with them would flood my heart. Then it would help so much to offer both my grandchildren and my desires to the Lord Jesus as a love-gift. How much more enjoyable this was than to look at our separation as a sacrifice! By viewing loved ones not as mine but as a love-gift to the Lord, I received His gift of inner release. Then the memories of my grandchildren could bring joy instead of sorrow. Though they were half a world away, just the thought of them would nourish my heart when my love for them was centered in the Lord.

So by making the small investment of simply placing in God's hands my negative responses to trials, I find an open door to joy and freedom right now. I find a way to see past my troubles and pressures to enjoy the broad horizon of our vastly wonderful God and our eternal destiny, glorious beyond imagining. When I delay in making that investment, I drain away my energies (and who needs that kind of drainage?). When I retreat into self-protection as trials assail, I only deprive myself of rich benefits.

COMPENSATION FOR THE RAIN

It's easy to want our lives to be all beauty and no cost, all gain and no loss. When difficulties mar the scene we find ourselves focusing on our disappointment rather than treasuring life's delights. Job asked, "Shall we indeed receive good from God and not accept adversity?" (2:10, NASB). God wants us to receive both good and adversity with open hands and a trusting heart.

As I meditated on the birth of Christ one Christmas season in the late 1950s, the Lord gave me fresh light on trials. I needed this. By then the Lord had blessed our family and Gene and Mary's with two children each, ranging in age from six months to two years. We were on our first furlough, and this was the first chance to spend Christmas with the grandparents. But Dean and Gene wouldn't be there. The Lord had sent them to Kenya, Africa, for a very strategic ministry opportunity. So no daddies around for Christmas! As the season progressed, I began to feel sorry for myself as well as for the grandparents and children.

Then the Lord rescued me. He reminded me that the first Christmas, though beautiful, was costly. God gave special revelations and privileges, and He provided for and preserved Jesus, Mary, and Joseph in exciting ways. But in no sense did He coddle them. The cost included the arduous journey from Nazareth to Bethlehem, the far-from-glamorous birthplace, the hurried flight to Egypt to escape Herod. And for Jesus, much more:

> He left the heavenly hills above
> To die on Calvary's mountain,
> Left the eternal springs of love
> To taste earth's bitter fountain.

If our Father did not pamper His beloved Son, should we expect Him to pamper us? Jesus Himself assures us in John 16:33, "In this world you will have trouble [pressures, trials, tribulations, hardships, sorrow]. But take heart!

I have overcome the world" (NIV). We can choose to take heart, to cheer up, and therefore to experience His peace in the midst of the pressures and costly trials. Or we can dissipate our energies through negative attitudes and pockets of inner resistance.

Often when my feelings cry, "Oh, if only it would get easier," a quotation from Phillips Brooks, an Episcopal bishop in the 1800s, motivates me to choose a different attitude—to open my arms wide and receive what God gives me to do, along with His sufficiency to accomplish it:

> Do not pray for easier lives;
> Pray to become stronger men.
> Do not pray for tasks equal to your powers;
> Pray for powers equal to your tasks.
>
> Then your life shall be no miracle,
> But you shall be a miracle.
> Every day you shall wonder
> At that which is wrought in you
> By the grace of God.

Frequently my heart is touched by a prayer of George Matheson, the blind Scottish pastor who wrote "O Love That Wilt Not Let Me Go." Matheson has long been a model for me of being receptive and responsive to God in the midst of trials. He addresses his prayer to God as Spirit, who constantly desires fellowship with us. Here's the prayer. I trust it will mean as much to you as it has to me:

> O Thou Divine Spirit, that in all events of life art knocking at the
> door of my heart, help me respond to Thee. I would take the events
> of my life as good and perfect gifts from Thee; I would receive even
> the sorrows of life as disguised gifts from Thee. I would have my
> heart open at all times to receive—at morning, noon, and night; in

spring, and summer, and winter. Whether Thou comest to me in sunshine or in rain, I would take Thee into my heart joyfully. Thou art Thyself more than the sunshine, Thou art Thyself compensation for the rain; it is Thee and not Thy gifts I crave; knock, and I shall open unto Thee. Amen.

ABOVE AND BEYOND

One season of my life seemed extra-abundant in fresh, yet often painful insights for growth. During that time the Lord showed me anew the importance of praying not for a quick end to any trial but rather for Him to change me through it—"Lord, do not end this trial until You have done all You want to do in me through it."

The Lord reinforced this for me as I studied Psalm 119. Most of this psalm is a very personal prayer. And most of the requests are not "gimme" prayers but "change me" prayers; not so much "Do this for me," but "Do this in me." Even the do-for-me requests relate to the psalmist's desire to be more pleasing to God rather than to his earthly advantage. He prayed, "Do this for me (teach me, revive me, strengthen me, deliver me, be gracious to me...) that I may keep Your Word."

Paul described his agonizing trials in 2 Corinthians 4, then concluded, "Our light affliction, which is but for a moment, continues to accumulate for us a solid and eternal weight of glory far beyond any comparison, if only we fix our eyes on what is unseen, not on what we can see. The visible things are transitory; it is the invisible things that are really permanent" (4:17-18, a blend of KJV, Williams, Knox, and Phillips). So we're to look beyond the visible to the invisible, beyond the temporal to the eternal.

For the past several years, when we haven't been living or traveling in Asia we've headquartered in a delightful condominium the Lord provided for us in Colorado Springs. It has an extra-special feature, an answer to a bonus prayer request: a clear view of Pikes Peak from the living room and deck, plus a broad panorama of foothills and the Garden of the Gods. It's wonderful, but not quite perfect. Down across the foreground stretches the rear view of other condos and their garages. I was forewarned about this flaw in the vista, but I thought it wouldn't matter. For decades we've often had to look above and beyond the unattractive—sometimes even the ugly—to enjoy beauty in our surroundings. At least, I reasoned, the view of the other condos and their garages wasn't trashy.

Then it hit me: What if those condos and their garages do start to bother me? What if they mushroom in my mind and spoil my delight? I decided to use this very minor trial for good. I would let the flaws in our view remind me of what life is like in a fallen world: never perfect, never totally matching all my dreams or expectations. If I want real joy, I must always look above and beyond—above, to exult in our God of splendor and might (who is more majestic than the mountains), and beyond, to exult in the magnificent future we'll share with Him. I can also exult in my trials and stresses, for they prod me to look higher and farther, to let my thoughts dwell on the things above instead of the passing things of earth.

So if I look out at our gorgeous view and notice the garages, I choose to exult in the fact that the view is not quite perfect. I let it remind me to keep my heart fixed above and beyond. Why fix my attention on time pressures and other trials? I can let life's problems fill my whole view if I want to, or I can choose to live above them.

Why not pause before the Lord and let Him search your heart as you ask yourself, "Am I accepting my present trials as steppingstones to a deeper knowledge of God's love? Or am I resenting them, stumbling over them?" You may be facing huge trials that seem to rock life's foundations; or you may be facing what Annie Johnson Flint called "the tiny pinprick troubles that annoy, the squeaking wheels that grate upon our joy." Each trial, great or small, is God's love-gift in disguise. With each one He's knocking on your door, wanting intimacy, wanting you nearer, wanting to do something bigger and better in your life.

"Whom the Lord loves, He chastens" (Hebrews 12:6, NKJV). He uses trials to discipline every child in His family, including you. You are His eternal longings coming true, and He cares for you too much to leave you as you are. Trials are evidence that He loves you, proof of how precious you are to Him. They come to cut away the defects within you, to remove any malignant growths in your spiritual and emotional life. Trials keep you from settling for superficial, short-lived happiness, so that you'll live in His love more of the moments of more of your days.

Father, I love You. I praise and adore You for Your boundless love and wisdom. Thank You for Your perfect loving design for my life. Thank You for revealing Your love to me in Your Word, as time and again the Holy Spirit stirs my heart with the wonder of being loved by You.

Thank You that You have permitted every trial in my life as a steppingstone to knowing Your love more intimately. Thank You for every trial in my past and all that You've taught me through each one. Thank You, too, for the trials I face now and for whatever trials You have lovingly planned for my future. Give me grace to accept each one as a love-gift from You, as an invitation to closer, richer fellowship with You.

In Jesus' name…

Your personal gleanings for meditation, prayer, and action:

What Scripture or truth in this chapter do you feel the Lord is especially speaking to you about? What will you do to profit the most from this?

FIVE

So Vastly Wonderful

PERFECT LOVE—that's the way God's love is described in 1 John 4:18. And since His love is perfect, it cannot be improved. It will never become better, for it's already flawless and full and complete. God already loves us perfectly, so we never have to try to get Him to love us more!

His is the *only* perfect love. One verse in the Bible (1 John 3:1, Wuest) describes God's love as "exotic," as "foreign to the human heart." It's strikingly different, delightful, captivating. It's something extraordinary that's beyond our natural capacity to fully grasp. This means God's love is far better than any earthly love you'll ever find. Even your dearest friend or loved one cannot offer you love that is flawless, limitless, unmarred, and available around the clock every day of your life. God's love is the only perfect love.

There's a reason God's love is perfect: It is linked inseparably with everything He is. As I've thought about God through the years, I've been amazed at the wonderful blend of qualities we find in Him. I like to think of His strong side, and also of His tender side. Most people don't have a good balance of strength and tenderness, but God does. In Him they blend and mingle together perfectly.

His strong side means that He's powerful, majestic, holy, glorious, righteous, and sovereign. He's the supreme, almighty Ruler of the entire universe. And His tender side means that He is warm, welcoming, gracious, kind, good, merciful, and so understanding. As Ephesians 1:8 says in *The Living Bible,* "He has showered down upon us the riches of His grace—for how well He understands us and knows what is best for us at all times."

All these qualities—and scores more—are behind all of God's love. That's why we're not to pick and choose among His attributes, focusing on certain ones while ignoring others. All of God's attributes are intertwined, and they all undergird His personal, intimate, perfect love for you and me.

EVERYTHING ABOUT HIM

There's another good reason to ponder deeply all of God's attributes: By doing so we learn more about ourselves. For not only does God give us clear, direct statements in His Word about who we are, but also everything about *Him* reflects something about you and me as His children, His friends, His treasured possessions, His dwelling places who are one with Him in an intimate, inner union that will never end.

For example, in this book as we explore God's love, we can more fully realize, "This means that I am a person who is loved with a perfect love." And as we learn more about God's infinite power, we can be assured, "I am secure and nothing can truly harm me, for He holds me securely in His almighty hand."

As I've studied Romans 15:4-5 in several versions, I've discovered that God is the God of perseverance and encouragement. These are His own personal attitudes. He will always persevere in relating to us and working in our lives, patiently enduring our ups and downs. He will never get discouraged and give up. And He is the source of perseverance and encouragement for us. He gives us perseverance to run the race that lies before us, and He encourages us through Christ and through the Scriptures. No wonder the psalmist said, "My flesh and my heart may fail, but God is the strength of my heart and my portion forever" (Psalm 73:26, NIV). God Himself is our inner strength.

Everything about *Him* reflects something about *me.*

Because of who our Lord is we can feel loved and secure, for we *are* loved and secure. These are facts, and God wants us to know them and to see ourselves in this way. He wants us to know Him, because everything we know about Him does something to us inside: It encourages us and gives us confidence, the ability to hold our heads high—not in pride, but in the light of His love.

That's why we can find such excitement in exploring different truths about God revealed in the Bible, as we'll do briefly in this chapter. These truths enable us to appreciate His love more fully. They help us to look *at* Him in worship, praising and adoring Him. They also help us look *to* Him in dependence, putting our faith in Him. The clearer our understanding of what our God is like, the more we're able to trust Him and rest in the depths of His love.

ALTOGETHER DESIRABLE

One truth about God that deeply motivates me to explore His attributes is this: He is totally desirable. God is "the most winsome of all beings," as A. W. Tozer put it. One place in Scripture where we can especially focus on His winsomeness is Psalm 45.

Earlier I mentioned Dad Byus, the southern gentleman who radiated Christ when he came each year to speak in our college chapel services. One year he announced that we would spend an entire week on Psalm 45. *How could he?* I thought. *It's only seventeen verses.* But he was mining so many riches from this psalm that in a week's time he made it only through verse 3. He made me so thirsty for Psalm 45 that I've gone back to it and spent hours and hours in it, and I'd like us to spend time in it now.

In the background of this psalm is a young woman chosen to be the bride of an excellent, most admirable King, and she's been brought to the royal quarters for the wedding. She no doubt was the envy of every other young lady in the country, but what was she doing? She was moping because she was homesick. She was thinking about her own people and her father's house—couldn't get them out of her mind. She was not on course to be the kind of bride this wonderful King deserved.

The psalmist saw this situation and decided to remedy it. But did he reprimand her? Did he say, "You silly girl, get with it and start acting like a queen"? No, his response was not reproachful; it was positive. His goal was to make the young lady want to surrender to the King. So he spent the first nine verses describing what a wonderful person her bridegroom was.

This allegory extols a Person who infinitely surpasses any mere human, even the most magnificent earthly king. By highlighting the wonders of our heavenly King and Bridegroom, it seeks to draw us into a joyful surrender to Him. The psalmist is preparing us for his appeal in verses 10 and 11, which we might paraphrase as follows:

> Listen, O daughter, consider and take notice: forget your own whatever-it-is that hinders your response to your heavenly Bridegroom.
> So will the King greatly desire your beauty, for He is your Lord.
> Worship Him.

If we really see what our Lord Jesus is like, we can't help but be captivated. Jesus manifested this winsomeness even on earth. You remember, for example, how He came to Levi at his tax-collector's table and said, "Follow Me." Though despised by the Jews, Levi had a lucrative business and he probably walked in a rather wealthy social circle. He would be leaving a lot to follow Jesus. But there was something about this Person that drew him.

A poet put it this way:

> I heard His call,
> "Come follow."
> That was all.
> My goal grew dim.
> My soul went after Him.
> I rose and followed.

That was all.
Who would not follow
if they heard Him call?

If we get a good look at Jesus, I believe we'll be moved to want to follow Him with the total response of our being. Even if we've already made the commitment to be His very own with no strings attached, we all still need to be folded more deeply into the will of God. Over time He keeps invading new territory in our lives to make us more totally His in actual experience.

In verse 1 of Psalm 45 the psalmist tells us that his heart is bubbling up and overflowing with a beautiful theme as he addresses his words to the King. Then he says to the King, "You are the most excellent of men." What does this mean? It means that our King "excels in manly traits and beauty" *(The NIV Study Bible)*.

We know what it is to deeply admire someone. Imagine what would happen if you and I and all our friends were each to choose two people in our lives whom we most admired. Then imagine that we could take the single foremost character quality from each of them and transfer all those virtues into just one person. That person would be tremendous, don't you think? But he would still fall short of our wonderful Lord, for He is the most excellent of all human beings. Where they all leave off, He's still far above.

He is indeed the bridegroom described by the bride in Song of Solomon 5. Using the most elaborate terms she can think of, she compares Him to the costliest things imaginable, such as gold and ivory and precious stones. Then in verse 16 she concludes, "He is altogether lovely," or as the *Revised Standard Version* says, "altogether desirable."

This is the One who wants our love. He wants us to come to the Scriptures and find out how desirable He truly is. As we do this, something deep within us responds in worship, for He meets our deep, inborn need to adore someone without reservation, with no fear of finding ourselves disillusioned. We read in Jeremiah 10:7, "For among all the wise men of the nations and in all their kingdoms, there is none like Thee" (NASB). If we compared all the wise and great men of the nations from all time, they would all fall completely short of our King. He is the most excellent of all who have ever lived.

So the psalmist gives the bride in Psalm 45 a picture of what her wonderful beloved One is like, and we see that she's foolish to pout away in her room rather than going on to cultivate a love relationship with Him. Throughout the rest of the psalm he shows that with the King are favor and riches and beauty. In Him are joy and gladness, and His ivory-adorned palace is filled with fragrance and gold and music. All these desirable things about Him enhance our delight now, as we live in His presence here on earth. And they'll be ours in an infinitely fuller way when He calls us to live with Him in His heavenly palace forever. This incomparable King of ours does not plan to rob us, but to enrich us.

Our beloved King loves each one of us with a perfect love. Everything about Him tells us something about His love, and something about ourselves.

HIS PERFECT POWER AND GREATNESS

Our Lord's perfect love is undergirded by His perfect power, greatness, and exalted position.

Verses 3 and 4 in Psalm 45 are ones I especially like to use for tough times and difficult situations. These again are words that the psalmist addresses to the King:

> Gird your sword upon your side, O mighty one;
>> clothe yourself with splendor and majesty.
> In your majesty ride forth victoriously
>> in behalf of truth, humility, and righteousness;
>> let your right hand display awesome deeds. (NIV)

This is a favorite passage not only for prayer but also for worship and praise. It helps me mingle an attitude of praise with requests for victory, both for myself and others. It tells us several things about what our Beloved is like. For one thing, He's the mighty One. There is no one stronger. Don't we admire strength in a man, so that we know we can rely on him in times of need? That's what we have in our Beloved. He is the most mighty One, and we're able to lean upon Him in every way.

Another of my favorite passages on God's power is the prophet's cry to God in Jeremiah 32:17: "Ah, Lord GOD! Behold, You have made the heavens and the earth by Your great power and outstretched arm. There is nothing too hard for You" (NKJV). For One who stretched forth the heavens and the earth, nothing is too complex or troublesome or demanding. All power in heaven and on earth is His.

Ten verses later, God answers Jeremiah and affirms His might. Here He mentions something else besides His ability to create the universe. He says, "Behold, I am the Lord, *the God of all flesh.* Is there anything too hard for Me?" (NKJV). It's as if He says, "Yes, I am the God who fashioned heaven and earth, and that shows My power. But I am also the God who is deeply interested in people. I'm the God of all mankind, able to control people, able to protect you and take care of you. I'm down here involved in people's lives, with all My limitless power."

That's what we need, isn't it? Limitless power coupled with limitless love and dedicated to helping us as His people, so that no problem needs to seem too big.

As Corrie ten Boom said, "There's no panic in heaven." God never presses the panic button. It's all easy for Him. And prayer releases His power. "Prayer is the slender nerve that moves that mighty hand of God." As we turn our eyes to Him in prayer and present our requests, we discover that He is indeed unlimited in His power. We realize, as did the blind and prolific hymnwriter Annie Johnson Flint, that

> His love has no limits, His grace has no measure,
> His power no boundaries known unto men.

For out of His infinite riches in Jesus
He giveth, and giveth, and giveth again.

Psalm 45:3 also speaks of our mighty King's "glory" and "majesty." Today we're not as accustomed to royal majesty as people were in King David and Solomon's day. What great kings they were, and how splendid the majesty of their kingdoms! Yet today there's still something captivating about royalty, for the human heart longs for a majestic King to follow. And we have One! He is clothed with majesty; He is high and lifted up; He is glorious.

LAYING HOLD OF HIS GREATNESS

The psalmist implores this awesome King, "Gird your sword upon your side, O mighty one" (45:3, NIV). What kind of sword is this? From the New Testament we know that it's the very Word of His mouth, sharper than a two-edged sword. Before it no enemy can stand.

Next the psalmist appeals to the King with these words: "In your majesty ride forth victoriously in behalf of truth and humility and righteousness" (45:4, NIV). I like to use this in many situations that I—and others—face. I pray, "Lord, in this situation, in this life, ride forth victoriously. Defeat the enemy's evil purposes, and bring about Your good, acceptable, and perfect will."

Often I need Him to ride forth victoriously in my life because of an inner enemy that needs defeating—a fleshly attitude or desire—and He is more mighty than that inner enemy. Or I need Him to ride forth victoriously into circumstances with which I simply cannot cope or against some scheme or attack of Satan.

Notice that the psalmist asks the king to "ride forth victoriously for the cause of truth and humility and righteousness." We can't call upon Him to ride forth for the sake of our little preferences and petty hostilities. We can't ask Him to slap the other person, so to speak, for something he did that we personally don't appreciate, but that doesn't really involve the cause of truth or defending what is right.

But there are many times when we do need defense, and rightly. We need protection against the storms and battles of life, and against our spiritual enemy. We face temptations and struggles that we're not able to fight on our own. And God never intended for us to fight them on our own; He meant us to call upon our most mighty One and ask Him to ride forth victoriously to defeat what's wrong and defend what's right. So we ask Him, in His majesty, to do just that.

And we know that whenever the Lord rides forth, it's always victoriously. He has never yet been defeated, and never will be. He is Victor. The very name Jesus means "Jehovah Victor, Savior Victor." He is Victor over every enemy.

I once heard Corrie ten Boom say, "Jesus was Victor, Jesus is Victor, Jesus will be Victor—so don't wrestle, just *nestle*."

Some years ago I came across some lines from a poem by Sidney Lanier called "The Marshes of Glynn." In this poem Lanier portrays a marsh bordered by a forest of live oaks on one side, the sea on another, and the afternoon sky above. At first he stays in the gloomy woods, which he describes as a place "for the passionate pleasure of prayer for a soul that grieves." But at the end of the day, when a yellow beam slanting out from the setting sun is "like a lane into heaven," he's drawn out into the vast open space of the sandy marsh stretching along the seashore. "Somehow my soul seems suddenly free," he says, as the marsh in its simplicity and openness reminds him of the presence of God.

Then come these lines in the heart of the poem:

> As the marsh-hen secretly builds on the watery sod,
> Behold I will build me a nest on the greatness of God;
> I will fly in the greatness of God as the marsh-hen flies
> In the freedom that fills all the space 'twixt the marsh and the skies;
> By so many roots as the marsh grass sends in the sod
> I will heartily lay me ahold on the greatness of God.

In God's perfect love, we can lay hold of His greatness and find that it gives us security, a place to build our inner nest, a settling-down place. At the same time it also gives us freedom in which we can fly. But we've got to know anew how great He is if we want to have both the freedom and the security that we need in life.

The psalmist next requests the King to "let your right hand display awesome deeds" (NIV), or as the *New Living Translation* puts it, "Go forth to perform awe-inspiring deeds!" We're to leave our personal lives in the hands of this mighty One who cannot be defeated. Then we'll stand in awe at the wonderful things God does for us.

The psalmist continues his praise of the King:

> Your arrows are sharp,
>> piercing your enemies' hearts.
> The nations fall before you,
>> lying beneath your feet. (45:5, NLT)

Every enemy must fall before Him. In Psalm 66:3 we find these instructions for praise: "Say to God, 'How awesome are Your deeds! So great is Your power that Your enemies cringe before You'" (NIV). Picture that in your mind: every enemy cringing before His power.

This is the kind of King we can call upon. In His love He will always answer us out of the constancy of His greatness, a constancy on which we can utterly depend. Years ago I wrote this meditation while studying Isaiah 40, a soaring and breathtaking chapter on God's greatness:

Constancy

> All flesh is as grass
>> and all its constancy as the flower of the field.
> Generation after generation
>> springs up fresh and fragrant

then fades and withers
    as the breath of the Lord blows upon it.
Each flies away
    like a wind that passes
    and does not return.

But the Word of our God stands
    constant
    comforting
    as generations appear and vanish,
the Word of the living God,
the everlasting Creator,
    incomparably great,
    supreme in power,
    yet caring,
    and visiting His people
    as their mighty King and tender Shepherd.

He comforts and conquers,
He rules and rewards,
He gathers and carries and gently leads.
He measures the immeasurable
    and knows the unknowable
    and sees the minute vastness of our need
    as we wither and fade,
    as we grow weary and utterly fall.
He holds the world in the palm of His hand
    and keeps the galaxies in their courses
    and calls the stars by name
    and infuses strength into those who wait on Him.

An eternity is in His Word,
a finality in His forgiveness,
a comforting constancy in His plans.
As He has promised, so shall it be,
as He has purposed so shall it stand;
the plans of His heart endure to all generations.

Surely all flesh is grass that withers,
its loveliness a fading satisfaction,
its strength a failing support.
But the Word of our God stands forever.

OUR CHAMPION

All of these passages have taught me a great lesson. They're talking about God being our Champion.

I'm reminded of the story of El Cid from ancient Spain, a story that's half myth and half history. El Cid, a wonderful and admirable character, was the king's champion. If someone challenged the king, El Cid would go out and fight the battle for him. The king, rather shiftless and unreliable, didn't deserve to have this splendid man fighting on his behalf. But El Cid faithfully and loyally championed the king's cause, and in the end the king's character began to change because of El Cid's life.

As Deuteronomy 33:26-29 shows, our God is a God of majestic splendor—exalted and glorious—who comes rushing across the heavens to protect us, help us, and thrust out the enemy. "The eternal God is your refuge, and His everlasting arms are under you.... He...is your place of safety, and His arms will hold you up forever. He is your protecting shield and your triumphant sword!" (NLT, NCV). What glory!

Like Psalm 45, another psalm I've loved to soak in now and then is Psalm

68. Here David speaks of the Lord riding through the deserts and through the very skies as if on a huge eagle or on a horse with wings. And why does He ride like this, in awesome power? He's speeding on His way to help us.

Of course the Lord is always with us, daily bearing the burden of our lives. And as Psalm 46:1 says, He's an ever-present help in trouble, immediately available in tight places. But I also find it a blessing to think of Him in His high position of supreme authority, far above heaven and earth, far above all enemy powers. And then I pray that He, my mighty Champion, will "ride forth" from His vantage point, from His sure-to-win position, and work mightily.

Time after time, Psalm 68:4 has helped me pray with overtones of confidence and praise for this One who rides forth on our behalf:

> Sing to God, sing praises to His name,
>> cast up a highway for Him who rides through the deserts,
>> whose name is the Lord, and exult before Him. (NASB, early editions)

What a God we worship, so worthy of our praise, so heart-expanding as we exult before Him! The context in Psalm 68 shows Him involved in the deserts of human experience, meeting the needs of the fatherless, the widows, the lonely, the prisoners, the parched, the poor. It shows Him meeting needs abundantly: "When Thou didst march through the wilderness... Thou didst shed abroad a plentiful rain, O God" (68:7-9, NASB). The God we praise is deeply concerned about us and has committed Himself to care for us as we trust Him.

This psalm connects our praise with casting up a highway for our loving, mighty God who rides through deserts. A similar connection is found in Psalm 50:23—

> He who sacrifices thank offerings honors Me,
>> and he prepares the way
>> so that I may show him the salvation of God. (NIV)

Through praise and thanksgiving we can help provide a highway that lets Him speed along unhindered to rescue and provide.

Don't you like the praiseful, trustful attitude of these psalmists? With them we can say, "Lord, You are a wonderful, majestic, powerful, gracious, caring God. We can count on You to win victories and to bless abundantly."

I've often used Psalm 68 to lift my heart in praise and prayer, weaving in truths from other verses such as Psalms 63:1 and 97:3-5, Isaiah 57:15, and Matthew 5:3, where Kenneth Wuest translates "poor" in spirit as "destitute and helpless." I find that the Lord prepares my heart to pray with confidence when I begin with praise like this:

"Lord, I worship You as God Most High, the great King over all the earth. You are the high and exalted One whose name is Holy, who inhabits eternity—who dwells far above and beyond us, unlimited by time and space!

"I praise You as the One who rides—who soars—upon the highest heavens, who speeds through the skies in Your majesty to help us. You sweep down to the earth and ride through the deserts of our human experience, coming to the aid of the fatherless, the widows, the lonely, the prisoners, the poor and the needy. You ride forth to help us when we recognize how destitute and helpless we are in ourselves to obey You, when we're burdened and need deliverance, when we dwell in a parched and thirsty land where there is no water.

"And as You march through the wilderness, the earth quakes and the skies shake at Your presence, O God! And the heavens pour down rain—a plentiful rain that refreshes us, revives us, and meets our needs.

"And our enemies flee before You. As smoke is blown away by the wind, You blow them away, scattering them, making them flee. At Your Presence, mountains of satanic opposition melt like wax before a fire.

"You are the Most Mighty One, an awesome Warrior, splendid, majestic, triumphant—and loving! You are for us a God of victories! I exult before You and rejoice with gladness. And I pray that today You will ride forth and act on behalf of…."

Looking Often at His Greatness

Along with Jeremiah 10:7 (quoted earlier), I also love to use verse 6 to worship God for His greatness:

> There is none like You, O Lord.
> You are great,
>   and Your name is great in might.
> Who would not fear You,
>   O King of the nations?
> For this is Your rightful due.
> For among all the wise men of the nations
>   and in all their kingdoms,
>   there is none like You. (NKJV)

When it comes to greatness and power, as in everything else, "There is none like You"—and we need to look at the Lord often in His infinite, awe-inspiring greatness.

This includes taking a look at the Lord Jesus in His exalted position. This is so beautifully expressed in the Phillips version of Ephesians 1:20-22, where Paul was thrilled by the tremendous power of God available to us as believers:

> That power is the same divine energy which was demonstrated in Christ when he raised him from the dead and gave him the place of highest honour in Heaven—a place that is infinitely superior to any conceivable command, authority, power or control, and which carries with it a name far beyond any name that could ever be used in this world or the world to come. God has placed everything under the power of Christ.

That's what our Lord Jesus is like. And as we realize how great and exalted He is, it does something to stabilize us inside, because we're linked with Him in a union that can never be broken.

Another passage I've often used in worship is 1 Chronicles 29:11-12, where David pours out a beautiful description of God. If you don't already know it by heart, you'll profit greatly by memorizing these verses, for not many of us can match David in the power and magnificence of his words:

> Yours, O Lord, is the greatness,
> > the power and the glory,
> > the victory and the majesty;
> For all that is in the heaven
> > and in the earth is Yours;
> Yours is the kingdom, O Lord,
> > and You are exalted as head over all.
> Both riches and honor come from You,
> > and You reign over all.
> In Your hand is power and might;
> > in Your hand it is to make great,
> > and to give strength to all. (NKJV)

God most mighty, exalted as head over all, is the One who loves us. And we are now free to love Him in return. Yet how easily we forget what a privilege it is to adore and worship God. How slow we sometimes are to realize that as we worship, we offer sacrifices of praise and thanksgiving that rejoice His heart. We give Him something unique, something no one else in the universe can give: our own personal love and adoration. This deepens the intimacy He longs for. It helps complete His joy in being our Father, our Beloved, our Friend, our Brother.

We worship and offer praise in order to honor God and give Him joy. We worship to give—yet He turns around and gives us far more in return. His gifts include a richer experience of Himself, inner refreshment and transformation, and practical blessings as well.

Because praise increases our faith as we pray, it opens the way for God to bring a multitude of benefits our way. This in turn calls forth fresh praise. And praise helps us fulfill the chief purpose to which God has called us: to glorify God and enjoy Him forever.

My wonderful and glorious King, I bow in worship before You, rejoicing at the wonderful blend of attributes I find in You. How strong You are, yet how tender!

And how I rejoice and rest in the gratifying truth that everything about You reflects something about me. How privileged I am to be Yours!

I praise You for Your perfect love—love that is boundless, unchanging, and faithful, love that will endure forever. Love of every love the best! Thank You that Your love perfectly dovetails with all my needs and enriches me in countless ways every hour of every day. What a joy to know that I am someone who is loved with a perfect love!

And Lord, You are altogether desirable —in every way perfect and beautiful. I praise You for revealing Yourself in Your Word, so that I can behold Your beauty, delight in it, and let it fill my soul. Teach me to do this more and more.

I worship You as the most mighty One; nothing is too difficult for You. I worship You as the Victor, before whom every enemy must fall. And I praise You for the limitless power You bring to bear on my problems and difficult situations. You are truly my Champion, my ever-present Help in trouble. Ride forth victoriously, O Lord, in all that I face today, to defeat the enemy's evil purposes and to bring about Your good, pleasing, and perfect will. Help me more and more to heartily lay hold of Your greatness.

In Jesus' name…

Your personal gleanings for meditation, prayer, and action:

What Scripture or truth in this chapter do you feel the Lord is especially speaking to you about? What will you do to profit the most from this?

SIX

So Perfectly My King

WE HAVE SOMEONE to champion our cause. That Someone is our God of love—perfect love that is inseparably linked with His perfect power and greatness. He is the King of all the earth, the God who acts in behalf of the one who waits for Him; His eyes search the whole earth in order to strongly support those whose hearts are fully committed to Him (Isaiah 64:4, 2 Chronicles 16:9). This God of mighty love is eager to champion our cause.

How many times I have needed a Champion. Let me give you an example. While Dean was alive, he and Gene always did the vacation planning for their families—the whole thing. Gene continued to do this for the children and me after Dean's death, until he and Mary returned to Asia.

Then we moved to Colorado and were on our own. Occasionally the children and I took short getaway trips. That was fun, but I felt it would be nice sometimes to have a personal retreat. Yet I didn't really have the money for such a vacation, nor did I like the process of planning for it.

On one occasion a much-appreciated Navigator friend told me he was planning a vacation with his wife. "I feel she really needs to get away," he said; then he asked if their children could spend part of that vacation time with us. I counted that a privilege, but the enemy used it too, implanting this thought in my mind: "You don't have anyone who thinks *you* need a vacation. And you haven't had one in a long time."

Every now and then this would bother me. One day as I thought about having no one to champion my cause and plan a vacation for me, I came across Psalm 4:1 in the Moffatt translation: "O God, my champion, answer my appeal. When I was hemmed in, Thou hast freed me often. Be gracious to me now and hear my prayer."

"That's just what I need, Lord," I told Him. "I need You as my Champion."

Then I recalled Isaiah 41:14, again in the Moffatt version: "Fear not, puny Jacob, petty Israel; I will help you. Your champion is the Majestic One of Israel." *That's me,* I thought—*puny and petty.* Puny in not being able to look out for myself, and petty because so often I can't see beyond my own interests. So I prayed something like this: "Lord, I qualify. And how much I need Your help as my champion. I'm counting on You take care of a vacation for me, whenever You want me to have one. I commit my vacation problem to You."

I had to wait awhile—about another year, as I recall. Then a dear friend invited me to fly at her expense to her home in Tyler, Texas, to relax, spend time with friends, and attend some meetings they were having with a thought-provoking speaker. Not only did I get an expense-free vacation, but they also took me shopping and bought me a whole new winter wardrobe (it was November). I'd never had such beautiful clothes.

A friend from Dallas drove to see me while I was there, and as she left she pressed something into my hand, saying, "The Lord told me to give this to you." When I looked later, there was a two-hundred-dollar check—worth far more in 1963 than today.

At the airport, while I was waiting to board a flight for my return to Colorado, my friend's father also pressed something into my hand. After getting on the plane I looked at it: a one-hundred-dollar check.

Now, how often have you heard of someone going on a paid-for vacation and coming home with a free new wardrobe plus all that money?

The next spring my friend again flew me down to Texas for ministry meetings with women in her Bible studies. This time she took me out and bought me a whole new spring wardrobe.

So I concluded that the Lord is quite good at being my Champion. He can ride forth victoriously and undertake for each of His loved ones far better than we can for ourselves. And He does this if we ask Him to and if we allow Him to be Lord in our lives and circumstances.

The choice is ours. We can try to guard and protect ourselves, relying on our own puny defenses. Or we can give up our "rights" and instead have this wonderful King looking out for us, this Mighty One who always has our best interests at heart.

The fact is, He Himself has promised to look out for our rights. If it's something truly right, He has promised to take care of it. Psalm 37 teaches us to trust in the Lord without getting upset and to commit our way to the Lord, knowing that He will indeed act on our behalf. "He will bring forth your vindication as the light," we read in verse 6, "and your right as the noonday."

Whether on this earth (today, tomorrow, or years from now) or in eternity, God in His time will right every wrong—if we let Him, and give up looking after our own rights. As we willingly open our hands and let go of those rights, we drop them into the hands of our Mighty One, the Champion who rides forth victoriously for the cause of truth and to defend the right.

His Perfect Sovereignty

In Psalm 45:6 the inspired writer continues his praise for the King: "Your throne, O God, is forever and ever" (NKJV). Our Beloved will never be dethroned. He will always be ruling over all—He will always be sovereign. And He's not just a king; He's the King of kings! So we need never fear.

That's why even now we can actively enjoy the fact that we're on the winning side, though it may not look like it in our world today or in our personal situation. Our King is ruling behind the scenes, never losing a battle for each of His own, as we count on Him in simple faith. And soon the day will come when His rule and His sovereignty will be obvious. Then everyone will see and recognize that He rules forever.

Verse 6 continues, "The scepter of Thy kingdom is a right scepter" (KJV). It is a "scepter of justice" (NIV). The golden scepter with which He rules is right and just, so we can depend on Him never to make a mistake with our lives. We can count on His decrees and decisions to be always wise and always best.

The psalm continues, "You love righteousness and hate wickedness" (45:7, NIV). Our King is righteous through and through, and His love for us is altogether a righteous love. We never need to suspect any ulterior motives in His relating to us. He will never wrong us; He'll never do anything we cannot admire. So we can give ourselves totally to loving Him and depending on Him. With all the corruption in the world in places high and low, we find few people we can depend on unreservedly. But God is totally dependable. There will never be any corruption in His government. What a sense of peace this gives! He is so perfectly the kind of Ruler we need.

THE BLESSED CONTROLLER OF ALL THINGS

A couple of years ago I was in the garage unpacking one of the boxes we had sent from Singapore as we returned to the U.S. (It was another small, quick stab at a huge job that had begged for months to be done.) In one box I came across something a friend had made for us years earlier: a beautiful embroidery of a phrase taken from 1 Timothy 6:15 in the Phillips translation: "God is the Blessed Controller of all things." I hung it just inside our bedroom door where I would see it often. Since then I've meditated on this verse time after time, situation after situation, by day and by night. I say to Him, "You are *blessed*—warm and caring, generous, gracious. And You are *in control.* You are God Most High, and You work all things into a pattern for good for all who love You."

What a peace producer!

Some fifteen years ago, Warren saw this same quotation displayed in a home in India, and it had a similar impact on him. He wrote at the time,

This truth…has dominated my thinking and praying ever since I saw it, greatly strengthening my faith and praise. It has given me confidence and thankfulness at the way God orders events, influences, and chance contacts. It has also helped my attitudes and reactions toward those who, intentionally or not, inconvenience me, resist me, or make demands that seem unreasonable. This is a special cause for rejoicing because being gracious and patient is often hard for me, especially with the pressures of traveling in other cultures. What a rich encouragement the entire passage has become, reminding me that God is always in control, always seeking to bless us through what He sends and permits.

"God is the blessed controller of all things, the King over all kings, and the Master of all masters, the only source of immortality, the One who lives in unapproachable light…. To Him be acknowledged all honor and power forever, Amen!"

It's always God who's at the controls. Ephesians 1:11 says that He works all things after the counsel of His own will—*all things.* That circumstance in your life, which is causing you pain or dismay or confusion or worse, is not accidental. As someone has said, "With God nothing is accidental, nothing is incidental, and no experience is wasted." God is working for a purpose in allowing these things. He is looking out for us, and He won't let anything happen to us that He can't work together for our good, just as He has promised.

All this is far more than something to know; it's something to praise Him for. I'm reminded of what my godly friend Helen Morken used to say about the word *hallelujah:* "Use this word. When you are standing at the stove or ironing board, say 'Hallelujah, for the Lord God omnipotent reigneth.'"

Regarding God's sovereignty I especially like Isaiah 46:9-10, where He says He declares the end from the beginning, and from ancient times the things that are not yet done. From the very beginning of all things God knew what would happen all the way through to the end. Nothing can take Him by surprise. He never faces the temptation to panic or be anxious because of something He just hadn't considered or anticipated.

In verse 10 the Lord adds these words, "My purpose will stand, and I will do all that I please" (NIV). He has a beautiful purpose and plan for the broad picture of the centuries, and He will continue working it out until the day comes when He returns to rule visibly over all mankind. For now that plan is focused on calling out a people who will love and worship Him as He prepares them for that day.

I also like Daniel 4:34-35. This passage records words spoken by the greatest king on earth at that time, Nebuchadnezzar of Babylon. Before this time Nebuchadnezzar had seen in various ways how great God is and had verbally acknowledged Him. But in his pride he had refused to bow before God in his personal life. Then just as Daniel had prophesied, the king lost his sanity and for seven years became like a beast of the field. After God restored his reason, Nebuchadnezzar extolled and honored the God of heaven:

> His dominion is an everlasting dominion,
> and His kingdom endures from generation to generation.
> And all the inhabitants of the earth
> are accounted as nothing,
> but He does according to His will
> in the host of heaven
> and among the inhabitants of earth;
> and no one can ward off His hand
> or say to Him, 'What hast Thou done?' (NASB)

No one can hold back God's hand and say to Him, "Just a minute, God—what do You think You're doing?" We just don't have that privilege. Nor does the greatest man on earth. God is sovereign, and His purposes are being accomplished.

This does not mean that everything that happens in the world meets with God's approval. God has sovereignly given humans free will, and they often exercise their free will to bring about many ugly things in this fallen world.

But if we belong to God we are protected by His sovereignty. He can stop anything from happening to us if He knows it won't be for our ultimate good, as well as the good of others. He lets many things happen to us that cause disappointment or distress; and our natural response is, "I wish He hadn't let that happen." But He assures us in Romans 8:28-29 that He works all things together for something more beautiful in our lives: to make us more like Jesus.

I also love David's words about God's sovereignty in Psalm 31:14-15, which was such a help to me when Dean had cancer. It's the passage that includes the familiar statement, "My times are in Your hand" (NKJV). In *Psalms for Today* the passage reads, "But I have complete confidence in You, Lord; I have said, 'You are my God.' My destiny is under Your control."

Knowing that our destiny is under God's control cannot help but do something for our inner stability.

One of the most beautiful stories in Scripture about the sovereignty of God is the story of Joseph. I would dare say that in the circle of people you're around most often, you occasionally hurt one another. It happens because we're human. Sometimes we don't understand, or we don't hear or observe accurately. Often we do the best we know how from a heart that wants to be helpful, a heart that does care. But we make mistakes. So on many of the occasions when we hurt one another, it's not intentional.

But Joseph's case was different. You know the story, which begins in Genesis 37. First, bitter malice on the part of his brothers thrust Joseph into years of slavery in Egypt. Then, because the Lord was with him, he finally worked his way up to a high position in his master's household. Later he became the victim of deceit by his master's wife. This time it meant years in prison.

But at the right time God gave Joseph the second highest position in the greatest nation on earth, a position that allowed him to save his father and brothers and their families—and many others—from starvation.

Through his heartbreaking past, Joseph had learned something that his brothers hadn't. "You intended to harm me," he told them in Genesis 50:20. "But *God intended it for good* to accomplish what is now being done, the saving of many lives" (NIV).

When Dean and I lived in Hong Kong, we heard a godly Bible teacher from Taiwan tell how God took the blackest fragment, the blackest piece in the lives of Joseph's brothers—selling their brother into slavery—and made it central in a beautiful picture of salvation for them and countless others. That's also what God did at Calvary, the speaker reminded us. God took the worst, most hateful, most despicable thing man had ever done—killing the Son of God—and made it central in a beautiful picture of salvation for all mankind. Because of Calvary, we can claim that God will somehow work even our failures into desirable end results.

To illustrate this point, the speaker related what a Chinese jade carver does when he finds a piece of jade that is large and extremely valuable but has a major flaw. He doesn't try to disguise and hide the flaw. Instead he carefully studies it, then makes it central in a perfect design. This is what God does for us. We serve a God who's able to bring beauty from ashes. As we yield to His loving sovereignty, He works even our failures and mistakes, our weaknesses and our inadequacies—as well as the mistakes or malice of other people—into something beautiful, for His glory and our good.

He did this for Paul when he was under house arrest in Rome in about A.D. 60. He wrote joyfully, "What has happened to me has really served to advance the gospel" (Philippians 1:12, NIV). Such a wonderful thing to know!

THE CIRCLE OF HIS SOVEREIGNTY

In a practical understanding of God's sovereignty, I've been especially blessed by Romans 11:36, "For from Him and through Him and to Him are all things. To Him be the glory forever. Amen" (NASB).

Everything in all creation (including all that we are, all that we have, all that we need) comes from Him, is held together by the word of His power, and rises back to Him to His glory. All has been assigned one integrating and exalted purpose: His glory and pleasure.

I like to imagine a huge circle, starting with God, coming down to creation, and returning to Him—all things coming from Him, all things existing through Him, all things rising back to Him for the glory of His name. Only fallen beings refuse the upswing of the circle, veering off in self-centered downward spirals.

This challenges me to recognize more consciously and consistently that all things are from Him and through Him, with me simply a receiver. I then consent to the upswing of the circle by lifting my heart in grateful worship and a simple "I'm Yours" response.

What a joy—and what good sense—to respond this way, cooperating with the principles by which life runs well. Anything less (as E. Stanley Jones wrote) is singing off-key or marching out of step with the rhythm of all creation.

What praise our God deserves! We are here in this setting of earth and cosmos by His creative genius, endowed with incredible resources. We are sustained by His Word and power. And our high privilege is to enjoy Him as the focal point of our aspirations and adoration. "To Him be the glory forever, Amen."

Our Lord Jesus perfectly enacted this Romans 11:36 circle. He came down to earth to fully experience the human scene. At every moment He lifted His heart to the Father in dependence, adoration, and obedience. He descended even to the depths of our degradation and death, then rose and ascended to the Father.

Now we have a resource that did not exist before: the indwelling life of God-as-man who perfectly depended on and glorified the Father. He is in me, life of my life, to enable me to do the same. Only through Him can I consent to the full circle, with its humble receiving from God and its outflow of love back to God and out to people.

What a relief it is to rely on Him! It's clear to me that my life needs much transforming so that my responses will bring God greater joy. But many times I'm not clear just what changes are needed. For example, am I too intense in some things, yet in others do I hold back from giving myself to meet needs? When am I preserving my life for what I prefer? Perhaps God does not offer me a tidy, generalized answer. Maybe instead His answer is an indwelling Person to live out through me what is pleasing to Him.

I find it a joy to simply pray, "Lord, You are always zealous to do the Father's will, but never over-intense. You are never anxious, never threatened, never self-preserving. You are always full of trust, always relaxed in spirit, yet given to humble and diligent service. Thank You that You are in me! You alone perfectly please the Father, and You are my life. Through You, this hour, my gratefulness and service can rise as a fragrant aroma to the Father."

HIS PERFECT JOY

We've seen that God is able to demonstrate His love through meeting our needs because of His perfect power and greatness and sovereignty. His perfect love is backed by all that He is as the strongest Strong One, exalted far above all other powers.

God's perfect love is also linked with His perfect joy. In Psalm 45:7, the psalmist says to the King,

> You love what is right and hate what is wrong.
> Therefore, God, your God, has anointed you,
> pouring out the oil of joy on you more than on anyone else. (NLT)

In the *King James Version,* this oil is "the oil of gladness." There is more joy and gladness with Him than with anyone else.

Isn't it refreshing to be in the company of a glad person? A glad person can walk into a room and brighten up the whole atmosphere. And isn't it discouraging to be in the company of someone whose spirit is always low, someone who's always griping and complaining and trapped in a mindset of gloom?

But this One whom we love is anointed above all others with a contagious joy and gladness in His countenance. He's not long-faced, moody, or glum, and He doesn't want us to be that way either.

We can pray with David, "In Your presence is fullness of joy; at Your right hand there are pleasures forevermore" (Psalm 16:11, NKJV). We can rejoice as David did that God's people can feast on the abundance of His house and drink from the river of His delights (Psalm 36:8). That sounds like a rather happy situation, doesn't it? Our God is full of joy, and His love is full of joy—joy that spills over into our hearts as we, too, love what is right and hate what is wrong.

His Perfect Wisdom

God's perfect love is guided by His perfect wisdom. Scientists will never finish assigning numbers to all the stars, but He who created all the billions of blazing suns also calls them all by name and keeps them all running in perfect order. Certainly He's also wise enough to make plans for my life, too wise to ever make a mistake.

Romans 11:33 is one of the most beautiful verses on God's wisdom. J. B. Phillips translated it like this: "Frankly, I stand amazed at the unfathomable complexity of God's wisdom and God's knowledge. How could man ever understand His reasons for action, or explain His methods of working?"

So we can say, "All right, Lord, You are wiser than I am. My mind is like a tiny cup of water, while Yours is like a vast ocean. I can't expect my limited little mind to contain all Your reasons and understand all that You do. But You are all-loving as well as all-wise, so I'll just rest in You."

HIS PERFECT GOODNESS

God's perfect love is interwoven with His perfect goodness. These two attributes, along with all the others, are inseparable. God is good; this is one of the most beautiful truths about Him.

Often we think of goodness in contrast to being bad. When we say a child is good, it's likely that we primarily mean he isn't being bad. But when the Bible speaks of God's goodness, it refers more to His good motives, His kind intentions, His habit of pouring good and beneficial things into our lives.

James 1:17 says, "Every good and perfect gift is from above, coming down from the Father of the heavenly lights, who does not change like shifting shadows" (NIV). He is invariably good. He can be or do nothing but good.

Often we cannot understand the Lord's process for bringing about good results. The things He does do not always seem good. He says in Isaiah 45:7, "I bring prosperity and create disaster; I, the Lord, do these things" (NIV). But even when He sends or allows severe trials, it is always for good purposes. Such trials are "severe mercies," to use C. S. Lewis's expression.

Psalm 84:11 was one of the first passages I learned about God's unshadowed goodness. "For the Lord God is a sun and shield," the verse begins. The sun brings warmth and light to us, and a shield brings shade and protection. God, in His perfect goodness and love, is both.

The verse continues, "The Lord will give grace and glory; no good thing will He withhold from those who walk uprightly" (NKJV). To those who are walking in a right relationship to Him, God keeps back nothing that is good. As I mentioned before, I learned this verse early in my Christian life. I had been afraid to let the Lord freely control my life, thinking I'd miss out on what I wanted in life. I found out of course that the opposite was true. After I gave my life to Him, God began filling it with good things.

No wonder God's people in Bible times so often extolled Him for His love and goodness, using words similar to Psalm 106:1: "Give thanks to the Lord, for He is good; His love endures forever" (NIV).

HIS PERFECT FAITHFULNESS

God's perfect love is inseparable from His perfect faithfulness. Again and again the psalmists link God's love with His faithfulness (or, as some versions say, His truth). For example, Psalm 36:5 says, "Your love, O Lord, reaches to the heavens, Your faithfulness to the skies" (NIV). The Lord's faithfulness exceeds by far any human faithfulness.

The Lord is always faithful and true—true to His Word, true to His character, true to each of His loved ones. He is never unfaithful, never untrue. He is faithful to bless us and faithful to chasten us: "In faithfulness You have afflicted me" (Psalm 119:75); "Before I was afflicted I went astray, but now I obey Your Word" (119:67).

God is faithful to sanctify us completely, keeping our spirit, soul, and body sound and blameless until Christ returns (1 Thessalonians 5:23-24). He is faithful to forgive us as soon as we confess our sins (1 John 1:9). His forgiveness is always glad and instant, never grudging or delayed. He never says, "Well, we'll wait and see how much better you do." He is faithful to fulfill all His promises: Not one single word of all His good promises has ever failed (1 Kings 8:56). And He promises to love us forever. Nothing will ever separate us from His love (Romans 8:37-39).

One of my favorite Scriptures on the Lord's faithfulness is Lamentations 3:21-24. Jeremiah had been going through prolonged and traumatic trials; finally all his hopes had been dashed. After recounting his bitter afflictions, he says in verse 21, "This I recall to my mind, and therefore I have hope." What did he remember that gave him hope in a hopeless situation? He tells us in verses 22-24: "The steadfast love of the Lord never ceases, His mercies never come to an end; they are new every morning; great is Thy faithfulness. The Lord is my portion therefore I will hope in Him" (RSV).

The writer of Psalm 42 also turned his mind to God and His constant love. The psalmist was in exile—mourning, oppressed, weeping day and night. His heart was disquieted, discouraged, downcast. His solution? See verse 6:

"O my God, my soul is cast down within me. Therefore I will remember You." And what did he remember? The Lord's constant and faithful love: "The Lord will command His lovingkindness in the daytime, and in the night His song shall be with me" (NKJV).

I have found, that no matter how discouraging or hopeless or pressing my situation may be, there's something about God that can encourage me, give me hope, and bring me through triumphantly—when I remember Him, calling to mind what He is like. When I turn my mind and heart to Him, focusing on who He is according to His Word, He is faithful to restore my soul. He repairs and heals my inner person. He refreshes me as water refreshes a dry, wilted fuchsia plant.

Often through the years, beginning in the days when Dean was suffering from cancer, the Lord has used the following lyrics by Katharina von Schlegel to quiet and reassure my soul:

> Be still, my soul: the Lord is on thy side;
> Bear patiently the cross of grief or pain;
> Leave to Thy God to order and provide;
> In every change He faithful will remain.
> Be still, my soul: thy best, thy heavenly Friend
> Through thorny ways leads to a joyful end.

HIS LOVINGKINDNESS

To close this brief two-chapter study of our vastly wonderful God, look with me at a delightful word. It is one of the best terms in Scripture for helping us understand God's perfect love.

One year I did a study, largely in the Psalms, on the Lord's *lovingkindness*. The *New American Standard Bible* uses this expression for an amazingly rich Old Testament word. Other translations render this word as "mercies," "steadfast love," "covenant love," "unfailing love," "kindness," or simply "love." It's a tender word, showing the compassionate side of the Lord as He is actively involved with us, bestowing on us a "multitude of lovingkindnesses." It is also a strong word, for embedded in its meaning is durability. The most-used sentence of praise in the Bible reinforces this: "His lovingkindness endures forever."

I discovered that God's lovingkindness is good, abundant, marvelous, precious, and better than life. It extends to the heavens, and the earth is full of it. It is from everlasting, and it will be built up forever. It is mine for all the days of my life and for all eternity. The Lord shows it to those who trust Him, who fear Him, who call upon Him. It follows us, surrounds us, and crowns us. By it we enter His house, by it we expect answers to prayer, and through it we will stand unshaken, for it will hold us up when our feet slip. It satisfies us and is the one unfailing basis for rejoicing and being glad all our days. It is infused into all God is and into all He does (as you can see in Psalm 136).

The Lord wants me to pray about experiencing His lovingkindness, to rejoice in it, and to give thanks for it. He wants me to trust His lovingkindness and to hope in it, expecting Him to be loving and kind. He wants me to speak of it, to declare it to others.

All these truths (except one, taken from Isaiah 63:7) brighten up the pages of the Psalms, along with many more insights into His amazing lovingkindness. They have helped me so much.

Psalm 103:4 speaks of the Lord's "lovingkindness and tender mercies." This takes me back to Luke 1:78, which reminds us of the tender mercy of our God by which the Sunrise from on high has visited us. Indeed, the Light from heaven, our Lord Jesus Christ who lived and died for us, was the supreme demonstration of His lovingkindness!

Psalm 32:10 says, "He who trusts in the Lord, lovingkindness shall surround him" (NASB). Just think of His tender love encircling each of us, blessing and protecting us on all sides! This reminds me of a song that says, "I'm overshadowed by His mighty love"—but it is not merely above me but also all around me like fresh air and warm sunshine.

Then in Psalm 52:1 we read, "The lovingkindness of God endures all day long" (NASB). It never lessens or wears thin as the day wears on, as our human love and kindness often do! All day, every day, it flows from His heart and envelops us, as He constantly cares for us.

No wonder the psalmist said in 59:16, "I shall joyfully sing of Thy lovingkindness in the morning" (NASB). This joyful singing in the morning can result from praying as the psalmist did in 143:8, "Cause me hear Your lovingkindness in the morning, for in You do I trust" (NKJV). What a good way to start the day: listening to His lovingkindness and singing about it! This brings pleasure to God. "His joy is in those who reverence Him, those who expect Him to be loving and kind" (Psalm 147:11, TLB).

I'm also reminded of Psalm 36:7-9 (NIV)—

> How priceless is Your unfailing love!
> Both high and low among men
>   find refuge in the shadow of Your wings.
> They feast on the abundance of Your house;
>   You give them drink from the river of Your delights.
> For with You is the fountain of life....

As we have seen earlier, the shelter of His wings offers not only protection but also abundant provisions from His vast reserves, along with delightful, refreshing living water. Our hidden relationship with God connects us with an abundant flow of life, both for us and for others through us.

BE THAT TO ME

We've been considering God's attributes, some of the qualities we find in Him. We have seen that He is so awesome and adequate: altogether desirable, perfect in power and greatness, our Champion, the Blessed Controller of all things, perfectly wise and good. Now the question is, *What is God to me?* What are the various relationships He has toward me that show me what to expect of Him?

The most important truth in my life is that God wants me to know Him in intimate, personal experience. Yes, He wants me to know the true concepts about Him in His Word. But He wants me to take each of those concepts and allow Him to *be that to me* in personal experience. If we want to be realists, if we want to live realistically, we must know what God is and let Him be that for us.

So often there can be a sort of psychological distance between us and God. We can know and say, "God is my heavenly Father, He is a refuge in the storms of life, He is the source of deepest satisfaction"—but do these truths really mean much to us? Is our knowledge largely mental knowledge? It's possible to see these truths but not experience them.

But God wants us to see ourselves linked with Him in the whole picture of our life. And He wants to reveal Himself so personally to us through the Bible that we can with our whole heart respond back to Him and say, *"My* Father, *my* Refuge, *my* Satisfaction." I've found through the years that this is what happens as we become more and more aware of what He is to us.

To really know God means that we see what He is in relationship to us, and then more and more, in the experiences of daily life, we let Him be that to us—*we count on Him to be that.*

I have found Psalm 31 very helpful in this. In verse 2 David prays, "Be my rock of refuge, a strong fortress to save me" (NIV). Then in verse 3 he says, "Since You are my rock and my fortress...." At first I thought this sounded like double-talk: Be to me a rock, because You are my rock. Then I realized what it means. It's as if David said, "I have chosen You to be my rock; now be that to me in my situation right now. Be to me now *what You are.*" Isn't that great?

Be to me what You are. You are my best love—be that to me now, for I need that today. You are the water of life—be that to me at this time, because my soul is thirsty.

Here's where praise comes in, turning our eyes to what He is and giving Him thanks and praise. Then our experience begins to line up with these truths, and He begins to move in with a growing reality of Himself.

So we can keep running to Him, saying, "Be my Strength and my Redeemer…my Sun and my Shield…my Joy…my Counselor…my King…" Oh, there are so many more! We could devote many pages to listing them, and we still wouldn't begin to exhaust the wonders of who He is.

You remember how often, in John's gospel, Jesus said the words "I am." Here are some of them: I am the Messiah (4:25-26). I am the Father's Son, the Son of God (5:22-26). I am the bread of life (6:35). I am the light of the world (8:12). I am the door (10:7). I am the good shepherd (10:11). I am the resurrection and the life (11:25). I am Teacher and Lord (13:13). I am the way, the truth, and the life (14:6). I am the true vine (15:1).

For each of these I believe He wants us to say, "Thank You, Lord—You *are!* You're the Bread of *my* life, You're the Light of *my* world, You're *my* Door and *my* Good Shepherd, and *my* Resurrection. You're *my* Teacher and Lord. You're my Way, my Truth, my Life, and my True Vine." That's faith. And it helps our knowledge seep down into our experience. It frees us up to let Christ dwell within us more fully.

Think also of Christ's offices to us: He is Prophet and Priest and King. For each one He wants us to know, "I'm that to *you.*" And we can respond, "Yes, Lord, thank You that You're my Prophet and my Priest and my King. Now, today, during this hour, this moment, be to me my Prophet, be to me my Priest, be to me my King."

Jesus also said, "I have called you friends" (John 15:15). He is our Friend. *Yes, Lord, You are! Be my Friend now, in my actual experience today.*

NO LONGER GRASPING

God takes all the most fulfilling and beautiful relationships we know in human life—bridegroom to bride, husband to wife, father to child, friend to friend, brother to brother or sister—and for each of those relationships He says to us, "I am that to you. You belong to Me, and I want to be that to you in your day-to-day experience. Won't you let Me be that to you in its perfect form, in its ideal form, in a better way than any human being ever could?" He fulfills each of these relationships in ways so far above the perverted form of them that we often hear about in this life. And so far above the mediocre form that we more often observe. And far above even the best and strongest forms of these relationships that we ever encounter here on earth. He says, "I am that to you, and more. Let Me be the very best of fathers to you, the very best of friends, the very best life partner." And He wants us to reply, "Thank You, Lord; *You are,*" and then to allow Him to be just that.

This is one of the most beautiful aspects of getting to know God better and letting our relationship with Him grip us in a new way. We find out what He is, then accept in our heart that He's that *to me!* Then we can say with ever-growing delight, "You are my Shepherd, my Beloved, my Bridegroom, my Father."

It's essential not only to see Him with our minds but also to embrace Him with our hearts—just as we did at the time of our salvation. We realized with our mind: He is the Savior, who died for our sins. And we responded to Him in faith with our hearts and said, "You are *my* Savior!" Regardless of the precise words we used, this is what happened deep within us.

And so God's perfect love fulfills every ideal that the human race has ever searched for in a relationship. As the godly Shirley Rice put it, "Once you've been loved by God, you are loved completely, and you do not need to grasp anymore."

O Lord my Champion, Your majesty and glory and sovereign power are mingled so beautifully with Your warm love and goodness and mercy. I rest in the perfection of who You are and of how perfectly You love me.

I also exult in Your perfect sovereignty. "Your throne, O God, is forever and ever." I praise You as the Blessed Controller of all things everywhere—and of all things in my life. Thank You for the peace You give as I trust in Your perfect control over all that has happened in my past, over everything I face today, and over all that the future will hold.

And I'm so grateful as well for the example Your gladness is to me—Your full, contagious joy—and for the privilege of sharing in it with You. Thank You that Your wisdom is perfect. You have never made a mistake in anything You've allowed to touch my life, and You never will. And thank You, too, for Your perfect goodness. Your every thought and intention is entirely good— purest and highest good—and You will never withhold anything good from me as, by Your grace, I walk uprightly. How grateful I am.

Thank You especially for Your lovingkindness that surrounds me and overshadows me. Your lovingkindness is better than life itself.

So I worship and praise You, for "there is none like You, O Lord." Today, in new ways, display Your love and power to me, and through my life to others.

Meanwhile I rest in the fact that I am loved so completely and never need to grasp anymore.

In Jesus' name...

Your personal gleanings for meditation, prayer, and action:

What Scripture or truth in this chapter do you feel the Lord is especially speaking to you about? What will you do to profit the most from this?

SEVEN

So Utterly and Completely Delightful

THEY SAY THAT GOD loves for a woman's reasons. When a woman is asked why she did or said something or why she thinks or feels a certain way, she may well answer, "Just because." To her that's a reason, and a good one. Her inner sense, her intuition gives her insights that she may find difficult to put into precise words. Warren recalls his mother telling his father, "But you can't expect me to be logical—I don't have to be!"

God loves us "just because." His love defies human logic. It doesn't make sense. Our human minds cannot figure it out. We cannot uncover reasons for it that to our way of thinking seem adequate. It is darkness to my intellect. We have to accept that it's *just because.*

And yet there *are* reasons. I think of at least two: First, God loves us because He *is* love. It's His nature to love.

Second, He loves us because He made us. Sin has destroyed some of the beauty of His design that He must now work to restore; but He made each of us with great skill, and we have unique value to Him as His special work-manship—one of His originals. Because He made us for Himself, in His image, we have the potential of intimate relationship with Him, which is extremely important to Him. He highly prizes us and wants us for Himself. He loves us for what a love relationship with Him can mean to us—and to Him—now, in this life. He also loves us for what He knows we'll become for all eternity—beautiful, living works of art, bringing glory and pleasure to Him as He continues to lavish His riches on us. He eagerly awaits the delights in store for Him and us when we will dwell with Him forever in joyful unbroken fellowship.

We read in Deuteronomy 7:7 and 10:15 that God set His love upon His people—He "fastened" it upon them, as *The Berkeley Version* says. I like that. There's a gentle but unyielding persistence about the love of God, a tenacious tenderness toward each person who has responded to Him. He loves us and holds on and won't let us go.

Now if someone who was not generous and loving fastened himself onto you, it could make you uncomfortable. But God is incredibly generous and loving, and His tenacity makes us secure.

I realize that much of what I share in this book is not really new to you. But I know that as we look at God anew, as we gaze at Him with concentration and focus, He will strengthen our hearts, and our knowledge of Him will become truer and deeper. What's more, if we then let our hearts praise and adore and worship Him, something will happen deep in our emotional nature. It's like the feeling that comes when you pause and fully appreciate a sunset, when its beauty overwhelms you and your heart rises in admiration. That's why it's so important that we often take a closer look at God—important both to Him and to our own well-being.

Essentially, this entire book is an endeavor to answer the question, What is God's love like? But in this chapter I want to respond directly to that question. Then we'll devote the rest of the book to discovering two truths: what God's love can mean personally to each of us and how we can enjoy it more.

FROM EVERLASTING TO EVERLASTING

The tenacious love of God is both eternal and changeless. These two concepts are wonderfully linked.

"The steadfast love of the Lord is from everlasting to everlasting on those who fear Him" (Psalm 103:17, RSV). *From everlasting to everlasting.* That's a long time, isn't it? Let's look at this phrase more closely.

From everlasting, way back before I ever existed, God loved me. Long before I was born He looked ahead and fastened His affection upon me. His love for me began in His foreknowledge of me. That means He didn't love me because I earned it, for when He decided to love me I did not yet even exist. His love is not mine because I merit it, for He fastened His love upon me before I ever did one thing good or bad, before I ever merited anything.

Therefore in the midst of my failures and struggles when I feel so undeserving, I never have to think, *Oh dear, does He still love me?* He never started loving me in the first place because I deserve it. He just loves me. His love for each of us is never rooted in our worthiness, but rather in His own nature.

God is saying to us, "It's not because you earned it or worked so hard for it that I have loved you. And I don't continue loving you because you manage to maintain a high enough standard in my eyes. No, I simply made a permanent choice to love you."

That choice will never change. He loved me *from* everlasting and will love me *to* everlasting. His love for me—and for you—will never end. It's a lifelong, eternity-long relationship, now and forever available to meet our every need as we seek to know Him better.

God has always known all things. Before we were born He already knew the worst about us, and nothing that happens now can surprise or disillusion Him. He has never had any illusions about anyone or anything. He doesn't suddenly discover some truth about one of us and think, "Oh, why did I ever choose to love *him* or *her?*" I like what J. I. Packer says in *Knowing God:* "God's love to me is utterly realistic, based at every point on the prior knowledge of the worst about me, so that no discovery now can disillusion Him about me in the way I am so often disillusioned about myself, and quench His determination to bless me."

In Isaiah 54:10, God says, "For the mountains may be removed and the hills may shake, but My lovingkindness will not be removed from you, and My covenant of peace will not be shaken" (NASB). His lovingkindness is an unshakable love that will always be mine. This truth makes me feel secure; it also makes me want to love Him in return.

The Berkeley Version of the Psalms speaks of His love as a "covenant love." The One who cannot lie and cannot change has made a covenant—a binding, unbreakable agreement—to love us. He has given us His word that He'll always continue to love us; He has committed Himself to it. And He will never change His mind. God will never divorce us, because He's given His promise and He cannot break His word. It's an attitude and commitment God has freely chosen, and He will never, in any way, go back on it.

Deuteronomy 7:7-9 tells exciting truths about God's love for His people Israel. If we belong to the Lord we are now His people through the new, everlasting covenant He has made with us in Christ. So we can claim these truths in an even greater way than the Israelites of old could. In this passage we read that God set His love upon His people and chose them, but not because of their greatness. In fact He reminds them that they were the least of the nations. He chose them to be His valued possession simply because of His love and His promises. Likewise God has chosen us simply because He loves us, and He has made promises that guarantee that love for all time and eternity.

The Psalms speak often of the Lord's "steadfast love" and "unfailing love." In the *Revised Standard Version* of the Psalms we frequently see together the words *steadfast love* and *faithfulness*. His love is always steady, with no fluctuations. It is connected with His incredible faithfulness: He will never let us down. His love is solid ground for us to build our lives upon.

Hebrews 13:8 says that Jesus Christ is the same yesterday and today and forever. When Jesus walked on the earth, He was a living demonstration of God's love for us. Remember the love Jesus exhibited, the kind of intimate involvement He sought with people, the intense concern and care He showed in meeting people's needs? He is the same today. His love is rooted in His nature, and it will never change. It is everlasting and will never end (Jeremiah 31:3).

Even When We Rebel

We see God's unchanging love in an especially beautiful way in the book of Hosea. There God declared that He still loved His people "though they turn to other gods" (3:1, NIV). Throughout the prophet Hosea's message the Lord shows how constant is His love for His people even when they spurned Him and persisted in rebelling against Him.

I once came across a new version of Hosea in a booklet called *Just as Now,* where God speaks these words to His people in Hosea 11:8— "I cannot just cut you off. My heart recoils within me. How can I let you go?" The *Good News Bible* says, "How can I abandon you? My heart will not let me do it! My love for you is too strong." And the *New Living Translation* puts it this way, "O, how can I give you up? How can I let you go? My heart is torn within me, and my compassion overflows." This was His attitude toward them even though they had persistently rebelled against Him. God had patiently sent them warnings over the centuries, but so often they refused to listen. Finally He had to send severe chastening. They needed it, and He gave it. But even that chastening was evidence of His love, just as it is in our lives. Throughout it all His attitude was still, "How can I let you go?" He cannot give us up. He cannot abandon us. His love for us is too strong.

How that relieves my heart! Even when I'm letting something else be more important to me than God, God is still loving me. Even when He must discipline me, He says, "I won't go one bit farther than I have to for your good, and I would never cut you off from My love. My heart would never allow it." He recoils at the very thought of ever withdrawing His love for us.

The Wuest translation of 1 John 3:1 reads, "Behold what exotic love the Father has permanently bestowed upon us." His love is something bestowed, something He has given us—not because we could ever deserve it, but simply because we said yes to Him. By that simple, believing consent we were born into His family and are now called His children. And His children is what we are and forever will be, because His love is unchanging and eternal, permanently bestowed. What joy is ours as we understand this more deeply!

The Lord also wants us to find great joy in the human loves He brings into our lives. But these loves may not be lifelong. Nor do they in any way measure up to His love. Our deepest and most satisfying love will always be our Father's love, and we can count on it to be lifelong and eternity-long.

Psalm 73:26 begins, "My flesh and my heart may fail"—yes, this will happen to us in different ways all through life. Our bodies and souls may grow weak, may waste away, may droop like a wilted flower. And worse than that, we may inwardly and outwardly fail to trust and obey the Lord. But we can come right back to Him, confess how we have failed, and let the Lord love us. Then we can go on to personalize the last part of this verse, saying with the psalmist, "Lord, You are the strength of my heart, the source of my stability; and You are my chosen portion forever."

"You remain the same," David says to God in Psalm 102:27, "and Your years will never end" (NIV). Because God remains constantly and forever the same, we can say also about His love, "Your love will never end. You will always have the same love for me, the same heart-involvement with me!"

God's love holds on—and this perfect, permanent love gives us deep stability. Many times I've told Him, "Lord, that's the kind of love I need—love that never fluctuates, never falters, never fails. If You didn't have that kind of love, You surely would have given up on me long ago!"

In one of his books, Paul Tournier draws our attention to the change that comes about when a young man and young woman fall in love. Suddenly the young woman's personality blossoms, and beauties unfold that no one knew were there. This goes on for quite a while, perhaps until after the wedding and the honeymoon. Then sooner or later, in most relationships, the man and woman gradually begin to pick at each other. Little by little they become critical here, critical there. The bloom disappears. Old and ugly traits come out again.

But as we're getting to know God's love we can be confident He'll never begin picking at us, He'll never start viewing us with a condemning, critical attitude. We can know that our personal beauty will continue to unfold before Him, to His delight.

LOVE WITHOUT LIMITS

When we talk about God's love it seems impossible not to use big adjectives. His love is really beyond words. The words we use only hint at it, yet they can lead us into a greater experience of it.

God's love is incalculably great. His love is abounding, vast, infinite. His love has no limitations, no boundaries. In both duration and extent it is limitless. We'll never be able to get out of it, or away from it, or beyond it.

Notice again the description of God's love in Ephesians 3:16-19. Paul speaks of how the Spirit within us strengthens us so that we can, in fuller measure, have Christ dwelling within us. Then he says, "I pray… that your life will be strong in love and built on love" (NCV). He goes on to pray that we will know in actual experience the greatness of Christ's love—that we will understand more fully its boundless dimensions—how long and wide and high and deep it is—though it is far greater than anyone can ever know.

We can never fully grasp with our minds how immense God's love is, but to a wonderful degree we can experience it in our hearts. One poet, realizing how needy and undesirable he was in himself, how undeserving of such love, wrote these words:

> How Thou couldst love me as I am
> and be the God Thou art,
> is darkness to my intellect
> but sunshine to my heart.

God's love can warm our heart, though it is so great we will never know it in all its fullness. Yet we can press on to know it better.

God's love is limitless. This means there are no bounds to the encouragement and hope and strength it can give us. Once I found myself under unusual pressure while Warren was gone for almost a month. Situations arose that were difficult for me to cope with, especially without a man's objective counsel. In those stressful weeks the Lord deeply ministered to me through 2 Thessalonians 2:16-17: "Now may our Lord Jesus Christ Himself [!] and God our Father [!], who has loved us and given us unending encouragement and unfailing hope by grace, comfort and strengthen your hearts in every good work and word" (NASB and Phillips).

Here is His personal, loving touch: encouragement and hope that never fail because they are by grace, not based on my deserving. My heart—and yours—may often fail and our resources prove to be inadequate. But the Lord Himself, who loves us, is always ready to inspire us with courage and confidence, as Phillips puts it.

In Psalm 103:11, David says that "as high as the heavens are above the earth, so great is His love for those who fear him" (NIV). What a wonderful picture this is of God's overflowing, limitless, ever-present love.

The Lord does not parcel out little dabs of love—"Well, you've been good children today, so I'll love you a little bit." No, His love flows freely. It overflows, coming to us in an abounding way. We read in Romans 5:5 that God's love has been poured out in our hearts by the Holy Spirit. "It floods our hearts," as James Moffatt translates it. It's a tremendous outpouring of love—not in skimpy measure, but rather in a flood, an inundation. And He has put right within us the source of this abounding love—the Holy Spirit—so His love can be poured out abundantly throughout our whole being. We don't have to settle for trivial little insights into His love. We can experience vastly more of it than we do at present, if we truly want to—if we open ourselves to Him and His Word, seeking and yielding and trusting.

We read in John 3:16 that God *so* loved the world. Perhaps there's no better or simpler statement of the greatness of His love than this. He so loved. God's love is *so* intense, His love is *so* great, His love *so* deep. He loves us so much that He gave His Son, submitting Him to unimaginable, unprecedented agony for our sake. This is how God so loves us.

His love is "broader than the measure of man's mind," as the hymn says. No man's understanding is great enough to measure God's love. I've often ended letters to my children with the line, "I love you more than you know." God loves us far more than we know, and far more than we'll ever know. His love is so great that we'll never completely comprehend it.

This means there's always more about His love for us to discover and enjoy. What a privilege!

It also means we can always count on His love. It's always big enough to meet the deepest needs of our heart. Even in the best of earthly relationships, human love cannot always be what we'd like it to be. In our own marriage, Warren's love wears thin once in a while and so does mine. But God's never does. As A. W. Tozer says in *The Pursuit of God,* "How completely satisfying to turn from our limitations to a God who has none."

THE GRACE BEHIND HIS LOVE

Chapters 5 through 8 of Romans have often focused my attention on a favorite theme—living by grace through faith. Both our justification and our Christian living are by grace. We do not have to balance any scales to show ourselves "worthy" to experience His total forgiveness, His warm attitude of favor, and His inner sufficiency. It's all free for the believing! For decades this truth has been a blessing both practically and emotionally, ministering to me in new ways at different points in my life.

God's love is linked inseparably with His grace, His attitude of unmerited favor toward us. Grace is the basis on which He first chose us in His love, and His overflowing grace is the basis on which He continues to lavish His love upon us.

We read in Romans 5:20 in the Wuest translation that where sin abounded, "grace superabounded with more added to that." There are no words to adequately convey the abundance of God's grace. So we can just say that it "superabounds—with more added to that"!

God's love is so great that no sin is too great for Him to forgive. We can always approach His throne of grace and receive forgiveness, whether for a large, obvious, even scandalous sin, or for any of the mass of little failures that get us down so that we think, *Oh, do I have to confess that again?* It is all grace—just as I am, I come.

One initial condition, and one alone, is necessary in order to enjoy His love. We've met that condition if we have simply opened our lives to Jesus—if we have made the simple choice: "Yes, come in and be my Lord and Savior. You died for me, and I receive You into my life." Then we're linked in a permanent personal relationship with Him through His never deserved, never ending love.

In Ephesians 2:13, J. B. Phillips says that in Christ Jesus we are "inside the circle of God's love and purpose." We were outside that circle before, shutting ourselves off from our God of love. But we stepped inside by responding to Him in humble faith, admitting our sinfulness and opening ourselves up to experience His love.

OPENING OR CLOSING THE BLINDS

In no way do we ever need to earn God's love; He loves us—period. The flow of His love never stops. His love always shines forth undimmed. But our response determines whether it gets through to us. We can pull the blinds—or we can open them. We choose what we'll let ourselves be filled with, and God respects our choice. He does not force His love on us. But at all times His love flows and shines—perfect, unwavering, available to meet our needs.

We see this unchanging flow of God's love portrayed in the story of the prodigal son in Luke 15. The father was waiting for the son to turn his back on his rebellion and return home. And when he saw him coming, he didn't have to think twice about responding with fervent love. The flow of his love had never lessened, though the son had strayed to a far country and into terrible sin.

All of us need this grace. All of us have to confess sin. We *are* sinners—not, we *were* sinners. We're forgiven sinners and sin is no longer part of our core identity. But we still sin. The Lord gives us victory over certain sins and enables us to grow in holiness. But we still fall short of perfect holiness. As we mature through the years we see shortcomings and areas of neglect in our lives that we didn't know were there. We always need God's grace.

So often, when we feel we're doing well (if we've been victorious and had our quiet time every day and learned Bible verses and been nice to our family and our neighbors), then we think, *God surely loves me today.* Then we drop into those low times—we're sure there's no way He could love us now. So at the very point where we need His love most, we don't even dare come before Him to seek and experience it. We forget that He has always loved us even when we had absolutely no use for Him at all. And He will always loves us—just because.

What qualifies us to receive God's love? We qualify simply because we need it. I'm reminded of C. S. Lewis's words: "Our whole being, by its very nature, is one vast need; incomplete, preparatory, empty yet cluttered, crying out to Him who can untie things that are now knotted together and tie up things that are still dangling loose."

David understood this. Psalm 40 reveals his honest heart as it portrays the kind of person God thinks about and demonstrates His lovingkindness to. David knew what it was to be in a slimy pit, in the mud and the mire. He cried out,

> "Do not withhold Your tender mercies from me, O Lord;
> let Your lovingkindness and Your truth continually preserve me.
> My iniquities have overtaken me,
> so that I am not able to look up;
> they are more than the hairs of my head;
> therefore my heart fails me.

I am poor and needy;
    yet the Lord thinks upon me." (40:11,12,17, NKJV)

To the person with desperate needs who is willing to admit them, God shows His love.

Do you qualify? I know I do. I qualify because I have needs—desperate needs. And He has made me willing to admit them and let Him meet them. When I fail to recognize how needy I am, He graciously works to remind me (at times in painful ways). And He renews my willingness to say, "Lord, I'm so messed up, so needy, so unable to obey You and to handle life in my own strength. So I bring my deep needs to You."

I find it so helpful to pray with the songwriter,

Dear Lord,
Take up the tangled strands,
Where I have wrought in vain,
That by the skill of Thy dear hands
Some beauty may remain.

We qualify for the benefits of God's love because we are needy.

HIS LOVE IS SACRIFICIAL

When it comes to human love, we like to see action as well as words, don't we? Words, of course, are important. A wife never tires of hearing her husband tell her again, "I love you." God gives us plenty of words to tell us He loves us, but He also acts upon that love. As we have seen, His greatest action was sending His Son to suffer humiliation and anguish for us when we still had no use for Him. He was willing to pay the highest price possible so that we could belong to Him, so that He could have a loving relationship with us.

His love for you and me is a costly love.

By contrast, human loves seldom go beyond gimme love or exchange love, unless the person's heart has been filled with God's love so that it overflows to others.

A gimme love, the most immature kind of love, pops up at times in all of us. It thinks only of our own need. Being self-centered, it does not really give to the other person. When we're caught in gimme love, we expect people to love us just because we exist—or because we're clever enough, manipulative enough, or angry enough to make the other person meet our needs in just the ways we have in mind.

In exchange love our attitude is, "I'll love you *if* you love me. If you go this far, I'll go this far. I'll go a little further if you go a little further. But if you back off, I'll back off." When we love with exchange love, we carefully measure it out to make certain everything is kept fair.

God's love is different. Entirely different. In the Wuest translation of 1 John 4:7 we read that God's love is "divine and self-sacrificial." This, again, points us to the Cross—the ultimate sacrifice. Such love is foreign to our nature. Humans love like this only when their love comes from God.

And yet human love can also be a picture that helps us to better grasp God's sacrificial love. Perhaps you've heard the story of the railroad man who was taking a walk along the tracks with his five-year-old son on a Sunday afternoon. They were enjoying the trees and flowers and birds near the railroad. They came to a place where a trestle carried the tracks over a deep ravine. There the keen eye of the railroad man noticed a separation where one rail section joined another. The rail had somehow loosened, leaving a gap wide enough to cause a derailment that would send any oncoming train into the ravine.

The man knew that a passenger train would soon be approaching. As his son played nearby, he feverishly went to work looking for a heavy limb to use as a lever. If he could manage to hold the rail in place long enough for the afternoon train to pass safely by, he could then alert a work crew to permanently repair the break.

Then he heard a whistle and saw the approaching train. He quickly muscled his body into place, and with all his might applied pressure through his lever to hold the rails together.

At that moment he looked up and saw to his horror that his son had wandered out onto the trestle—too far out to be rescued or to make it back on his own before the train would cross.

The man had a choice. He could save his son simply by not holding the rail in place, allowing the train, with all its passengers, to plunge into the ravine. Should he save his son? There was just enough time. Or should he save all those people on the train?

The man chose to save the train, and he watched his little boy die.

Afterward, some of the passengers who were saved heard of the man's deed. They wrote letters to thank him and sent him gifts. Others were overheard saying that the man was a fool for doing what he did to his son. But most of the passengers were simply not affected. They forgot the incident and went on with their lives as if it had never occurred.

This is a small picture of God's love for us. He let His Son suffer the agonies of death and separation from Him so that He could rescue us. The Son was not a little boy who couldn't save himself—He was Jesus, God the Son, who purposely went through that torment for us. "He was crushed for the evil things we did. The punishment which made us well was given to Him" (Isaiah 53:5, NCV). He went through incalculable pain and grief and suffering—all because He loves us.

The passengers on the train were strangers to the railroad man who lost his son to save them. God likewise sacrificed His Son for us when we were strangers. But we were strangers by choice. We were His deliberate enemies, going our own way instead of His. Knowing this, God still sent His Son to die for us.

All the passengers were helpless to do anything to save themselves. Only the railroad man, who alone was fully aware of their danger and was there at just the right time, could save them. Likewise we read in Romans

5:6-8, "You see, at just the right time, when we were still powerless, Christ died for the ungodly. Very rarely will anyone die for a righteous man, though for a good man someone might possibly dare to die. But God demonstrates His own love for us in this: While we were still sinners, Christ died for us" (NIV).

And because of this sacrifice, "we also rejoice in God through our Lord Jesus Christ, through whom we have now received reconciliation" (Romans 5:11, NIV).

Jesus says, "Greater love has no one than this, that one lay down his life for his friends" (John 15:13, NIV). A human love will conceivably die for a friend—though only the greatest of human loves would ever dare to do it. Jesus, however, died for His enemies, so that He could make us His friends, bringing us into intimate relationship with Himself. That's how much He desires to have us near Him.

Only God is the source of such love. His is truly the greatest love of all.

LIVING LIKE KINGS

In this, as in all that God gives us, He is immeasurably generous. His love gives and gives and is never depleted, because His power and resources are unlimited. He never has need to give in a grudging way. As Ephesians 3:20 says, He's able to do exceeding abundantly above all we can ask or think—beyond our fondest dreams. He's a total giver who loves to give, who delights to do good for us, so that we can live truly abundant lives.

I came across these lines in a women's magazine:

> Life is so full of a number of things,
> most of them so chaotic,
> that those of us who are as happy as kings,
> must either be boobs or psychotic.

But there is a way to live as happily as kings without becoming psychotic: living plugged into the privileges and resources God has given us because of His amazingly generous love.

Romans 5:17 speaks of what Christ has done for believers and how "by their acceptance of his more than sufficient grace and righteousness" people can now "live all their lives like kings!" (Phillips). We have this possibility of living royally because of the abundance of God's grace. As we have seen, grace means "unmerited favor," favor that we don't have to earn, favor that we don't deserve. In fact we deserve just the opposite!

And whose favor is it? The favor of the King of kings. Favor that flows out from Him toward us. And as we receive it, realizing we are highly favored by the only truly important Person who exists, it does something in our hearts.

I'm reminded of Queen Esther's story. She had a weighty, life-and-death request to bring before the king. But he had not called her in to him for thirty days, and she was far from certain what his response would now be. In fact she was afraid, because by law she would be killed as she approached him if he did not hold out to her his scepter.

But she bravely went in. And look at her king's response:

And it happened when the king saw Esther the queen standing in the court, she obtained favor in his sight; and the king extended to Esther the golden scepter which was in his hand. So Esther came near and touched the top of the scepter. Then the king said to her, "What is troubling you, Queen Esther? And what is your request? Even to half of the kingdom it will be given to you." (Esther 5:2-3, NASB)

The king's favor and generous offer serve as a vivid illustration of the Lord's attitude toward us, but with one big difference. As we approach our King, we don't have to experience the kind of fear Esther had. If we belong to the King of kings, we can be sure of His favor whenever we approach Him. He consistently looks upon us with favor. As the Phillips version of Ephesians 1:6 tells us, God's "glorious generosity... has made us welcome in the everlasting love he bears toward the Son." His welcome is assured, so we can come to Him with confidence. As I come before Him I can picture Him extending His scepter toward me and saying, "Queen Ruth, what is your request? It shall be granted to you, even to half the kingdom." God loves to honor our requests and bestow His favors upon us.

Making Us Rich

God delights to do the things that delight us, and so He gives to us lavishly. In his book *Forever Triumphant*, F. J. Huegel put it like this: "When God gives it is always in a multiplied fashion, something akin to the unnumbered millions of shining worlds in the boundless firmament of heaven." God certainly didn't have to put so many stars in the sky—but isn't it just like Him to fill our night skies with so much beauty for us to appreciate and admire with astounded awe?

He is not a stingy God.

Of course His intention is not to make us all rich materially. In His life on earth Jesus was not wealthy materially, but He was rich in all that truly mattered. And in leaving so much behind in heaven as He came to this earth, His purpose was to share with us His true and eternal treasures. "For you know the grace of our Lord Jesus Christ, that though He was rich, yet for your sakes He became poor, so that you through His poverty might become rich" (2 Corinthians 8:9, NIV).

As part of these riches God has already made available to us everything we need here on earth for a full spiritual life and a satisfying emotional life. "His divine power has given us everything we need for life and godliness through our knowledge of Him who called us by His own glory and goodness" (2 Peter 1:3, NIV). This is all ours to enjoy as we seek to know Him better.

And as God works in our lives to encourage and strengthen us, to develop and train us, even in this He's ultra-generous. He does more than we would expect Him to. This has been an important lesson for me, because for a long time in my early years I had a wrong concept of God. I mentioned earlier my fear of missing out on what I really wanted if I'd turn my life over to God. So for several years in my early teens I held on to my life in fear. But as I became more and more miserable trying to work out my own wonderful plans, I at last told God that He could do anything He pleased with my life. For the first time I began finding satisfaction on a truly deep level. I began to realize that His plan is good, that He brings the very best into our lives. His love means that His heart is filled with good will toward us, and with good plans: "Thy wonderful purposes are all for our good" (Psalm 40:5, NEB).

Psalm 68:6 says that God "leads out the prisoners into prosperity" (NASB). Usually a newly released prisoner must scrounge around and start life over again from nothing, or in fact from less than nothing, as he tries to make something of his broken life. But when God brings us out of our spiritual and emotional prisons, He brings us forth to prosperity. He gives us a whole bank account of spiritual resources, so that we're rich. We're not just free; we're spiritually prosperous.

Psalm 68:6 continues: "Only the rebellious dwell in a parched land." It's our inner rebellion— our fear of submitting to God and giving Him first place — that causes spiritual dryness and lack of satisfaction in our lives. This is not God's desire or plan for us. His intention is spiritual prosperity—life in all its fullness.

I think again of Psalm 84:11—"No good thing does He withhold from those who walk uprightly" (NASB). He won't hold back a single blessing from us if we relate to Him as Lord of our life.

Ponder again these words in Romans 8:32— "He who did not spare His own Son, but gave Him up for us all—how will He not also, along with Him, graciously give us all things?" (NIV). He gave us the very best, letting His beloved Son suffer agony so that we could belong to Him. How much more will He give us everything else that's necessary for our true joy, both in time and eternity! If we've become His friends by letting Him come into our heart, will He not take care of us throughout this life and forever?

He will!

Not Like a Computer

Years ago I learned to relate to an incredibly structured new helper—our laptop computer. I quickly grew to love its word-processing abilities. But at times I felt so frustrated when it allowed absolutely no leeway for human error, taking no note of my good intentions. If I didn't do everything precisely right, the computer refused to work.

This led me to rejoice in the ways God is *unlike* a computer. He, too, is structured—unchanging in character and precise in how He runs the physical universe. Yet how amazingly flexible He is with us! He doesn't make us follow exact procedures in relating to Him. He doesn't refuse to work if we fail to do everything precisely right. Isaiah 52:12 speaks of God as our "rear guard"; our friend Lorne Sanny pictures God as "sweeping up after us when we make mistakes." Warren likes to add, "Sometimes He does this with a dust pan; sometimes He needs a giant, front-end loader."

Psalm 103:8 (Berkeley) says that God is "patiently considerate." He never says, "Oh, you stupid thing! Why did you do that?" Do you sometimes call yourself "stupid"? Should you talk about yourself that way? Of course you do some "dumb" things, and you have areas that need improvement, as I do. And at times we all need to confess sin. But you are very precious to God as His child, and He doesn't want you talk that way about His child. He wants you to value yourself, because *He* values you.

Whatever our failing, He always understands. He's always sympathetic. Though God never excuses sin, He never condemns us (Romans 8:1). "The Lord is like a father to His children," we read in Psalm 103:14, "tender and compassionate to those who fear Him. For He understands how weak we are; He knows we are only dust" (NLT).

And we want compassion, don't we? We want to be understood. So many times other human beings simply don't understand us, and frequently we can't even understand ourselves. But God does. I think again of Ephesians 1:8— "How well He understands us and knows what is best for us at all times" (TLB).

BOTH TENDER AND TOUGH

God's love toward us is both tender and tough. In Hosea 11:4, God speaks to His people in the imagery of a father bending down to pick up his child and hold him against his cheek (TEV). What a picture of the intimate relationship we can enjoy with Him and of the feelings He has about His involvement with us!

Yet God's love is as tough as it is tender, because He's working to make us fully beautiful, with the beauty of Jesus. Therefore He sends a mixture of blessing and trial. He doesn't hold back even if it hurts us.

Sometimes our ideas about what's best for us are based only on what looks easy. But the easiest thing isn't always the best. Sometimes the easy thing might actually harm us, so God takes it away with one hand because He has something better to give us with His other hand. Sometimes the "something better" can seem quite difficult or even tragic.

We read in Lamentations 3:33 that God "does not willingly bring affliction or grief to the children of men" (NIV). He doesn't enjoy our pain when He brings into our lives things that are so hard. Instead He cares for us like a kind surgeon who knows that if he doesn't cut, it may cost us our life.

In whatever adversity the Lord lets us endure, He's always there with us. He feels our distress and understands our weakness. In Isaiah 63:9 we read, "In all their affliction He was afflicted" (NKJV). He was reminding His people that whenever they went through something difficult, He felt it with them.

It's not that God is up there wringing His hands, overcome with anxiety as we sometimes are when our children face difficult situations. But He is like we are when we feel with our children in their painful struggles more than if we were going through the struggles ourselves. God really feels with us. Because He loves, He is vulnerable to our pain and He hurts when we hurt. Even when He must deal with us severely, with tough love, His heart is loving and tender.

God's love is also tough in the sense of being a strong love that gives us inner support. His love is like the steel in reinforced concrete, providing enough strength inside so that the jolts of life don't crack us. How grateful I am for the reminder in Colossians 1:11 that in Christ we can be "strengthened with all might" according to God's glorious power. This can be translated "made strong at all points" or "given strength of every kind."

What would we do without the physical, emotional, and spiritual strength He has made available to us?

Psalm 91 pictures in a powerful way both the tough strength and the tenderness of God as He relates to us. The psalm's opening lines call Him the "Most High" and the "Almighty"; then immediately we see Him tenderly covering us with His feathers and under His wings. A pastor in the Philippines paraphrased the first two verses of this psalm as follows, expanding them to include the meaning of the names of God used in the passage:

> He that settles down in the hiding place of the strongest strong One, possessor of heaven and earth, shall abide under the all-protecting shade of the all-sufficient God who is enough. I will say of the Lord, my everlasting Redeemer, who promises and keeps His Word, "He is my high place of hope, my fort-castle. In Him will I trust."

Our God is tough, but oh so tender.

BETTER THAN WINE, BETTER THAN LIFE

I like the way three verses in Song of Solomon portray God's love: "Your love is more delightful than wine" (1:2), and "We will praise your love more than wine" (1:4), and "How much more pleasing is your love than wine" (4:10, all NIV). Wine in the Scriptures is often a symbol of joy. It offers release from inhibitions—sometimes too much!—and relief from fears and anxieties. But anything wine can do for a person, God's love can do better, and without the side effects. You can take in all of His love You want without worrying about a headache the next morning. His love is better— and we find this to be so true if we just take a drink of His love as often as we need it.

We know we've begun to go deep into God's love when we can say to Him the same words David prayed in Psalm 63:3— "Your love is better than life" (NIV). Wouldn't you rather give up being alive in this world than to be separated from the love of God?

His love *is* better than life.

O my God and Father, Your love reaches to the heavens. It is too high and wonderful for my mind to grasp, but my heart rejoices and rests in it.

I praise You that You are love. I cannot understand adequate reasons for Your loving me; yet I thank You that the perfect reasons are there in Your nature and in Your heart, and always will be.

Thank You for loving me eternally, for fastening Your love upon me before the foundation of the world.

And I celebrate with glad wonder the truth that Your love never changes. How grateful I am for the steady overflow of Your love to me even though You know so well all that is worst about me. I especially want to thank You for loving me even when I've been disobedient and rebellious toward You. How incredible is Your faithfulness to our relationship, Your loyalty and commitment to it! How it relieves my heart to remember that You have never turned away from me, and never will. I praise You for making Your love to me an enduring gift, permanently bestowed.

Father, I confess that I desperately need Your love, and always will. Thank You for the many ways You have met my needs… for the many times You have flooded my heart with the reality of Your loving presence. I exult in the grace You have lavished upon me in delivering me from sin and death… and welcoming me into Your inner circle of love… and drawing me into growing intimacy with You. I rejoice that I will enjoy this intimacy throughout all the future—that ours is a life-long, eternity-long relationship.

I thank You especially for all that Your love for me has cost You—for the way You watched Your Son suffer and die for me when I was a stranger to You, and an enemy.

I glory in the truth that You delight to do the things that delight me. Thank You for making me so rich in the blessings that matter most.

I choose also to thank You for the trials and discipline You bring my way because Your love is tough. Thank You for not holding back, and for continuing Your tender care even when You're putting me through refining fires.

Thank You for the hope and encouragement that are mine because I can always keep coming back to these wonderful truths. And I praise You that exploring Your boundless love is an adventure that will last forever…that I will never stop experiencing it in fresh and different ways.

In Jesus' name…

Your personal gleanings for meditation, prayer, and action:

What Scripture or truth in this chapter do you feel the Lord is especially speaking to you about? What will you do to profit the most from this?

EIGHT

OUR PRICELESS PRIVILEGE

WHAT PRIVILEGES mean the most to you in this life, on the human level? As you think about this, your answer probably includes relating to people who mean a lot to you. To have access to people who are truly important to us and to have a pleasing, loving relationship with them—this is what most of us value more than anything else. Perhaps family members and close friends come to your mind; or mentors, pastors, teachers; or others you deeply admire and want to be close to.

The highest privilege life can offer is to know God and become more intimately acquainted with Him, an acquaintance made possible through knowing His Son, Jesus Christ.

We first "know" Christ when we open the door of our hearts and say, "Lord, come in. Be my Savior and Lord." We put our trust in Him; He forgives our sins and enters our life. So we've been introduced. We no longer just know *about* Him, but we've met Him. We've become acquainted with Him. Then comes the lifelong pursuit, the lifelong joy of knowing Him more intimately—our life's highest calling.

I wonder: What is your chief pursuit in life? What do you really want?

What do you actually *demand* from life? What comes to mind when you think, "I must have this"?

I remember sitting in our third-floor apartment at Glen Eyrie years ago when

I was a widow. I began to feel fearful about what the future might hold, in contrast to what I'd like it to hold. Then I sensed the Lord asking me, "Ruth, what is it that you really demand from life?"

There were several things I wanted Him to do. But this question was narrower, more directed, more focused: "What is it you really demand?"

I answered, "Lord, there's only one thing I demand out of life, though sometimes my feelings don't agree. This one thing that I demand is *You*. I have to know You better, to experience You more fully."

A REAL CHOICE FOR REAL REWARDS

A few years later my daughter came home from school one day and told me that the other kids had been teasing her by saying, "You don't have a daddy, and we do."

After we had talked about how this made her feel, I said, "You know, Doreen, what those children are saying is not really true. You have your daddy in heaven. But you also have a heavenly Father—and He's a King. So what does that make you?"

"Well, that makes me a princess." This helped her feel less afraid or worried about her schoolmates' teasing.

It's good for us as well to keep remembering this truth: God has told us we're His sons and daughters, children of the King. And He's told us so many other good things about who we are. So now we have a real choice in how we see ourselves. And the first step for a lasting change in our sense of who we are is to embrace the priceless privilege of getting to know God better. We won't consistently see ourselves as God sees us unless we cultivate a close relationship with Him.

Hebrews 11:6 says that God is a rewarder of those who diligently seek Him. And in Jeremiah 29:13, God says, "You will seek Me and find Me when you search for Me with all your heart" (NASB). We cannot be halfhearted in our pursuit of Him, spending time with Him now and then, when it happens to be convenient. To the best of our knowledge we're to seek Him earnestly and let Him be first. Then He begins to satisfy our longing soul and fill us with His perfect love and goodness. This changes how we view ourselves.

One summer in Singapore was especially busy. We had just moved into a different home, and at the same time we were leading an eight-week orientation program for new missionaries to Asia. One day, "dying" for some time alone, away from it all, I slipped away to a nearby coffee shop. There I had a great time reviewing Hebrews 11 and recording my thoughts while sipping the delicious local milk tea. I had been blessed for several days through soaking in this chapter. Through it God seeks to focus our hearts on the things hoped for and the things not seen—on wonderful, invisible realities that far surpass anything in our present lives, anything we hope for in our earthly future.

As in all of Hebrews, the word *better* stands out in chapter 11. I'm to keep my eyes on the better things God has provided spiritually, and the even better things He promises for eternity. God wants me to focus on the reward, on the riches greater than any earthly treasures, and most of all on the Rewarder. He created and framed all visible things from that which cannot be seen; He is the Builder and Maker of the continuing city that we seek; He is faithful; He is able even to raise the dead. He is a God of wondrous long-range purposes that extend beyond our little lives, our generation, our millennium. *This* God has given us utterly reliable promises regarding life today, life tomorrow, and life forever.

So we are to endure as "seeing Him who is invisible" (11:12), assured of the joy set before us, grateful to be part of the city of the living God and citizens of a kingdom that cannot be shaken (12:22-28).

In God's hall of fame in Hebrews 11, some of His people of faith won great and obvious victories; others went through disgrace and defeat in terms of visible success and advantages. So the rewards God has promised are not only for those who do great things that make the headlines. The rewards are for all who diligently seek Him and, by faith, simply do His will. That encouraged me! And it still does.

SIMPLY TO BE USED

Knowing God better includes walking close to Him day by day and serving Him as He desires, whether in lowly tasks or in great ones. Whatever my situation, whatever duty may call, the following poem has repeatedly helped me. It reminds me to rest in the Lord by faith and to invest my life with contentment. It helps me fix my eyes not on earthly significance but on significance in the eyes of the One I serve, on the Rewarder and the ultimate, invisible rewards He promises:

> I would be simply used,
> Spending myself in humble task or great,
> Priest at the altar, keeper of the gate,
> So be my Lord requireth just that thing
> Which at the needful moment I may bring.
> O joy of serviceableness divine!
> Of merging will and work, dear Lord, in Thine,
> Of knowing that results, however small,
> Fitly into Thy stream of purpose fall.
> I would be simply used!

This reminder of my simple "serviceableness divine"—of being useful in God's eyes—frees and uplifts my heart. It prepares me to head back joyfully to practical duties and opportunities (large or small) with people, assured of the invisible rewards He has promised. These rewards include the honor of seeing myself as the servant of the living God who rules over heaven and earth.

Many treasured rewards have already become mine. By the time you read this, I'll have reached my seventieth birthday. It's a good age, for I know the Lord a bit better than I did at thirty, or forty, or even sixty. So I'm a lot wealthier than when I was younger. And I pray I'll know Him a lot better when age seventy-five or eighty-five rolls around.

But pursuing the Lord with all my heart doesn't necessarily get easier. I just have a different set of distractions than when I was thirty or fifty. Pursuing Him is a priceless privilege, but nevertheless one that requires continual effort, continual wisdom in my daily choices. Fortunately, as we keep pressing on to know Him better and deepen our relationship with Him, our experience of God's love keeps growing. We also grow in our capacity for experiencing that love and in our desire to experience it even more. So it doesn't involve less work; it doesn't become easy. But it does bring greater rewards, greater motivation to know Him better, and a greater sense of loss and longing when it dawns on us that we've grown slack in seeking Him.

I've found in my own life—and I need to keep remembering this—that to know God better and love Him the way He wants me to, I have to set God-centered goals for my life. I can set other goals too, but these must be my primary goals. Then no matter what happens, no matter what loss I may face, no matter what trial or hindrance may come my way, I can say, "Thank You, Lord, that this is going to lead me closer to fulfilling my real and deepest goals."

We touched on this earlier, but let's remind ourselves once more: What are our most important, most strategic goals if we want to live God-centered lives? I think of my primary goals as these: I want to know God better and love Him more. I want to worship Him the way He deserves. I want to do His will. And I want to glorify Him in all I am and say and do.

I like to keep these goals before me, but Satan has many schemes for drawing me away from them. So I need to pray often about consistently fulfilling the goals I've set.

What are your primary goals in life? I encourage you to give this some prayerful thought, to write down your goals, and to pray about them often.

TAKING HIM PERSONALLY

Our priceless privilege of pursuing a deeper relationship with God involves taking personally what we see and learn about Him and His love.

The more personally we take the messages of God's love, the more His love will change our lives.

In fact, it's impossible for me to take God *too* personally. He actually wants me to take His love very seriously. He longs for me to experience Himself and His love, and He wants my experience of Him to constantly grow more rich and full.

As we have seen, to know God is not just to accumulate facts about Him, but also to experience who He is in our daily living. That's why He's called Himself things like Bread, Water, Light—things that we so greatly need. He knows we're familiar with the ways these things meet our needs on the physical level, so He says, "I am that to you as far as your inner being is concerned—bread to satisfy your hungers, water to quench your every thirst, light to dispel all your darkness. Let Me be these things to you."

This is what He wants. And He wants it to start now, because He loves you personally. Pause quietly and hear Him say those words: *I love you. I long to meet your needs.*

We've looked closely—perhaps more closely than you ever have before—at what God's love is like, this beautiful, vast ocean of delight. But how can we learn to swim in it, to relax and enjoy the feel of it?

As a start, allow the following truths to soak in more deeply than ever, and express to God your gratitude for them: God in His grace has made His love available.

Every believer can have an experience of His love that continually grows deeper. It is ready and waiting to transform our lives.

God wants to give each of us not just fleeting impressions of His love, but a strong, settled, growing sense of it. He wants us to know how dearly He loves us and to feel this warm love everywhere within us (Romans 5:5, TLB). He wants us to enjoy a genuine, deep, constant experience of His love.

But such a relationship is ours in experience only to the degree that we get intensely involved with God. E. M. Bounds wrote that God does not reveal Himself to the "hasty comer and goer." If we settle for a casual relationship we won't experience His love deeply. It's not that anything about His love changes when we neglect Him. His love is still just as full and flowing, just as wonderful and powerful. But we're blocking it out when we don't pursue a deeper, more constant relationship with Him.

GOD'S PRIMARY VALUE

A relationship with God (like any close relationship) takes time and teamwork. It won't become deep if we are distracted or indifferent or erect barriers. It takes the willingness to bare our souls and pour out our hearts to Him. As in human relationships, it takes time to really listen, to develop trust in the other person, then to learn to trust him or her still more.

I've already mentioned how I learned early in life that God wanted to be my first love. The Lord uses those same words in Revelation 2. He commended the church in Ephesus for their perseverance and for working hard and holding to the truth. But He had one thing against them: "You have left your first love" (Revelation 2:4, NASB).

Isn't it amazing that this was the most important thing to His heart? Of course He still wanted them to persevere and be hardworking and keep their hold on the truth, but He especially longed for them to rediscover and return to their first love.

Think of how delighted and focused a young lady is when she first falls in love—so eager to be with this man she adores, so eager to please him. But when it comes to adapting to him and his ways day after day, the first love can lose its glow.

In our relationship with Christ, it's so easy to lose our glow, to lose our first love. The Lord wants us to be focused on Him and captivated by Him in our hearts; that's part of our "first love." But He wants more than the passing feelings of enchantment—more than emotional highs when we sing or listen to praise songs. He wants love that delights in time alone with Him, love that has a passion to bring Him joy and become more like Him. And He wants us to go beyond our first love to a deeper, more mature love—love that enters into His purposes regardless of what this may cost us. This is what I pray for in my own life—the freshness of my first love and the depth of an ever-maturing love.

How assuring and stimulating it is to see that love is so primary in God's value system. We're called first to a Person. We're also called to serve Him. And we're called to our spouse, our children, and other human relationships. But above all we're called to a relationship with the most important Person of all—our God. We're called to live in His love.

That's why it's so exciting to me that God wants me to spend plenty of time coming to Him in His Word and taking what I see of Him there very personally—that He's *my* Savior, *my* Shepherd, *my* God, *my* Champion, *my* Friend, *my* Beloved. Only then can He minister to my deepest inner needs.

Choosing Him to be our first love—to be our best life partner who is also our Lord—is a lot like marriage: one big yes and a whole lot of little uh-huhs. Jesus desires that one big yes, and a host of other daily yes's as well. Each yes is a confession and an affirmation: "Lord, I can't do it on my own, and I don't want any barrier to shut me off from Your love and blessing. I need You. And I'm Yours."

With each yes we can review in our hearts some of the reasons why our Lord is worthy of being our first love. We can pray as George MacDonald did:

> All that I can imagine of the wise, the lovely, the beautiful, is in You, only infinitely more than I can imagine. In You is all the wise teaching of the best man and more; all the gentleness and truth of the best child and more; all the tenderness and devotion of the truest woman and more. Therefore I must be all Yours. All my aspirations, all my worship, all my honors, all my loves, must center in You.

The hymn "Jesus, Thou Joy of Loving Hearts" includes these words: "From the best bliss that earth imparts, I turn unfilled to Thee again." Life brings many joys and loves; marriage in God's plan brings deep satisfactions, as do relationships with other loved ones and friends. But the heart that has tasted of God's love will always turn back to Him with longing and say, "Only *Your* love can meet my deepest needs."

Think again of the wonder of it: The supreme Ruler of all the universe actually *wants* a loving, intimate relationship with you. The almighty and eternal God is saying, "I am your Friend, and I want you to be My friend. You are My beloved child, and I love to hear you say, 'Father, my dear Father!' You are so precious to Me, so treasured, so deeply loved."

And we ourselves determine whether or not we experience a truly intimate and life-changing relationship with Him. If we respond to Him, His love is powerful and transforming. It cannot help but revolutionize our lives in a phenomenal way.

Then you'll find in your heart the kind of longings that Hudson Taylor expressed to the Lord:

> Lord Jesus, make Thyself to me
> a living bright reality,
> more present to faith's vision keen
> than any earthly object seen.
> More dear, more intimately nigh
> than e'en the sweetest earthly tie.

GIFTS TO HELP US RESPOND

In an earlier chapter I mentioned five exceptionally important love-gifts that God provides to help us draw nearer to Him. Do you remember them? I feel it's good to turn our thoughts to them again, for they make it possible for us to enjoy our priceless privilege of a strong and growing sense of God's love.

The first love-gift—*the Word of God*—is one we can daily take advantage of with ever-increasing rewards. The Holy Spirit has filled the Scriptures with God's love messages, which He uses to change our lives.

The Lord longs to reassure us day by day through the Word of His grace. When we take time to listen and then believe what He says, He transforms our minds. He causes us to grow in grace as well as knowledge, enabling us to love and obey and serve Him out of sheer gratitude.

By taking time alone with God in His Word and in prayer, we come to know and believe the love of God. His Word teaches us how to live in His love—how to truly abide in it and let it fill our being.

The sense of worship that comes when we behold God through His Word and let Him love us is something very close to enjoying a sunset. When you're thrilled by a sunset, it isn't because you sit down in a room, decide you want to be thrilled, and then imagine a spectacular display in the western sky (though if you have a vivid imagination you might succeed at this). When a sunset thrills you, it's because you're actually looking at one, and your heart rises in enjoyment and awe.

Likewise, when we want to enjoy God we don't just sit back in our quiet time and think, *Now let's see, I should love Him and I should worship Him.* No, we take a look at Him in His Word. We gaze at Him there. Then the love flows and the worship rises from our heart. This brings something far better than enjoying a sunset. It brings the profound pleasure—the inner release—of enjoying the love of God and all that He is. You can't take a good look at Him without realizing: How worthy He is of my adoration, my worship, my love!

The second of those love-gifts is *His Spirit living in us.* As we let the Lord have His way in our lives—His loving way that always results in our good—then the Spirit of God pours the love of God throughout our being. It's not that He provides love as something apart from Himself. No, He *is* love, and as we let Him enter every area of our lives, filling our very self with Himself, we're filled as well with His warm and satisfying love.

This is a process because God doesn't hit us with everything at once, but deals with us in a wise, timely, gradual way. It's a process because of barriers within us that must come down. Perhaps the Holy Spirit has shown you some of those barriers in your own heart and has already removed them. Or He's in the process of doing so. One stanza of "Just As I Am" goes like this: "Just as I am, Thy love unknown has broken every barrier down. Now to be Thine—yea, Thine alone—O Lamb of God, I come." God's love is powerful. It melts down inner barriers as fire melts wax. The more we come to Him and let Him love us, the more those barriers melt away. Then the Spirit can control our lives more fully and deepen our experience of God's love.

Ephesians 3:16-19 is one of my favorite passages on the Spirit's part in our experience of God's love. You may want to pore over it in two or three versions—and memorize it so you can use it often in prayer and praise.

The third love-gift—*the body of Christ*—is also one we dare not neglect if we want to deeply experience the Lord and His love. Other fellow believers help us grow spiritually as they channel to us the Lord's love and truth through their Christlike qualities and their spiritual gifts. This takes place when we fit closely together, as members of our physical bodies do, with each individual part of the body meeting the needs of the others. So living in harmony with other members of Christ's body is not optional; the Lord commands us in Ephesians 4:2-3, "Accept life with humility and patience, making allowances for each other because you love each other. Make it your aim to be at one in the Spirit" (Phillips).

Nor is it optional to worship together: "Let us not hold aloof from our church meetings, as some do. Let us do all we can to help one another's faith, and this the more earnestly as we see the final day drawing ever nearer" (Hebrews 10:25, Phillips).

The fourth love-gift is *the circumstances of our daily life,* all of which God orchestrates. It's often the trials of life that cause us to let God love us. They help us see how needy we are and motivate us to seek His face.

Romans 5 is so good in showing how both the Holy Spirit and our trials bring about a growing experience of God's love:

We can rejoice, too, when we run into problems and trials. For we know that they are good for us—they help us learn to be patient. And patience develops strength of character in us, and helps us trust God more each time we use it, until finally our hope and faith are strong and steady. Then when that happens we are able to hold our heads high no matter what happens, and know that all is well, for we know how dearly God loves us, and we feel this warm love everywhere within us because God has given us the Holy Spirit to fill our hearts with His love. (5:1-5, TLB)

God longs for us to trust Him with sincere gladness in every situation we face. In order to do this in all our joys or trials, we must make some choices. Have you honestly come to the conclusion that you cannot find true satisfaction apart from Him, and therefore you won't even try? We have to make Godward choices such as: "Your will: nothing more, nothing less, nothing else." I first discovered this quotation hanging in my sister-in-law's kitchen. It's an excellent prayer of dedication.

Here's another basic choice:

> My goal is God Himself,
> Not peace, or joy,
> Or even blessing,
> But Himself, my God.

Is our desire to know Him strong enough so that we can tell Him honestly, "At any cost, dear Lord, by any road—and through any circumstances You want to use in my life"? Do you want to know Him that badly?

Remember the Lord's special instructions in James 1:2-3— "When all kinds of trials and temptations crowd into your lives, my brothers, don't resent them as intruders, but welcome them as friends! Realize that they come to test your faith and to produce in you the quality of endurance" (Phillips). Then tell

Him, "Lord, I believe You have my best interests at heart; now show me Your love in this adversity, and let me be comforted by You."

I don't want to imply that it's always a hard road. God brings many delightful roads as well, and so many joys. As we accept these from His loving hand, they also deepen our knowledge of Him. But if we really want to know God and His love, we have to open up our lives for Him to take us along paths we ourselves would never choose. As we do this, we know His heart of love better, and we understand more clearly and with greater certainty how much He has our best interests at heart.

Then there's *the path of obedience,* the fifth love gift. God allows us to choose between two basic paths in life. One is the path of disobedience. Smog and heavy clouds hang over it, letting very little of God's love shine through. On that dangerous, potholed road, our experience of His love is cold and meager.

On the path of obedience the clouds and smog are gone, and God's warm love shines down undimmed to meet our needs. Our daily time of hearing God speak to us through the Bible helps us to see and choose the right path. And when we stray or take detours, the Scriptures help us return to the path of obedience as quickly as possible. On this road we're walking through life with the Lord, and our experience of His love becomes increasingly warm and rich. And through our obedience we allow God to love us more intimately, with a glad heart rather than a grieved heart.

It's not that spending time in God's Word and obeying Him make us more deserving of His grace and love. It's so dangerous to think God's love is only for those with imposing spiritual qualities, or only for those times when we feel we're "successful Christians." This kind of thinking is dangerous because it makes it easier for us to get discouraged. It's easier for us to give up in our struggle against temptation and just go on sinning. But once you really taste God's intensely personal love that's there for every Christian, it meets such needs in your heart that you *want* to please Him. A response of love wells up in your heart so that out of sheer love you want to obey Him. And you realize that whenever you willfully sin, you're pulling that dark cloud back over your head, obscuring the sunshine of God's love and robbing yourself of its warmth.

In John 14:21 Jesus says, "He who has My commandments and keeps them, he it is who loves Me; and he who loves Me shall be loved by My Father, and I will love him, and will disclose Myself to him" (NASB). This does not mean that we earn God's love by our obedience. Rather, we're simply choosing the path where His love shines unhindered.

So a rich, ever-deepening experience of the love of God will be yours as you take advantage of these five love-gifts.

Why not pause now and ask the Lord for five things: (1) that you will spend more time in His Word, seeking to know Him better; (2) that the Holy Spirit will increasingly fill and control you and flood your heart with God's love; (3) that, as a member of Christ's body, you will take full advantage of your opportunities to experience and express God's love; (4) that you will receive each of life's circumstances as love-gifts from Him, and (5) that you will constantly choose the path of obedience, where you'll enjoy His love more and more.

So many passages in the Scriptures can help us articulate our love-response back to God, who has so generously given these five love-gifts and countless others. One of these Scriptures is the first verse Dean ever shared with me, long before I knew he had any interest in marrying me. David says in Psalm 27:4, "One thing have I desired of the Lord, that will I seek after; that I may dwell in the house of the Lord all the days of my life, to behold the beauty of the Lord" (KJV). As we hear God express His love to us, we can respond with love back to Him: "Lord, there is nothing I want out of life more than to live in Your presence and behold Your beauty. I want to know You better and experience Your love. You're so wonderful and Your love for me is so vast—and I love You."

Psalm 27:8 gives us another response that brings joy to God. David says to Him, "My heart has heard you say, 'Come and talk with me, my people.' And my heart responds, 'Lord, I am coming'" (TLB).

And I think again of Psalm 73:25— "Whom have I in heaven but Thee? And there is none upon earth that I desire beside Thee" (KJV). The truth of that verse doesn't mean that I say to Warren, "I don't desire you or need you, because I've got God." We all have legitimate human desires, desires that please God. But measured against our desire for God, our desires for others should be so much lower that there's no comparison. Every now and then Warren and I say to one another, "I love you so much, but you're second."

ARE YOU TAKING ENOUGH TIME?

I'm sure you can see by now that taking God's love personally requires a commitment of time. There is no other way. *I must take time to enjoy Him and let Him love me.*

Are you taking enough time? Most of us must consistently prune back other activities to truly have enough time for Him. What pruning have you already done? Is there more you need to consider?

It takes time for love to get deeper. If you really love someone and desire the closest possible relationship with him or her, you want to see this person every day. You want some time alone together every day. Of course God is with us all the time, so we can enjoy His presence even more than that. But a daily time alone with Him becomes especially rewarding as day by day—if possible, in the morning—we let Him tell us through Scripture how much He loves us.

But let's not just "do our quiet time things." Let's not come to the Scriptures merely to do our Christian duty or ease our conscience. Take time to fellowship, take time to really absorb who and what God is, letting your roots go deeper into the soil of His marvelous love. Come with the purpose of knowing Him better, of cultivating the intimacy He longs for. Find out for yourself what He says about you and how much He loves you, and pause now and then for quiet communion.

I've mentioned my friend Helen Morken, a godly woman who influenced me deeply—a real foundation stone in my life. During one of the last times I talked with her before she died of cancer, we were visiting in her kitchen as she put the final touches on lunch. "You know, Ruth," she said, "so many people are talking about communication these days. What about *communion*? What's happened to that?"

By *communion* she meant intimate, sweet, quiet fellowship with the Lord. She meant taking time not only to think about the truth we see in His Word, but also to respond to God in praise—to say, "Thank You, Lord, that You're like that"—and then to rest in silence before Him, quietly enjoying His presence.

Many times I've missed the sweet consciousness of my secure protection in the Lord and the enjoyment of His abundance. This happens not necessarily through glaring sin but through taking Him for granted, through neglecting to pause for conscious, intimate communion with Him in my quiet time, as well as frequently throughout the day. So I say, "Lord, increase my thirst for You! Draw me often each day into sweet communion with You."

During our times in God's Word, we can pray as David did in Psalm 143:8— "Cause me to hear Your lovingkindness in the morning, for in You do I trust; cause me to know the way in which I should walk, for I lift up my soul to You" (NKJV). We can ask the Lord to cause us to hear Him: "I've got to hear it from You, Lord, through Your Word, again and again. Then I can love You, and others, the way You want me to."

Psalm 143 is one of several Scriptures that connect the morning time with taking a look at the love of God. It's the best time of day to hear His lovingkindness, to listen to His words of love through the Scriptures, to let Him love us, and to express our love back to Him. I encourage you to let your mornings be the time when you tune up for the day with God, so that the hours can go by with His love gripping your heart and meeting your needs. If there's no way you can get adequate time in the morning, take at least a few minutes to begin your day with your Beloved One. Then have the rest of your quiet time later in the day. Have a definite plan as to when and where—and keep it!

And have you learned the value of setting aside half a day every month or so for a date with God, an extended time of prayer and meditation on His Word? If not, plan ahead for it and put it on your calendar. When you're approached by someone with a pressing request to do something else during that time, you can answer, "I'm sorry, I already have an appointment." When the day comes, go to a quiet place—perhaps a quiet restaurant where you can have a cup of coffee or tea, or a library, or a park, or the beach, or even a parking lot—some place where you can be quietly alone with God and focus on Him in the Scriptures, in prayer, and in praise.

Remember, "God's acquaintance is not made in a hurry" (E. M. Bounds).

FOR AN ORDERED, FOCUSED LIFE

Giving priority to time with God—this is part of an overall attitude of being wisely selective in what we do and what we leave undone. I continually need prayer for this—for wisdom to follow the Lord's guidance and priorities and not let the immediate and the urgent crowd out things that are more important. So I pray, "Lord, keep my life from being cluttered and scattered! In a new way let my ordered and focused life show forth the beauty of Your peace." What a challenge it is to live this way!

I'm reminded again of the words my dad often quoted:

Little is much if God is in it;
Man's busiest day isn't worth God's minute.

I've found Psalm 84:10 a good reminder as well as a comfort in respect to time—"A day in Thy courts is better than a thousand outside" (NASB). Think of it: One day lived in His presence, under His blessed control, has more blessing and consequence than three years of mediocre Christian living!

My heart often runs to Psalm 57:1-2— "In the shadow of Thy wings I will take refuge, till the storms of destruction pass by. I cry to God Most High, to God who fulfills His purpose for me, who accomplishes—completes—all things for me" (RSV, NASB, and Berkeley). God completes all things for me. He guides and enables me, then puts on the finishing touches. He fills in the gaps in my far-from-perfect performance, making up for my inadequacies. I don't have to do every single thing that might possibly help me accomplish my personal goals and serve others. Yes, the Lord wants me to minister to people—to share the Word, to listen, to counsel, to encourage, to help in practical ways—but He's the One who infuses my service with life and power. He's the One who blesses people, who changes lives, who continues to work through my work long after my part is finished. In every area of life, the big share of the doing is always His. "Little is much if God is in it." Yes, He completes all things for me.

Look at His promise in Psalm 138:8— "The Lord will perfect that which concerns me" (NKJV). This is surely His loving answer for us when we pray the prayer in Psalm 90:17— "Yes, give permanence to the work of our hands" (NASB marginal reading).

And let's make sure that the work of our hands is God's will—nothing more, nothing less, nothing else. God is not a slave driver, whipping us into frenzied, ceaseless activity.

MUDDY THUMBS IN THE GLASS

For years I've been impressed with Psalm 103:13-14. Let's take another look at it. "As a father pities his children, so the Lord pities those who fear [reverence] Him" (NKJV). This word *pity* means that He is tender and sympathetic toward us. He knows our frame, as verse 14 goes on to say; He remembers that we're dust, so He does not expect perfect performance.

I'm reminded of a Dennis the Menace comic strip. His dad had been out mowing the lawn, then came inside hot and perspiring. Dennis watched him sink into a chair, and he thought, *Daddy's thirsty.* Off he went, poured some lemonade, and brought it to his daddy—with his muddy thumb hanging over the rim of the glass into the lemonade.

Now if the father had not been kind, he might have said, "Get your filthy thumb out of there! Can't you do anything right?" Or if a waiter in a restaurant had served him lemonade that way, he would have refused it. But instead the father was so delighted by the love behind his son's action that he thanked him and drank the lemonade with joy. Theirs was a loving relationship, a true father-son relationship.

Our heavenly Father does not expect us to do everything perfectly. Even at our best we've still got our dirty thumbs in the glass. That's true in all our service. We'll serve Him perfectly in heaven, but never here. But God understands. He accepts imperfect service because it's a love relationship. He's a Father who's delighted that we love Him and want to please Him.

We've got a wrong idea about God when we feel He'll be angry if we're less than perfect in what we do, or that He may suddenly turn around and attack us for some sin we aren't even aware of. This is wrong thinking that keeps us from enjoying His mercy, forgiveness, and tender love.

I'm glad God doesn't give up on me because of all my imperfections! Instead He is constantly and personally calling me upward. And He not only calls me to holy living, He has committed Himself to sanctify me wholly—to make my life harmonize with His call. This promise is in 1 Thessalonians 5:23-24— "Now may the God of peace Himself sanctify you entirely. Faithful is He who calls you, and He will also bring it to pass" (NASB).

Isn't the Lord wonderful! He's always the answer to our need, the all-sufficient solution! And aren't you glad He has revealed Himself in His wonderful Book, where He repeatedly enables us to fix our eyes on Him!

DRY EARTH

Something else is just as important as reserving the right amount of time for seeking God. That is having the right mindset—or perhaps we should call it "heart-set" or even "life-set," since it involves more than just a way of thinking. It's closely related to our emotional life. It means being honest before God, accepting both our overall inherent weakness as well as all our separate little weaknesses, and pouring out our hearts before Him. But it's also a commitment to pursuing Him, a commitment we can maintain even when our feelings don't agree. Because it's the basic bent of our heart, we can go back to it and be firmly anchored in it, in spite of what our feelings may be telling us.

Most of all it's an openness. It's being receptive toward God. We open our inner eyes and turn them to Him. We see who He is, let our hearts drink it in, and then let Him be to us what we need as the hours go by.

So our part is to need and receive. We can resent being weak or feel humiliated, and then put on an appearance of strength. Or we can humbly—even gladly—face our bankruptcy and inability. "I am poor and needy," sang King David. Paul gloried in his weaknesses. Inadequacy qualifies us to receive God's sufficiency.

Receiving is like dry earth soaking in rain. It's like a child absorbing his mother's love and soothing words, relaxing in her arms. As sunshine floods a room open to its brightness, so God's favor fills and warms the heart that is genuinely open to Him.

Simply and basically, what we've got to do is to *let Him love us.*

Let Him love you. Let Him speak to you His words of love through the Scriptures. Let Him fill you with the Holy Spirit and control you, and have His way with you, so the Holy Spirit can pour out His love in your heart. Let Him bring into your life anything He wants, and don't resist Him when He allows something difficult or distressing. As you let Him work in any way He desires, you'll find yourself more and more filled with His love.

Think back again to the prayer written by George Matheson, the blind Scottish pastor of the 1800s:

O Thou Divine Spirit, that in all events of life art knocking at the
door of my heart, help me respond to Thee.... I would have my

heart open at all times to receive—at morning, noon, and night; in spring, and summer, and winter.... Knock, and I shall open unto Thee.

Being open at all times, in all circumstances, to receive—what better attitude can there be toward our loving Father who is ready at all times to give? Kings of old offered gifts to those they favored—as the king did to Esther, "even to half the kingdom." God, our Father and our King, has opened *all* His riches to us—including unlimited forgiveness, strength, security, joy, wisdom, and love beyond measure. Plus joint inheritance with His Son!

Our wonderful bridegroom "richly supplies us with all things to enjoy" (1 Timothy 6:17, NASB). He opens His hands and satisfies the desire of every living thing (Psalm 145:16). Every satisfied desire that you and I have ever experienced has come from the hand of this One who loves us.

And I wonder: As He bestows His gifts, do we with gratefulness turn to Him and let Him be central in our joys so that they cement our heart closer to His? Sometimes we can be like the woman in Hosea who failed to remember that her beloved husband had provided her with grain and wine and the delightful things in life. Instead of gratefully responding to her husband, she went off after other lovers.

How often do we let God's blessings become more important to us than He Himself is? Then we end up with a divided (and eventually dissatisfied) heart. Of late an old poem has often come to mind, one that I frequently prayed to the Lord years ago:

> Have I an object, Lord, below
> Which would divide my heart with Thee?
> Which would divert its even flow
> In answer to Thy constancy?
> O teach me quickly to return
> And cause my heart afresh to burn.

FOLLOWING HIS LEAD

"We love Him, because He first loved us" (1 John 4:19, NKJV). This was true at the outset when we first realized how much Christ loved us by dying for us. We responded and began to love Him by receiving His gift of salvation. But it's just as true all throughout the Christian life—His love is first, He's the initiator. And if we want to be able to love Him back, we've got to keep letting His love penetrate and soak in.

Our love is always secondary. Our love is always a response. That's why it's essential that we first experience His love in order for us to love Him as we ought. C. S. Lewis said that our love to God rises on the wave of His love toward us. Let God love you, and you'll find yourself responding back to Him with a tremendously satisfying love response.

My final suggestion to you in this chapter is to pore over the Scriptures on God's love that really mean something to you, the passages in which your heart has truly heard God's voice and recognized His love. Soak in them awhile. Go back to them often. Memorize them, think about their meaning, let the Holy Spirit grip you deeply inside with their truth. Then you can return to them again and again to find rescue and enrichment.

O God, my Reward and my Rewarder, I must know You. You Yourself are truly the one thing in life that I demand, the one and only thing I cannot live without. I choose to diligently seek You, to earnestly pursue my relationship with You. You are my first love. My goal is You—not the peace or joy or blessings You give, but You Yourself.

Thank You, Lord, for making available to me this great privilege of knowing You. Thank You for giving such a satisfying way for me to invest my time and energy and thought.

Now, Lord, continue to increase my capacity for seeking and knowing You. I plead with You to make me more thirsty.

Lord, it is so encouraging to reflect on how seriously You want me to take You and Your love, and how personally. So I choose to see myself through Your own all-knowing and all-loving eyes. I ask especially that You will cause me to hear Your voice of love in the morning as I open Your Word and come to You. Through Your Holy Spirit, let the waters of Your love wash over me. Let me swim in the truth of Your love. And change my life as a result.

Give me grace, Lord, day by day, to seek You first and foremost—to faithfully set apart time to be alone with You. Enable me to say no (or not yet) to secondary things that so easily crowd out time with You.

Thank You especially, Lord, for accepting my imperfect service. This motivates me to want to serve You more. You are worthy, O Lord, worthy of my all and my best. Help me respond to You in ways that bring You increasing pleasure.

In Jesus' name...

Your personal gleanings for meditation, prayer, and action:

What Scripture or truth in this chapter do you feel the Lord is especially speaking to you about? What will you do to profit the most from this?

NINE

THE POWER OF HIS PERFECT LOVE

THE GOSPEL is very old truth. But it can never be only old truth for us. Romans 1:16 says that the gospel is the power of God for salvation, and salvation has three tenses: I have been saved from the penalty of sin (past tense); in this life now I am being saved from the power of sin—through victory over sin and forgiveness when I fail (present); and in eternity, I will be saved from the presence of sin when I appear before Him in glory with my indwelling sin gone forever (future).

So we read in Romans 8:1 those bold and freeing words, "There is therefore now no condemnation for those who are in Christ Jesus." The Phillips version expresses it this way: "No condemnation now hangs over the head of those who are 'in' Jesus Christ."

A deep man of God, David Morken, has had a great influence on my life for many years. (I mentioned earlier my friendship with his wife, Helen). One of the many things he has said that I repeatedly profit from was this: "God loves me and the devil's a liar." Another: "God is not in the business of condemning His children."

Now that's good news. But how can God refrain from condemning me, with my assortment of besetting sins? Is He a spineless, compromising God who winks at sin and simply says, "Never mind, that's okay"? How can a righteous God say to me, "You're not condemned"?

He can say this because when Jesus died on the cross, He paid for all my sin. He bore all the guilt of my whole life—past, present, and future from my current point of view. The Lord "laid on Him the iniquity of us all" (Isaiah 53:6, KJV). All the sin of all people for all time was compressed like a heavy weight, then it fell on Jesus and crushed Him. On the cross He took our sins into Himself. He bore the intensity of all the guilt and suffering and pain of all the wrongdoing that all of us have ever done or ever will do. He was condemned; He became accursed for us (Galatians 3:13).

Therefore if we have trusted Christ, all the guilt and condemnation of our sin has been removed. Even when we sin now, the condemnation is not placed back on us, for God would not be fair if He required the condemnation twice. So what happens when we sin? Our fellowship with God is broken, so sooner or later our peace is disturbed and our joy evaporates. But we're still His children. And God never condemns us because He is just and the penalty has been paid in full.

This is our legal righteousness. The account book has been closed. The whole debt's been paid. He has pronounced us free, and no longer counts our sins against us.

I like the fresh and pointed way Romans 8:33-34 is rendered in the Phillips translation: "Who would dare to accuse us, whom God has chosen? The Judge Himself has declared us free from sin. Who is in a position to condemn? Only Christ, and Christ died for us, Christ rose for us, Christ reigns in power for us, Christ prays for us!" The Judge has pronounced us free—the Judge of the Supreme Court of the Universe. There's no court that can reverse His judgment. It is final.

Only Jesus has the right to condemn us—and He does not and will not. So there is no condemnation for us.

In John 5:24 we read these words from Jesus Himself: "I assure you, those who listen to my message and believe in God who sent me have eternal life. They will never be condemned for their sins, but they have already passed from death into life" (NLT).

A DANGEROUS LICENSE?

I can recall a few times in my life when God really delved in and brought conviction and repentance on a deeper level than usual. And I think we need those times now and then. Yet even when those times come, we must remember that God does not hold us guilty for those things, though He does hold us responsible to confess and renounce them. Jesus bore all the guilt of those sins before we ever committed a single one of them.

Some see a danger in teaching such total forgiveness. They're afraid people will think they're free to do anything they want, and then come back and receive automatic forgiveness just by saying, "Please forgive me." Then it's back to sinning again.

But it doesn't work that way because God has given us a new life that can never again be happy in sin. It's like being changed from a pig to a lamb, two animals with such different natures. If you bring a pig inside and wash it up and tie ribbons on it, then open the door, the pig will head straight for a mudhole and lie in it contentedly. But if a lamb happens to slip into the mud, it gets out as quickly as it can. It has a nature that doesn't like mud. If a lamb likes to spend much time in the mud, take a close look at it. It's actually a pig—in sheep's clothing. If we have no desire to please our Father and avoid sin, we do well to examine ourselves and make sure we really belong to Christ (2 Corinthians 13:5).

So as Christians we can never be truly comfortable wallowing around in sin again, for we have a new life. We have the Holy Spirit who reproves us. And we have a Father who loves us so much that He'll spank us if He needs to. When we insist on going our way, He will lovingly discipline us to bring us back. He will not let us go.

That's why God's full forgiveness doesn't give us license to sin. We have safeguards against it.

I'M ALL RIGHT AS A PERSON

The total forgiveness that comes from God means above all that we are righteous—not we hope to be righteous some day or that we wish we were righteous, but we are righteous now. For not only has Christ removed our guilt, but His righteousness has been *imputed* to us. It's been credited to us, put to our account, so that in the court of God's judgment we do indeed have righteousness—Christ's righteousness.

And God has not only imputed His righteousness to us legally, He has also *imparted* it to us spiritually. When we put our faith in Christ, He came to live within us. A union took place deep within us—a union of His life with ours. Now we are spiritually alive with His life. And because His life is a righteous life, we are righteous with His righteousness. This is not figurative or imagined, but actual. It's true. We are now new persons in Christ, so we can say, "I'm alive with the life of Christ! And I'm righteous with the righteousness of Christ! Lord, how can I thank You enough!" Later we'll discuss this more fully.

One way of looking at righteousness is the definition, "being all right as a person." In Christ, because of God's gift to us—"the gift of righteousness" (Romans 5:17)—we are all right as persons now and forever. We must let this truth grip our hearts, for we live like the person we see ourselves to be. The more we realize who we are in Christ, the more we can live according to the new image of ourselves that we carry around within us. If we still carry within ourselves a basic image of being guilty and condemned and enslaved to sin, we'll be far more prone to live fleshly lives. We'll be much more likely to give in to sin. And we won't attract others to this wonderful person Jesus. But as we allow the Lord, through the Scriptures, to engrave on our hearts who we really are in Christ, then we can experience Romans 5:17; by our acceptance of His overflowing grace (His unmerited favor) and His righteousness, we can reign in real life through Christ. We can live like kings and queens.

God is at work in us to this end. He is putting us through a process that enables us more and more to reign with Christ day by day. He is a God of loving power who cannot fail. So with confidence and joy we can look forward to becoming all He has in mind for us to be. He's going to keep on working until this happens. He'll allow the necessary circumstances to come into our lives. This includes the difficulties that mold our character, make us more like Him, and cause our faith to grow stronger and steadier. As this process continues, "we are able to hold our heads high no matter what happens and know that all is well, for we know how dearly God loves us, and we feel this warm love everywhere within us because God has given us the Holy Spirit to fill our hearts with His love" (Romans 5:5, TLB). The more we know who we are in Christ—that we're in God's favor and all right as persons, forgiven and clean and dearly loved—the more we can hold our heads high in every circumstance, knowing that all is well.

In Romans 1:17 we learn that in the gospel (the good news of Christ's death and resurrection) the righteousness of God is revealed *from faith to faith.* For me that faith began when I was ten. It has continued as I've come to better understand and trust the truths of the Cross and the Resurrection. One of those truths is that I have been made righteous. Romans 5:1 elaborates on this: "Therefore having been justified by faith, let us enjoy the peace we have with God" (NASB and Moffatt). How wonderful this is! I've been justified— made "just-as-if-I'd" never sinned. I'm just as if I'd always done the things I ought to have done. I'm just as if I'd never done the things I ought not to have done.

"Having been justified *by faith…*" the verse says. It's by faith alone, not by our works, not by our earning or deserving it. And since that is true, God now wants us to enjoy our peace with Him. He wants us to enjoy with deep assurance how He views us: We are acquitted and justified, and we possess far greater value in His eyes than we can measure or fully understand.

Did you know that God's fundamental attitude toward you is one of peace? There is no enmity in His heart, no resentment. Even when You disobey Him, He does not feel exasperated or indignant toward you. Instead He feels deeply grieved because He knows that this sin will hurt you and that it will break your fellowship with Him. He wants you to repent, and He's ready and longing for you to come back to Him.

So the attitude of peace is always there in Him, for us to enjoy.

I mentioned earlier those months and years when our son Brian's faith seemed so crippled as he struggled in the grip of modern philosophies. During that time the Lord prompted me to do a great deal of healthy heart-searching. He made me aware of things in my life that perhaps I had never faced before, and I confessed to Him specific ways I had failed as a mother. I didn't blame myself for Brian's situation; I knew he had made choices that led to it, choices rooted in things beyond my control. But I did feel really bad that in some way I no doubt had contributed to his problem. So I wrote to him from Singapore, asking his forgiveness. He wrote back to say he'd forgive me of course, but that he didn't even remember those things.

But Satan tried to ride in and color my whole motherhood black. I knew that wasn't true, yet the enemy would feed accusations into my mind. I would feel a sense of blame on top of deep regrets that I hadn't been a better mother. The thought that I was to any degree responsible for this pain in Brian's life would at times overwhelm me. Then I would turn it over to the Lord and realize that He was somehow going to work out His good purposes through it all, in His time.

During this period Warren and I returned to the United States on furlough for a few months. One day as I was driving Brian back to the university, once again he talked about his struggles and doubts. As I drove away after letting him off at his dormitory, I felt so full of regret that I couldn't continue home. I found a little coffee shop where I could sit at a table facing the wall and drink coffee, and I sat there feeling horrible, with tears rolling down my cheeks.

Then I suddenly realized that I was jealous of Jesus, because He has never had to regret anything. Not one single thing.

At this point the Lord reminded me: "Ruth, whose righteousness do you have?"

"Jesus Christ's."

"And how much righteousness do you have?"

"Well, since I'm righteous with His righteousness, I'm really righteous. I'm totally clean!"

"Then if He doesn't have anything to regret, why should You be sitting there full of regrets?"

What a relief this was! I realized afresh that because I'm righteous with Jesus' righteousness, and He never needed to regret a thing, I need have no regrets either.

That doesn't mean I don't have to confess my sins and at times make restitution to clear things up. But I don't have to live in regret. If I harbor regrets, I'm not living by faith in what God says.

GOD LOVES TO FORGIVE

Satan loves to lie to us about God, and one of his common lies is that it doesn't really matter what you do as long as you're sincere. You can choose your own lifestyle and establish your own values, and as long as you live up to what you think is best for you, then that's fine.

That's a lie because God is a righteous God who hates sin. He loves each of His children in a unique way, and so He hates our sin because it's a poison that destroys. He loves the sinner, but He abhors the thought of our being involved in sin, much as we parents hate the thought of our toddler sampling something toxic or our teenager getting into trouble with the law.

Some people believe Satan's lie that because God is a loving God, He would never place restrictions upon us. He wouldn't want to limit our freedom and spoil our fun. They have difficulty accepting that God has communicated some very specific commands and that these are for our good. So they encounter unnecessary trouble in life. They're like the son who runs away from home to have his own way, then finds out it doesn't work out the way he imagined. The fact is, we need restrictions and loving controls on our lives. God knows that and supplies our need.

Another of Satan's lies is to portray God as a severe judge who condemns His children when they sin, and who is hesitant to forgive. Satan would have us think of God responding to our sin by saying, "Won't you ever learn?" Then when we ask for forgiveness, we imagine Him saying, "Well, first I'll see how you do; I'll be glad to forgive you if you do better in the next few days. Show Me you really mean business." Satan the accuser likes to use this strategy to attack our confidence in our salvation and destroy our fellowship with the Lord.

Of course it's true that whenever we saunter off in a sinful direction God wants us to do an about-face, which is repentance. He wants us to come to Him and say, "Lord, I've been tolerating this sin, but now I turn from it and I turn back to You. I let go of it and I receive Your forgiveness. I thank You that Jesus is in me so I can become victorious over this."

Then God loves to forgive us. When we make this about-face from our sin and turn to Him, He welcomes us fervently just as the prodigal son's father welcomed him, leaving no room for the son to plead for his father's forgiveness (Luke 15:18-24). After we return, God wants us to simply depend on Him and on His life in us. Then we won't stray from Him as quickly or as often— though from time to time throughout our entire life we'll still need to confess one sin or another.

The story of the prodigal son is a great comfort to me. Sometimes we think it applies only to unbelievers who finally come to Christ. But I think it applies especially to the Christian life, for this runaway rascal was a *son* and had enjoyed the privileges of being in his father's family before departing for that far country. Sometimes our own trips away are just one "little" sin, or sometimes we let many sins pile up. Eventually we realize how futile it is to go our own way, to do our own thing, as the prodigal did when he was feeding pigs and longing to fill his own stomach with the husks they were eating. We discover that sin pays poor wages.

Perhaps you've felt like telling God what the son decided to tell his father: "I am no longer worthy to be called your son." But that's as far as his father let that conversation go.

Didn't the son realize that his sonship had never been a matter of his being worthy of it? He was a son because he'd been born into the father's family. And so the father, who had been looking and longing for the opportunity to forgive and restore his son, immediately reinstated him. He wouldn't hear of his son's plan to become a hired servant and earn his way back into the family. Nor did the father preach a sermon to his son: "Have you learned your lesson? We'll give you a little time of probation, and see if you've really learned anything." No, the father ran to him, hugged and kissed him, and welcomed him right back into the love and riches of the family. There's no evidence that this father was the least bit resentful toward his son. So it is with God. Even when we're coming to confess sin, "we can run right into the throne room and find His arms wide open," as Kay Arthur says.

This is God's attitude when we sincerely ask His forgiveness for the things He so strongly disapproves of. He is never reluctant to forgive. He always accepts us as persons, as dearly loved children, regardless of how strongly He hates and rejects our sin—an important distinction to make.

A story from generations ago comes to mind. A young man living at home became increasingly rebellious against his parents' rules and moral standards. He just couldn't be comfortable living there. He caused quarrels and always seemed to be doing the wrong thing. Finally he decided to leave. Like the prodigal son he traveled far from home.

At last he was able to do whatever he wanted without anyone's disapproval. This was a dream come true. But as time went by he encountered problem after problem, and his life became more and more tangled, miserable, empty. Finally he considered taking his life. But then he thought, "My only hope is to go home. I've caused my parents so much heartache—I doubt they would want me. But still…"

So he wrote a letter home. He told his parents all he had done wrong, asked them to forgive him, and expressed his desire to come home. Assuring them that he'd understand if this was not agreeable to them, he offered a plan. The train he would travel would pass close to their house. He proposed that, if they were willing to have him back, they would hang a white handkerchief on the big tree in their backyard. If he saw the handkerchief as the train passed, he would get off at the next station. Otherwise he'd just keep going.

As the train rumbled toward home, he told his story to the passenger beside him. Then as they approached his parents' home his apprehensions grew. He turned to his fellow passenger and said, "I'm afraid to look. Would you watch out the window for me?" As they finally came near, he buried his face in his hands.

Suddenly he heard the other man cry, "Look! Just look!" He raised his head and looked out. The tree in their backyard was totally covered with white handkerchiefs. There was no doubt what his parents wanted.

That's how the Lord's forgiveness is. Whether we're coming to Him for the first time to receive Him into our life, or whether we're coming for the millionth time to confess a sin, He's got white handkerchiefs all over the tree. He ardently welcomes us home, back into His fellowship.

MERCY FROM GOD THE FATHER

The entire Trinity—the Father and Son and Holy Spirit—is involved in giving us this privilege of not only being forgiven but also feeling forgiven. All three are involved in ensuring us a life that is liberated, confident, conquering, and increasingly conformed to the image of Christ.

One of the big things the Bible tells us about the Father is that He is merciful. *Mercy* means that God does not give us what we deserve, while *grace* means that God gives us what we don't deserve. So instead of the wrath and punishment we rightly have coming to us, God gives us all kinds of blessings that we're not even remotely entitled to receive on our own.

But we can't really enjoy all these rich blessings of His grace if we do not understand and lay hold of God's mercy—if we're caught in the prison house of guilty feelings, with a cloud of self-condemnation hanging over us. Before we can go on to enjoy our spiritual riches, we have to know God's mercy and really believe that He doesn't give us what we deserve.

When I think of God's mercy, a Scripture I especially like is Psalm 103:10-12: "He has not dealt with us according to our sins, nor punished us according to our iniquities. For as the heavens are high above the earth, so great is His mercy toward those who fear Him" (NKJV). He's given us not just a little bit of mercy, but great mercy. In a very grand and extravagant way He chooses to deal with us in ways we don't deserve.

Another of my favorites is Psalm 130:3-4. Many times I have to use this passage when Satan wants to make me feel that God is marking down a list of things against me. The verse says, "If You, Lord, should mark iniquities, O Lord, who could stand?" (NKJV). Not one person in God's family could stand before Him if He kept track of our sins in some celestial account book. Then the verse continues, "But there is forgiveness with You, that You may be feared." He's looking for people who will fear Him—who will revere and obey Him— and He wouldn't find any if He was not merciful.

Another verse that has been such a blessing to me is Psalm 23:6— "Surely [not maybe, but surely] goodness and mercy shall follow me all the days of my life, and I will dwell in the house of the Lord forever" (NKJV). This is from David's shepherd psalm, and we can think of goodness and mercy as two dogs following along behind the sheep to help the shepherd protect them.

Both God's goodness and His mercy follow us in this way—His goodness that prompts Him to pour out all the good things He brings into our lives, and His mercy that keeps Him from giving us the punishment and emptiness we deserve. If a sheep runs away instead of following the shepherd, then falls over a cliff, what does the shepherd do? Does he let him lie there to suffer the fate he deserves? No, the good shepherd searches for the sheep, lifts it to safety with his staff, and lovingly brings it back to the warmth and protection of the fold. That's mercy.

The psalm says that goodness and mercy shall surely follow me all the days of my life—all the days: when I was twenty, when I was forty, when I was sixty, and when I'm eighty or a hundred, if I live that long—all those days His goodness and mercy will follow me. I'll always need His mercy because I'll never be perfect until I get to glory. And I'll always have it.

But doesn't God get tired of being merciful toward us? No, for Lamentations 3:22-23 tells us that the Lord's mercies are new every morning. He's got fresh, brand-new mercies for us every day.

MERCY FROM JESUS THE SON

God longed to justify man, to make him just as if he'd never sinned. That's because He is merciful. But He is also just. Justice says that if sin has been committed, the penalty must be paid. "The soul who sins will die," we read in Ezekiel 18:4 (NASB). How can God be just and still justify people, counting them righteous? That's a huge problem to the human mind. But God had it all figured out before He ever created Adam and Eve. He had a wonderful plan in which He would remain just, and yet be free to totally forgive us without our having to pay the penalty for our sin. That's where the second person of the Trinity comes in.

Satan had gained control of this world; he's called the god of this world. Satan had led the world in rebellion and herded mankind into his kingdom of darkness, condemnation, terrible guilt, and fear of death. So when Jesus, the Son of God, was born upon this earth, He was a warrior invading enemy territory. He came to defeat Satan. And He did this by dying on the cross and taking on Himself our sinful nature and the penalty for all our sins.

God so longed to see us free from the condemnation of our sin, He so longed for the privilege of giving us this totally free forgiveness, that He was willing let Jesus His Son go through immeasurable anguish. In Isaiah 53:10 we read that it *pleased* the Father to bruise Jesus, to hurt Him and let Him suffer. Why did it please Him? Because God saw that through this suffering, countless people would be justified—just as if they'd never sinned.

Hebrews 10:14 says that "by one offering He has perfected forever those who are being sanctified" (NKJV)—which means those He has made clean and set apart for Himself. In our innermost person we've been perfected forever. That means I'm all right as a person, and I always will be because of Christ's sacrifice.

How does Jesus really feel about our weaknesses and failures? In Hebrews 4:15-16 we learn that He is touched with the feeling of our weaknesses. He's not a distant high priest. He's not an unfeeling lawyer who says, "I just can't understand that—why did he (or she) do it again?" He sympathizes with us and feels our weaknesses. And the next verse tells us why: He Himself was tempted in every way just as we are, except that He did not sin. And the fact that He did not sin doesn't mean that the temptation wasn't hard for Him, for continuing to endure a temptation without yielding to it brings more suffering (at the time) than does giving in.

Jesus knows the feeling of temptation, and He understands. Therefore He doesn't condemn. Hebrews 7:24-25 says that Jesus, as our permanent High Priest, is able to save us completely because He's always living to intercede on our behalf. And 1 John 2:1 says that "if anyone sins, we have an Advocate with the Father, Jesus Christ the righteous" (NKJV). Jesus Christ rises to our defense in court, pleading our case.

In Hebrews 2:17, Jesus is described as "a merciful and faithful high priest in the service of God" (RSV). And the mercy of Jesus will continue to come our way all through life, leading us forward to our perfect life in eternity. In Jude 1:21 we find the command to keep ourselves in God's love—to stay always within the boundaries where it can reach and bless us—as we wait for the mercy of our Lord Jesus Christ to bring us to eternal life.

Paul said in 1 Timothy 1:15, "Christ Jesus came into the world to save sinners, of whom I am chief" (NKJV). As I pondered these words one day, I was suddenly able to identify with Paul's admission in a new way. If I were to list the evidence I know against myself up to this present moment, the list would be a longer one than I could make against anyone else I know. But Christ bore all the charges against me for every sin of my entire life. "He took this list of sins and destroyed it by nailing it to Christ's cross" (Colossians 2:14, TLB). God is never waiting to condemn, but to forgive. Knowing this, I can humbly and fearlessly admit with Paul, "I am a sinner"—not, "I was," but "I am."

IN HIS BODY

Our friend David Morken served years ago as a missionary on the island of Sumatra in Southeast Asia. With a native helper he traveled to many places in Sumatra to preach. His missionary journeys included a leper village where everyone had leprosy, some quite severely.

He felt he was making no headway in the leper village. He just couldn't break through with the message of God's love and the good news of what His Son Jesus had done for them.

One day as they approached the village, his Indonesian helper asked, "Mr. Morken, could I talk to them today?" David agreed, thinking this man could do no worse than he'd been doing.

When the people were gathered, the Indonesian helper told them a story about a man who once came to visit a leper village much like their own. He was very kind and began to help them, and they loved him for it. He stayed overnight in the village and helped them again the next day. It looked as if he might settle there. So they became worried, knowing that leprosy can be contracted through exposure to it over time. "You have to leave," they warned him. "We like having you here, but if you stay you'll get leprosy." But the man stayed and kept serving them.

Eventually the time came when they noticed a white spot on him. "Now you've really got to leave," they told him, knowing that with medicine the illness can be checked in its early stages. "You must go!" they insisted. But he wouldn't. He stayed, and his leprosy grew steadily worse.

But now they began to notice something strange. As the leprosy spread on the man's body—up his arms, onto his face, down to his feet—the villagers' leprosy began to diminish. By the time he was fully leprous, the other people's bodies were fully free from the disease.

At this point David's helper concluded, "Now there's no village on earth where that exact thing happened. But this is a picture of what Jesus did when He came to earth. He bore our sins in His body on the cross so we could be free from sin and guilt and have eternal life."

A DEBT NO LONGER MINE

I especially like Colossians 2:14 in the Laubach translation, which is written in basic English for those who have just learned English as a second language. It says, "God crossed out the whole debt against us in His account books. He no longer counted the laws we had broken. He nailed the account book to the cross and closed the account." So now there's no longer any place to write down our sins. Our account has been closed.

In our society today a person can legally declare bankruptcy for himself or his business so that others cannot collect the debts he owes them. But in generations past, a person with insurmountable debts often faced the options of either paying them or going to prison.

I'm told, however, of an old Jewish custom. If a man had more debts than he could possibly pay, he could write down a list of them and post the paper on his gate or outside his prison door, with one tack at the top and another at the bottom. If a kind and wealthy benefactor walked by and took pity on the man, he would take out the bottom tack, fold up the list under the other tack, then write his name on the outside of the paper. By doing this he was saying, "I personally assume the responsibility for these debts." The debtor would then go free.

That's what Jesus did on the cross. Imagine a list of every sin of our entire life—Jesus has doubled it over and written His name there to say, "I personally have paid the penalty for every one of these sins. I personally assume all the responsibility for them."

The story is told of how King Frederick the Great of eighteenth-century Prussia liked to disguise himself at night and go walking among the people, listening to what they were saying—especially to what they might be saying about him. Late one night while returning to his quarters from one of those walks, he passed by the room where his royal accountants worked. Looking in, he saw one of them still there, asleep at his desk with his head on his hands. This particular accountant was one Frederick knew well and liked. He stepped closer, looked over the man's shoulder, and saw a list of amounts of money, with a large total at the bottom. The man had somehow been involved in embezzlement, and next to the total he had written, "So great a debt! Who can pay it?" The king quietly took the pen, dipped it in the ink, and wrote, "I, Frederick." The king himself assumed the debt.

Next to all the sins of my life—future, present, or past—Jesus has written, "I, Jesus—I paid for that. I, Jesus, have assumed that debt."

What good news!

MERCY THROUGH THE HOLY SPIRIT

What part does the Holy Spirit have in all this? We've already seen what God the Father and God the Son have done and are doing for our forgiveness. That would seem to be enough. With all that they do, we have more than enough reason to say, "Praise God! I'm free! I don't have to go around feeling guilty or condemned."

It's the Holy Spirit who brings those truths home to our heart so that we can truly experience and express those very feelings.

In John 16:8-10, Jesus told His disciples that He would send the Holy Spirit to convince the world of sin and righteousness and judgment.

The Spirit would convict "in regard to sin," Jesus said, "because men do not believe in Me" (NIV). Failing to believe in Jesus is the sin that condemns people.

Jesus said the Spirit would convict "in regard to righteousness, because I am going to the Father, where you can see Me no longer." Christ rose from the dead and has ascended to the Father, demonstrating that His payment was acceptable and that righteousness is truly available to anyone who will receive it.

"And in regard to judgment," Jesus said, "because the prince of this world now stands condemned." Satan has been judged. He's under condemnation. And if he comes to accuse you, you can say—respectfully, but with firm faith—"God says that you are judged, Satan, and I don't have to listen to you. You are not my judge."

To bring us to Christ, the Holy Spirit opened our eyes to the fact that we had sinned and needed a Savior. Even now in our Christian life He convicts us of sin. He's living in us, and when we do something wrong He lovingly points it out—not to condemn us but to help us. He's like a friend riding in the car you're driving, and when you head down the wrong street he says, "You know, that was a wrong turn back there. This is not the right way to go." The Holy Spirit alerts us when we make wrong turns, so we won't waste our life on wrong roads. He does this graciously, not condemningly. He brings that gentle feeling of guilt that's a great and trusted friend to us, pushing us like a goad back to the right way, making us uncomfortable until we confess and repent, returning to the right road.

When we sense such guilt, how do we know if this is the Holy Spirit convincing or Satan accusing us? For one thing, Satan brings a general cloud of condemnation while the Holy Spirit points out something specific to confess. And Satan does it in a harsh way, while the Holy Spirit does it in a loving and a gentle way.

How does the Holy Spirit feel about us? In James 4:5 we read that the Spirit yearns jealously over us. He has a *longing* for us to be holy. And in Ephesians 4:30 we read that when we sin, the Spirit is grieved. Not angry or resentful—but *grieved*. That's a love word.

Remember also that sin in God's sight is not just disregarding a list of do's and don'ts. Sin includes pride, self-will, self-reliance, unsurrendered dreams and ambitions. It includes harboring such attitudes as indifference, hostility, resentment, anxiety, and self-condemnation. It also includes unbelief—including failure to believe He has forgiven us after we have confessed!

WASHING US CLEAN, AGAIN AND AGAIN

The Holy Spirit applies to my heart the reality that I am justified. He's the One by whom I was born again. In Titus 3:5 we read about "the washing of rebirth and renewal by the Holy Spirit" (NIV). We have been washed by being born again. Through the Holy Spirit I was born out of the old life into the new life, and now I'm clean. I've been born out of the dirt into a new clean place in God's presence with a new clean nature. That's really clean!

Remember in John 13 how Peter protested when Jesus began washing his feet? "Lord," he said, "You're not going to wash my feet!" But Jesus answered, "If I can't wash your feet, then you don't have any part with Me." He was saying that we can't have fellowship with Him when we have "dirty feet." And when Peter responded, "Oh, then don't just wash my feet, wash my whole body," Jesus said, "No, if you've been bathed, then you're completely clean."

In a similar way the Holy Spirit uses the Word of God to wash our feet day by day, to cleanse us. The Bible compares both the Word and the Spirit to water (John 7:37-39, Ephesians 5:26). And water of course has great cleansing power. As we have seen, we who know Christ are completely clean through our new birth—we never need to repeat that. Now it's just the "dirt that soils our feet" as we walk through life that needs to be washed away day by day. The Holy Spirit by His mercy does this for us. How often do you praise God for this wonderful cleansing?

The story is told of a figure in ancient Greek mythology who was given the job of cleaning the Aegean stables. The stables were unspeakably filthy—a hopeless job to clean. But the person assigned to this task had a brilliant idea.

He simply diverted a river and ran it through the stables to flush them out. Water has power!

The Spirit uses the Word of God and flushes the dirt out of our lives. We don't have to try to clean ourselves up—"Lord, wait until I rub this spot off and then I'll have my quiet time." No, we come as we are, "just as I am," and we let Him do the cleansing.

Sometimes as we come to the Scriptures the Holy Spirit shows us some specific sin to confess. At other times He may use the Word to wash away something we don't even know is there. He also uses the Word to reassure us that we're clean and righteous by faith, not by how well we perform.

We've seen in Romans 1:16-17 that the gospel is the power of God for salvation to everyone who believes. Why? Because in the gospel—God's recorded good news—the righteousness of God is revealed, "a righteousness that is by faith from first to last" (NIV). All through our lives, it's *faith*. Just by believing God we have been made righteous through what Christ did for us on the Cross. The Holy Spirit uses the Word to assure us of this, and by faith we can respond, "Thank You, Lord, that through Jesus I am righteous."

FORGIVENESS AND MORE

Before we can have true righteousness produced in our daily living, we have to realize that we are righteous in Christ. Our actions and attitudes will flow out of how we feel about ourselves. So if we want clean thinking and living we must have a sense of being clean. The inner power to live a new life is ours through the Holy Spirit as God gives us this confidence that we are clean and forgiven.

And God does so much more than that. His forgiveness isn't like human forgiveness, where at times a person may be forgiven and then let loose on society to continue his wicked ways. God not only forgives, He also begins a transforming work in our lives through the Holy Spirit. The Spirit is better than a parole officer. The parole officer can be there only part of the time, and when he's not around the parolee can sneak off and do something wrong again. But the Holy Spirit is right here within us all the time to gently show us where we're wrong and give us power to live righteous lives. He's in us to bring us back to the right and to continually transform us, giving us new desires, new attitudes, new ways of living. So the gospel is good news of our salvation from the power of sin as well as from the guilt of sin.

We're not just set free from prison—we're being transformed. And that's exciting, heart-expanding good news!

Thank You, Father, for the wonder of Your tender mercies, which moved You to send Your Son to earth—the Sunrise from on high who dispels the darkness of my sin and guilt. Thank You that He chose to suffer the agonies of the cross, where He bore the compressed weight of all my sin—and that with Him as my Savior I bear no guilt.

I praise You that through my new birth You made me completely clean... that I have been rescued... and that now I am righteous in my innermost being, fully accepted by You. How good it is to trust in Your forgiveness—Your full and free forgiveness that is available every moment of every day.

How I rejoice that all three Persons of the Trinity work together to assure that I experience Your mercy and forgiveness in my daily life.

I lift my heart to You, Father, rejoicing in Your loving, tender attitudes toward me day by day, hour by hour. You are so forgiving—never reluctant to forgive, always eager. It passes all human understanding how You can be so merciful and gracious to me—not giving me what I deserve, and so freely giving me what I don't deserve. I praise You that I can come boldly before Your throne of grace and receive mercy for my failures and grace to help in time of need.

I thank You for Christ my High Priest, and for the great compassion and understanding and sympathy He has for me. What a joy it is to know that He feels completely my every weakness, and prays for me. And that He is my advocate, my lawyer, never condemning me but always interceding for me.

And thank You for sending the Holy Spirit to live in me. How grateful I am that He makes me aware of sins I need to confess… that He "washes my feet" day by day with the water of Your Word… that He cleanses me from secret, hidden faults and gives me power to overcome. Thank You for His tender yearning to draw me on to greater holiness.

Lord, cause me to stand on these truths more firmly, more constantly, and with ever-growing gratefulness.

In Jesus' name…

Your personal gleanings for meditation, prayer, and action:

What Scripture or truth in this chapter do you feel the Lord is especially speaking to you about? What will you do to profit the most from this?

TEN

IN HIS PERFECT LOVE, I'M TRULY ALIVE

AFTER TELLING GOD at age sixteen that I would do anything He wanted me to do, I found that I really wanted to please Him. And I tried to please Him, though looking back I'm sure I did this in Dennis-the-Menace style, with my very muddy thumb in the glass of water. Yet I suppose I did a lot of things that deeply pleased the Lord, knowing how gracious He is and how easy to please.

But there were certain sins that greatly frustrated me because they kept cropping up again and again. "Lord, forgive me," I'd say. Then I'd try hard to do better. But sooner or later (too often, sooner) I'd commit the same sin again.

I can recall walking along with a close friend toward the end of our high school days, discussing how disappointed we were with our Christian lives. Our conclusion: "There must be something more to the Christian life than this."

I knew the answer wasn't going forward at another church meeting. I'd done that so many times, and yet I'd still get angry with my sister—the sin that troubled me the most. We had a wonderful relationship but occasionally we'd really get upset with each other. When we quarreled, she would yell at me more than I did at her (no doubt because I provoked her more), but inwardly I would be just as angry, maybe more. I knew this didn't please the Lord, and I felt genuinely sorry about it. I begged for Him to help me.

In this chapter I'm going to share with You how the Lord has answered this prayer.

A FRESH INNER DAWNING

This chapter, perhaps more than all the others, covers truths that are ultra-vital for a life that pleases God and brings consistent enjoyment of His love. These are truths that we cannot possibly grasp unless the Holy Spirit opens our eyes in a special way. There's no way we can wrap our natural minds around them. So we're going to look at them from different angles, and with a degree of repetition—for repetition is spiritual glue that cements truth in our hearts and minds.

And I encourage you to plead with God for fresh, clear understanding of these truths. Pause now and pray that these truths will dawn like a fresh and beautiful sunrise in your heart. If the Lord has already done this for you, pray that you will experience the reality of these truths with greater constancy. Ask these same things for others who will read these pages.

Then as you read, pause often to thank and praise the Lord for things that stand out to you. Praise has a way of opening our hearts to experience God more fully.

After my high school graduation, I began to feed on the Word with a hungrier heart and I absorbed more of its truth. Along with Faith Luing, a close friend, I spent that summer in northern Minnesota teaching vacation Bible schools. Often in the evening I would pore over Colossians 3. I was struck by the word *let*—we're to let God do certain things. I wondered what the implications of that were. *Let* seemed quite different from *try.* I noticed verse 4 of that chapter as well, which speaks of "Christ who is our life." But at the time the rich truth of those words did not yet penetrate my heart. But when we pore over the Word, when we examine it carefully, letting its meaning soak in, this prepares our hearts to grasp its truths in a life-changing way.

The following fall, I came across this statement: "It's not only true that my life is Christ's, but my life is Christ." Suddenly I experienced an inner dawning, just as I did at age ten when Mother quoted John 3:16 and I responded to the Lord in simple faith. This truth that Christ is my life became a light within me—and what a difference it made!

Now I could grasp the meaning of those words in Colossians 3:4, "Christ who is our life." And I was able to personalize this truth: "Christ is *my* life."

I began to see something I didn't grasp at age ten when I became a Christian. I started to see that because Christ was in me, I was a new person in the core of my being. I saw the truth of 2 Corinthians 5:17, that if anyone is in Christ he's a new creature, a new creation, "a new person altogether" (Phillips). Each of us has a brand-new life—Christ's life infused into us. We are "not the same anymore, for the old life is gone. A new life has begun!" (2 Corinthians 5:17, NLT).

It's true that God had chosen me for this before the foundation of the world, but when I received Christ personally I took ownership of the right to be called God's child, as John 1:12 says. At that point I was actually born of God. What took place in me was a birth, not an adoption in the modern sense of the word (wonderful though that is!). I was *born* of Him, actually becoming a part of His own family by birth (verse 13). So I now possess a new life, a new heredity—new spiritual genes, so to speak. All this became mine because I was born spiritually: "Not a physical birth resulting from human passion or plan—this rebirth comes from God" (John 1:13, NLT).

I HAVE THE VERY LIFE OF JESUS

As believers whom God has made righteous, we have the actual life of Jesus in the core of our being. His life is ours now and forever: "He who has the Son has life" (1 John 5:12).

It's important for us to grasp that this is eternal life. John makes this clear in the verses on either side of the verse I just mentioned: "God has given us eternal life, and this life is in His Son.… I write these things to you who believe in the name of the Son of God so that you may know that you have eternal life"

(NASB). My eternal life began when I trusted Christ as a child. It won't begin when I die; it will simply continue when I'm forever with Jesus in the place He has prepared for me. Eternal life is new life now and new life forever. It's Christ's life in me now and Christ's life in me forever.

I like to think of this new and eternal life in Christ as being like the pages in a book. If someone gives you a book and you accept that gift, you also receive the pages bound together with the cover. Likewise when I received Jesus, I also received His *life*—His eternal life—within me. Having Him, I have eternal life.

Warren led a thirteen-year-old boy to Christ some years ago and wanted to help him be sure of his salvation. So they turned to 1 John 5:11-13, as Warren asked, "Did you receive Jesus into your heart?"

"Yes," the boy answered.

"Well then, read what this verse says."

So he read, "He who has the Son has life; he who has not the Son of God has not life."

Warren asked, "So do you have eternal life?"

"No...I don't think so."

Warren again asked him, "Did you receive Jesus? Do you have Him in your heart?"

"Yes."

"Read the verse again."

The boy read it once more: "He who has the Son has life; he who has not the Son of God has not life."

"Do you have Jesus in your heart? Did you ask Him to come in?"

"Yes."

"So, do you have eternal life?"

"Well, I don't think so."

"Let's read it again," Warren suggested. They did this three or four times.

Finally the boy said, "Oh, this is wonderful! It says I have eternal life if I have Jesus!" And he started bouncing in his chair.

As Warren tells this story, he smiles and says, "We don't have to bounce to have assurance, but we have to see what God says and believe it. And then it's good to tell Him, 'Thank You, Lord. I have eternal life because I have Jesus in me.'"

So Christ's presence within me means I have eternal life, but it also means more than the privilege of dwelling forever with God. Right now, we are alive—with capital letters and exclamation points. We're ALIVE!!! When we realize that we have life now—the vibrant, abundant, overcoming life of Christ Himself—we may well do some "bouncing" in our hearts.

There's one major difference between who I was before Christ entered my life and who I am now. Before, there was a union inside me between sin and me. I was a *sin-me* person. Sin was my nature and my master—so thoroughly united with me that we were like one-and-the-same person. I picture it like this:

Now there's a very different union within me—a union between Christ and me. I am now a *Christ-me* person. That's where the union is now! I picture it like this:

This is the real me now. This is my new identity, my true identity. Sin is still in me, but it's not a valid part of me; it is no longer my nature or my master. Sin still tries to pose as part of me, as my partner and "friend." But sin is actually a traitor in the camp and a liar. It is no longer part of the true me. Deep inside me, I've become a totally new person with Christ and His life in me.

THE RIGHT SIDE OF THE CROSS

The practical truth of this can be illustrated by the following drawing.

In the drawing—as well as in our lives—the Cross and the empty tomb form a dividing line. That line separates the Death side from the Life side.

On the Death side is spiritual death. Now death doesn't mean annihilation. Death for human beings is never annihilation. What death really means is *separation*. When my first husband died, he was separated physically from his life on earth and from his loved ones here, but he went to a better life. In the same way, spiritual death means separation from God—eternal separation for unbelievers who never turn to Christ as their Savior and Lord. Before I understood and believed John 3:16, my sins formed a barrier between me and God.

In this illustration, the Death side represents this spiritual separation and alienation from God. Guilt and condemnation belong on this side where Satan and our flesh like to keep us in our experience.

But the right side of the dividing line is the Life side, the God side. On this side is spiritual life, total forgiveness, and freedom. Strength and vitality come to us here because we're alive with His life. This is possible only because, through faith, we've been given a share in Christ's death and in His resurrection.

When Jesus hung on the cross, He took into Himself all our sin and guilt, all our condemnation and deserved death. In that sense "we were dead and buried with Him" (Romans 6:4, Phillips). Our real identity with Him continues because of His resurrection, "so that just as He was raised from the dead by that splendid revelation of the Father's power so we too might rise to life on a new plane altogether" (6:4, Phillips).

When I was born again, I was born out of the Death side and into the Life side, the Righteous side, the God side of the Cross. I received Christ into my spirit, into my inmost being, through the Holy Spirit who came to make me a new person by living in me.

Until Jesus returns or calls us home, indwelling sin will remain with us. This is what the Bible calls the sinful nature (Galatians 5:19, NIV). It is our old, former self with its sinful tendencies—the person we were before Christ came into our lives. It's the evil present within us. Many call it our "old nature." I like to call it my "former nature," for this helps me not to identify with it as my true self. It produces the "works of the flesh"—the practices of human nature without God, including both obvious sins and self-produced "righteous deeds," which are like filthy garments in God's sight (Isaiah 64:6). It takes over our day-by-day experience when we rely on our own natural desires and dictates and strength rather than relying on Christ in us.

Indwelling sin is like an ugly, smelly garbage can. Lots of obnoxious things come out of it—things like immorality, hostility that hasn't been dealt with, anger that's been handled wrongly, anxiety that we haven't renounced, plus envy, resentment, bitterness, self-condemnation, and the fear that deafens us

to God's "Be not afraid." Each of us has our own assortment of sins that most often shift our experience back to the garbage-pail side. And the most basic sin for all of us is failure to trust God and count on what He says in His Word about Himself, about us, and about how life runs well.

The left side of the Cross is what I experience whenever I sin, before I repent and confess and receive the Lord's fresh forgiveness. After being forgiven, I can return in my actual experience to my new identity on the right side of the Cross.

We need to ask ourselves, "Which side am I identifying with? Where am I choosing to live? And when my fleshly ways take over, how quickly do I use the lid of truth—Spirit-empowered truth—to put a stop to their outflow?"

Even after we confess our sin, Satan often comes to us and says, "How can you think you're forgiven? How many times have you done that same old sin and confessed it, and now you're back in it again. You're no different than you ever were! You're just not worthy to be a Christian." But God tells us in Romans 6:11 that we should consider ourselves dead indeed to sin and alive to God. This is the way we're to look upon ourselves, for it's the way God sees us. We're to count it true because God has said it.

So the dotted figure is the "unreal" me, a phantom figure rather than the true me. When I have sin in my life that I'm not ready to confess and renounce,

I've shifted my experience to the death side, the unreal side of the Cross. But what if I feel caught on that wrong side of the Cross, even though I've confessed and renounced my sin? I can escape by returning to the truth that I am in Christ, *in union* with Him, and by choosing to let Him live His life in me. That puts the lid back on the garbage pail.

Indwelling sin—the sinful nature—is not the part of me that's going to be with Christ forever. That part is going to be left in the grave, or left behind when Jesus comes. My former nature will drop off like dirty clothes. And in the present, it is not the part of me that the Lord fellowships with. He fellowships with the true me, the me that is full of life and vitality and shining with His radiance.

As a believer in Christ, the real me is always on the right side. This is the new person I really am deep inside. My inmost, core relationship with God is not altered in any way when I sin. I'm one with Christ, and I always have the privilege of enjoying freedom, joy, love, light, life, adequacy, total forgiveness, and best of all, fellowship with the living God.

But God gives us the freedom to choose which side we will experience.

So we need to ask ourselves, "Which side do I identify with? Where do I choose to live this moment, this hour, this day?"

This is the person who dwells with God now and forever—always on the Life side, alive with the life of Jesus and righteous with His righteousness.

Therefore you and I can daily reaffirm before the Lord, "Father, in myself—my former self—I am a sinner. Yet in Christ I am guiltless, clean, and pure. Thank You for the assurance You give me in Your Word: 'There is no condemnation at all for those who are in union with Christ Jesus. For the life-giving power of the Spirit through union with Christ Jesus has set us free from the power of sin and death' (Romans 8:1, Williams). And how I rejoice that I am worth more to You than I can comprehend. I can hold my head high in the light of Your love because Your Son has reconciled me to You!"

And we can listen to our Lord's reassurances: "As the Father has loved Me, so have I loved you" (John 15:9, NIV). "You are precious in My eyes, and honored, and I love you" (Isaiah 43:4, RSV).

It's my choice which side I'm going to live on. By simple faith I can put the lid of truth on that garbage can with all those ugly things coming out of it. I can confess my sin and know I'm totally forgiven. Then I can go on to say, "Lord, I am a new person inside, indwelt by Jesus Christ. I have the resurrected power of Christ, and through Christ I can do all things. Everything You want of me, I *can do* through Him."

I find it important to keep in mind that God has not only pronounced Me righteous, but has also bestowed in me the righteous life of Christ. So immediately after even my deepest times of repentance for sin, I can go forth with confidence and say, "I'm alive with His righteousness, and through Him I can change my ways of living and become more like Him."

I'm very aware that certain parts of my personality have not yet been changed. But gradually God is transforming me, bringing my faulty parts under His loving control more continuously. Because I have His life within me, I have God's power to live more and more the way Jesus lived. But for each of us, becoming Christlike is a process. The Holy Spirit transforms us into the Lord's image not all at once but from one degree of splendor to another (2 Corinthians 3:18). This takes prayer, knowing God better, trusting Him more—and time. God works on one thing after another. He doesn't put together a list of everything that needs correcting, then dump the whole thing on us. Rather He leads us on in growth so that bit by bit the beauty of Jesus permeates our personality.

God has a lot of work to do in cleaning up my fleshly ways. He'll be working on that until glory. But the real me has already been made clean and pure by being born anew. The real me is permeated with the very righteousness of Christ and filled with the Holy Spirit. The true new me, deep down inside, is clean forever.

MADE ONE

Colossians 3:3 often reminds me that my "life is hidden with Christ in God." What special closeness this indicates—an intimate relationship at all times, whether or not I consciously enjoy it. And the privilege at any moment of letting my heart and mind consciously rest in Him—in the secret of His presence, the special, secluded inner sanctuary where in Him my true life is hidden.

This reminds me of a song about our union with Him:

Tired and weary-hearted, I can find in Him my rest,
For His love is like a cool and shady bower.
He is like a crystal spring, and He will satisfy
Every need of every passing hour.

Dr. Maurice Wagner, a godly pastor-turned-psychologist, says it this way: "God and I are united in a love relationship in the business of living." United, He and I face life together.

It's not like putting two books inside a desk drawer. They're in there together, but they're still separate. They're side by side, not occupying the same space. But with God we have a true inner union in which His Spirit is infused into mine. It's not just that He's in there *beside* me. It's that in my inmost person I've been *made one* with Him.

I like to compare this to filling an empty room with two kinds of gases. If we pump oxygen into a room through an opening in one wall, and we pump carbon dioxide through an opening in the opposite wall, the two gases would not stay apart. Given time the molecules would intermingle, and the whole room would become filled with the union of these gases. That's the way God's Spirit intermingles with our spirits, except that ours is a permanent union.

Suppose you had a gold spoon and a silver spoon and wanted to unite them. You could try tying them together with good, strong string in a double knot. But you'd only be kidding yourself. That wouldn't be a real union, because with a pair of scissors you could easily separate them.

Or you might get someone to weld them together. Now that would be a strong union, one you couldn't pry apart. But the two spoons would still be side by side.

If you wanted to truly unite them, you would put them in a crucible, heat up the fire, and melt down both spoons together so that the molecules of gold and silver would flow together and intermingle. Then you could pour the mixture into a mold and have an entirely new piece of metal in which the two original spoons were now completely one.

We are one with God's Spirit in a way that's something like that. We are "in Christ"—or as Williams translated it, we are "in union with Christ." We're one with Him. That's why we're a new creation in Him—"a new person altogether."

That's also why *knowing who God is* becomes so powerful in our experience. I have been united with Him, and with all that He is, in an intimate, wonderful union. I've been introduced to this marvelous Person as my Savior, and now I have the delightful adventure of going on to know Him better, so that more and more I may truly live with His life.

In 1 Corinthians 6:17, God reminds us that in our spirit we are one with Christ—"He who unites himself with the Lord is one with Him in spirit"

(NIV). *One with Him in spirit!* Have you considered what a beautiful thing that is? We are one with Jesus in our innermost being, in our new person. To that I say Hallelujah!

How I love to meditate on the fact that I'm alive with the life of Christ deep inside me! I'm one with Him in a permanent, eternal union. My former nature is also inside me, but the true me that communes with God and that He fellowships with, the real me that He enables, is this inner me who is one with Him.

The prophet Isaiah foretold that our Messiah's name would be called "Immanuel—which means, 'God with us'" (Matthew 1:23, NIV). Jesus Christ is *God with us* in a way that only He can be. Therefore we can know that always we have *the best* with us and within us. We never need say good-bye to Him!

WEARING HIS RIGHTEOUSNESS

I'm alive with Christ's life and righteous with His righteousness. Doesn't this make everything that's meant by the word *righteousness* more thrilling than ever, because it's something each of us can experience? We see ourselves as belonging to Him, as dearly beloved by Him, as clean and pure with the righteousness of Christ, and as adequate to face life because we have Him and His power in intimate union with ourselves.

If we believe in Christ, He is the end of our trying to earn righteousness on our own. Romans 10:3 speaks about unbelievers who didn't understand this: "For they being ignorant of God's righteousness, and seeking to establish their own righteousness, have not submitted to the righteousness of God" (NKJV). These people chose to work on their own and in their own way to make themselves righteous. By this choice they were in fact rejecting the only righteousness that's possible for us to have in God's sight. The next verse continues, "For Christ is the end of the law for righteousness to everyone who believes." We don't have to earn this righteousness. It's ours for free. We have only to receive it and rejoice in it.

As a picture of our being made righteous in Christ, I like Isaiah 61:10—"I will greatly rejoice in the Lord, my soul shall be joyful in my God; for He has clothed me with the garments of salvation. He has covered me with the robe of righteousness, as a bridegroom decks himself with ornaments, and as a bride adorns herself with her jewels" (NKJV). Here Isaiah links righteousness with beautiful wedding garments, with joy, with delight. I heard of one godly man who said that when he woke up in the morning he liked to fling off the covers and say, "I'm robed in His righteousness!"

We have the opportunity every morning, by faith, to mentally put on our robe of Christ's righteousness. It is already in us, but we can decide consciously to remember this with joy and choose to "wear" it in our attitudes and actions. When the Bible speaks of spiritual clothing, it's not something we put on as though it were external to who we are. Our righteousness is not a cloak or veneer that hides from view the ugly sinfulness of who we really are. Our flesh (our natural, independent, self-dependent humanity) is sinful, but our real self in Christ is not. So our "robe of righteousness" is the beautiful outshining of what we are in union with Christ. We can exult in the fact that He has given us His glorious righteousness, has made it an actual part of who we are. We can thank Him that growing in righteousness is letting the reality of who we are shine out more and more. It is simply learning to be ourselves, our new selves, to His glory as our Maker and our Father.

Isn't it wonderful that God has actually given us *His* righteousness! It's not that He looks at us through Jesus-colored glasses so that He doesn't really see us, but only Jesus. No, we actually have His righteousness imparted to us so that we can say, "I *am* righteous, in my true self, in the core of my being. My spirit has been united with His Spirit, and I'm righteous."

Jesus had no sin, but in 2 Corinthians 5:21 God tells us that He made Christ to *be* sin for us, "so that in Him we might become the righteousness of

God" (NIV). In our union with Him, righteousness is ours personally and inwardly as well as in the legal system of our King.

THE REAL ME

God's way is the only way for us to become what God intended us to be in our entire personality. C. S. Lewis makes this point so well in *Mere Christianity:*

> The more we get what we now call "ourselves" out of the way and let Him take us over, the more truly ourselves we become.... He made us. He invented—as an author invents characters in a novel—all the different men that you and I were intended to be. In that sense our real selves are all waiting for us in Him. It is no good trying to "be myself" without Him. The more I resist Him and try to live on my own, the more I become dominated by my own heredity and upbringing and surroundings and natural desires. In fact what I so proudly call "Myself" becomes merely the meeting place for trains of events which I never started and which I cannot stop.... I am not, in my natural state, nearly so much of a person as I like to believe: most of what I call "me" can be very easily explained. It is when I turn to Christ, when I give myself up to His Personality, that I first begin to have a real personality of my own.

Our old and natural way of "doing our own thing" resulted in the repulsive rubbish in our garbage pail and the stench it emits when the lid is off. We get out of our garbage-pail living when we focus on Christ in us and see ourselves as He sees us, then choose His way.

CHRIST IS MY LIFE — CHRIST IS ALL

I've found the whole book of Colossians a delight on this topic, showing Christ as the focal point—the center of attraction, attention, and activity—of our spiritual experience and service, even as He is of the entire universe. "Christ is all, and in all" (3:11, NASB). He is our complete answer for wisdom and knowledge, for life and growth, for forgiveness and fullness, for deliverance from every hindrance to our spiritual lives. And since we are in Him and He in us, we have a fresh new identity. We have died to our old lives and have been raised with Him. So we are now alive with His resurrected life. We are chosen and holy and beloved. Through these truths He provides both the motivation and the power for a life fully pleasing to Him.

Chapters 6–8 in Romans are another rich source of truth on this topic. What a delight I've known as I've spent hours in these chapters, meditating on the life-revolutionizing realities of our union with Christ. In *31 Days of Praise* I've shared some of the life-changing truths the Lord taught me through these chapters.

And I keep finding new Scriptures that give a new, beautiful sense of what these truths mean.

One day I was reading John 4:14, where Jesus says, "Whoever drinks the water I give him will never thirst. Indeed, the water I give him will become in him a spring of water welling up to eternal life" (NIV). The *New King James Version* translates this as "a fountain of water springing up into everlasting life." As I personalized these words, I was thrilled by the thought, "I have within me a fountain of living water. I don't have to live a dry, wilted, dehydrated life!"

Ever since the Holy Spirit came to dwell in us, our inner being has been permanently linked with the vast reservoir of the living God, with its continual, inexhaustible supply of fresh, life-enhancing water. As we simply yield to the indwelling Spirit, His life springs up in us in a refreshing, invigorating way. It's a bit like children running through a lawn sprinkler on a sweltering day, except that it's inward and spiritual. Or it's like watering plants that are wilted and drooping, then watching them perk up. But we don't have to wait until we're wilted, depleted, or dying of thirst. The flow can be continual as we count on the Life within us, letting the Spirit of God revive us and give us freshness, enthusiasm, and vigor.

Then there's an overflow. "Whoever believes in Me," Jesus said, "…streams of living water will flow from within him" (John 7:38, NIV). The water springs up in our inner being, transforming our attitudes and outlook. Then it flows out to others as well, making us a fresh, vital, life-imparting influence for Christ.

When I Believe This, I Live Differently

In Ephesians 4:24, God tells us that through Christ we were created "to be like God," or "to resemble God," as another version says. Then in 5:1 we're commanded, "Be imitators of God, therefore, as dearly loved children" (NIV).

All this is possible because we actually have the life of Christ within us. His life is the only life ever lived just as God intended—and His life is ours! What exciting implications this has for positive changes in our daily living! And when I believe this, it makes all the difference in how I live and how I influence other people. It makes a difference because I go forth in faith that *He will be in me exactly what I need Him to be.* He has revealed to us His truth about His perfect love and His perfect presence in us so that He can change our lives from the inside out. As we more fully absorb the truth that His life is ours, then everything about who God is takes on a new meaning. I can let Him be that in me, to me, and through me.

Out of our inner existence as a new creation in Christ, the light and the life can increasingly flow into our thinking and our feeling and our choosing. The beauty of Christ can more and more flood our inner being and flow out. Then we can say with fuller meaning, "Thank You, Lord, that You are my life."

As we live by faith in who God is and who we are in Christ, God glorifies

Himself through us in both conscious and unconscious ways. This poem by A. S. Wilson, titled "Indwelt," has blessed me for many years:

> Not only by the words we say,
> Not merely by our deeds confessed,
> But in a most unconscious way
> Is Christ expressed.
>
> To me, 'twas not the truth you taught,
> To you so clear, to me so dim,
> But when you came to me you brought
> A sense of Him.
>
> And from your eyes He beckons me,
> And from your heart His love is shed
> 'Til I lose sight of you, and see
> The Christ instead.

FOUR STAGES OF INTIMACY

When Dean and I, together with Gene and Mary, returned from Asia for our first furlough, Dean and Gene went to the East Coast for a ministry trip. One of their meetings was in a church where Dr. Norman Grubb was speaking. They came back and shared with us something that especially impressed them from Dr. Grubb's message, and it has stayed with me ever since.

Dr. Grubb described several stages that we typically go through in our growing consciousness of our relationship with God.

In the first stage we realize that we have a Father in heaven. As new Christians we recognize with excitement, "I'm a child of God. This wonderful, exalted God is up there with all His love and power caring for me, watching over me, and listening to my prayers."

That's a realization we'll always need, and the truth that He is our heavenly Father takes on new meaning as life goes on.

In the second stage we realize, "God is not only in heaven, He's also beside me. He comforts and guides me as my Shepherd. He is my Friend to communicate with, and my Beloved who holds my right hand and says to me, 'Fear not I will help you.'"

This, too, is a truth we'll need all of our Christian life—He is present with us; we can communicate with Him and count on Him.

In the third stage we move even closer to God in our experience. We realize, "He is also living in me. He's not only with me out there as my daily Guide and Helper, but He's indwelling me, closer than any human relationship can ever be."

And that's wonderful. But even that falls short of the fourth stage, where it dawns on us that we have an inner union with Him. We realize, "His Spirit is dwelling in my spirit in an intermingled way. Amazing!"

By the Spirit

This enables us to experience the Lord's perfect love and power in a new way, for as new persons in Christ, our spirit is united with the Holy Spirit, who is the Spirit of Christ and the Spirit of God. And as we let Him have His way in our lives (His loving way which always assures our highest good), He pours the love of God throughout our being. He also strengthens us within, imparting the power to do His will, to devote ourselves to the work God gives us to do.

I've been helped by the reminder that we should "burn the oil, not the wick." We do this by consciously depending not on our own powers but on the Spirit in us. This keeps us from depleting our emotional and physical resources, and from exuding the smoky fumes of fleshly attitudes and reactions.

Along this line I find it helpful to pray the following prayer, which ends with a personalized version of Romans 8:11 (Phillips) and Colossians 1:29

(Weymouth): "Lord, You are the fuel my personality was designed to burn. Empower me today and shine through me, through my attitudes and actions, so that I will not 'burn the wick' by relying on myself. I choose to rely on You. By Your Spirit, bring to my whole being new strength and vitality. May I exert all my strength in reliance upon the power of You mightily at work within me."

So God has me here communicating with you, using a spiritual gift that He has given. As I write these words, the Holy Spirit is working, and His work continues as you read the same words. Likewise when you use your own spiritual gifts, He gives the same power as you rely on Him.

These truths about who we are through our union with the Lord are marvelous and life-changing. We must become clear about them and sure of them, letting them grip our hearts. If we neglect these truths, we're likely to find our lives constantly disrupted by our negative emotions and fleshly ways of living. We must also keep pressing on to know the Lord better and experience the intimacy of His relationship with us. Unless we know more deeply who He is, we'll miss out on much of the benefit of our wonderful, loving, intimate union.

It's who He is that makes me who I am. Because He is King of kings, I am a princess, the daughter of the King of kings. Because He is love, I am loved. In a similar way, each truth about Him says something about me, for who I am is rooted in who He is. The better I know Him and see myself in the mirror of His attributes, the more accurate and stable my sense of identity becomes. This provides a solid base for my spiritual growth and vigor.

When a woman marries, what her husband is like is very important to her. One reason is that he brings into that union many qualities and characteristics, and in response to these she finds a new sense of her own identity on the human level. His admirable qualities make her feel good about herself, because this man chose to marry her. And his loving attitudes toward her reinforce her sense of worth. His flaws and weaknesses and negative attitudes tend to do the opposite. The conclusion she comes to about herself may or may not be accurate, and may have both positive and negative effects on her.

A similar thing happens in our love relationship with the Lord, but in a much more profound and positive way. In Him we have countless resources for living like kings and queens and becoming more like the One who loves us. We discover these resources in two ways. First, we get better acquainted with our altogether desirable, permanent Life Partner; and second, we learn who we are—what our new identity is because we are one with Him.

This releases us from trying to build a stable sense of who we are on the flimsy foundation of human responses to us. It also releases us from trying in our own power to become more like Jesus in our living and our serving. We become more Christlike as we depend on the Lord more—as we trust Him, have faith in Him, lean on Him. And how does our faith grow? Simply by knowing Him better. We cannot help but trust Him when we see Him as He truly is.

A LOVING LIFE

So I have the life of Christ in me. What kind of life is this?

First of all it's a loving life. The first and foremost fruit of the Spirit is love. In our new life we have all that it takes to love God and to love others, and that's the heartbeat of true Christlikeness.

Again and again in Scripture the indwelling presence of Christ through the Holy Spirit is pointedly connected with love. In John 14:23, Jesus promised the experience of God's loving presence to anyone who loves Him and obeys Him: "My Father will love him, and We will come to him and make Our home with him" (NIV). Later as Jesus spoke of our abiding in Him as branches abide in the vine, He added, "As the Father has loved Me, so have I loved you. Now remain in My love."

When Paul declared in Galatians 2:20 that he himself no longer lived, but that Christ lived in him, he described Jesus as the One "who *loved* me and gave Himself for me" (NIV).

In the book of 1 John we especially discover the close relationship between

God's love for us, our own love for others, and God's indwelling life within us through the Holy Spirit:

> Dear friends, since God so loved us, we also ought to love one
> another. No one has ever seen God; but if we love each other, God
> lives in us and His love is made complete in us. We know that we
> live in Him and He in us, because He has given us of His Spirit....
> And so we know and rely on the love God has for us. God is love.
> Whoever lives in love lives in God, and God in him. (1 John
> 4:11-13,16, NIV)

Because God dwells within me, my experience of His love can surpass in intimacy any human love relationship. He *is* love, and as I let Him control my mind, emotions, and will, and believe Him to fill and saturate my inner being, He fills me with love.

We have a new source of love, a perfect love within us to deliver us from our own inability to love others as the Lord desires. In Colossians 1:27 we read that the secret of living is simply Christ—"Christ in you, the hope of glory" (NIV). And because He's in us, we can count on Him to give us the inner power to love. Whenever we have unloving reactions, we can turn to Him again and give Him permission to love through us with His love.

The sins I personally need to confess most often seem to be anxiety (with its distrust in the Lord) and various kinds of love failures, such as defensiveness or impatience. Recently in a conflict with Warren, something he said brought me face to face with a very unpleasant reality: I have a knack for justifying myself and making a problem appear to be all his fault—putting myself in a good light and him in a bad light. This greatly troubled me. This failure, though I hadn't really thought about it for years, has a long history. Once when we lived in Hong Kong, my brother-in-law talked to me about it. And I know this is what I often did with Mary as we were growing up. Hadn't I changed at all? Would I ever be free of this obnoxious tendency?

As I struggled with discouragement over this, I realized afresh that indwelling sin doesn't necessarily get reformed. God often (perhaps generally?) does not eradicate its traits, but leaves them intact to humble us and make us more dependent on Him. With most of our sinful tendencies, spiritual growth does not mean that we never fail, but that we sin less often and repent more quickly. Growth means that we spend less and less time on the death/defeat side of the Cross, more and more on the life/overcoming side. So I turned from my wrong-side-of-the-Cross discouragement to the joy of God's full forgiveness, asking Him for quick awareness of this particular sin and for greater, more consistent humility and love.

A POWERFUL LIFE

Having the life of Christ in me also means that I have power in my life, a revolutionary power that transforms my character and makes my service effective. The evidence is abundant that Christ is relevant to every need of every heart in every circumstance. I love how S. D. Gordon expressed it (I've modernized and simplified it a bit):

> No human imagination can take in the startling, revolutionary
> power that flows down from the crowned Christ, softly, subtly, but
> with unhindered sweep into the lives of needy and grateful people.
> This power flows through individuals wholly under the gracious
> control of the Holy Spirit—people who simply live in full-faced
> touch with Christ, taking that power as the need comes and as the
> sovereign Holy Spirit leads.

Why is it that we can live a powerful life, energized by the power of His resurrection? It's because Christ Himself was resurrected; and now His risen, powerful, victorious life is our life. It's because God is able to do "immeasurably more than all we ask or imagine, according to His power that is at work within us" (Ephesians 3:20, NIV).

REALLY BELIEVING I CAN

So we're to live on the right side of the Cross, simply believing this: I'm a new person, I'm indwelt by the Spirit, and I choose to yield to Him and let His gracious influence control my life. Then we have a new competence, for we're alive with His life, refreshed and empowered by His Spirit. If we really believe this, we have an "I can!" feeling.

Paul expresses his experience of this in Philippians 4:13— "I can do all things through Him who strengthens me" (NASB). I don't think he is speaking here in a sort of self-effacing, pseudo-humble manner. No, God had given him a strong *I can* conviction, centered of course in Christ: *I CAN do all things THROUGH CHRIST who strengthens me.* Paul counted on his inner union with Christ, and so he could face anything and was equal to anything that might come his way. This is true for us too. Not that we can do everything—we'd burn out if we tried. But we can do everything He wants us to do by His life within us.

I often go back to 2 Corinthians 3:5— "Not that we are competent in ourselves…but our competence comes from God" (NIV). Notice the present tense here. Our competence *comes* from God right now—not just *will come* after we grow some more. I like that. So I can pray, "Lord, as I just trust You, my adequacy right now is from You. You are in me with Your mighty power. I rejoice that in the future You're going to take possession of more and more of my life, and You'll cause the competence and beauty of Jesus to pervade my whole personality more and more. But even right now You *are* my sufficiency, and I thank You."

Jesus has told us, "Without Me you can do nothing" (John 15:5, NKJV). One day I said to Him, "Lord, I don't fully understand this. You said it, so I believe it; but here's what puzzles me. Without depending on You I can do a lot of things, such as washing dishes, writing letters, and even mothering my children. Without you I can yell at them of course, but I can even be sweet to them much of the time. So, Lord, what do You mean that without You I can do nothing?"

Then He reminded me that He is the One who passes out the grades. He alone decides whether all my efforts amount to anything, whether they are truly significant. And He is saying in John 15:5 that my grade is zero if I'm doing anything in my own power. I can then expect no rewards, because my words or actions are coming out of the wrong side of the Cross—out of my fleshly efforts. And I couldn't even do my fleshly works if He was not keeping me alive and breathing!

Doing all things through Christ does not, of course, mean I sit in my rocking chair and say, "Move me, Lord, when You want me to make dinner. I'm waiting here until the Spirit moves me." It doesn't mean we cook meals or go to work or relate to people only when God in some special way motivates us to do these things. God doesn't operate that way. There is work do be done on my part, and I'm to take the initiative and do it, depending on Him for strength, for wisdom, for love.

But the difference is like this: You can turn on your vacuum cleaner and vacuum your entire house. Or, if you want to, you can go through the exact same motions but leave the switch off the entire time. You do the same amount of work both ways, but with the second way you get none of the results. You merely shove the dirt around. You miss out on all the needed power.

On the other hand, when you do turn on the switch, you don't say, "Now, vacuum cleaner, move!"—then sit there and listen to it go "whoosh!" through every room, sucking up all the dirt.

So by faith we turn on the power. Then, using that power, we work.

One of Warren's favorite Scripture verses is 1 Corinthians 15:10, which describes God's work and ours and summarizes the secret of real success in anything—in our spiritual life, family, Christian service, relationships, employment, and everything else we do. This verse portrays a sandwich, with God's grace on the top and bottom and hard work in the middle. In the *New Century Version* it reads: "But God's grace has made me what I am. And his grace to me was not wasted. I worked harder than all the other apostles. (But I was not really the one working. It was God's grace that was with me)."

Betty Stam was a missionary in China, where she and her husband were killed by Communists in the 1930s. She was the author of these lines:

I cannot live like Jesus,
example though He be,
for He was strong and selfless
and I am tied to me.
I cannot live like Jesus;
my soul is never free;
my will is strong and stubborn;
my love is weak and wee.
But I have asked my Jesus
to live His life in Me.

Another poem that has blessed me for years was frequently quoted by Dad Byus, the southern gentleman who spoke at times in our college chapel services. He said this poem meant more to him than anything ever written, except of course the Bible. Here's the first verse:

Live out Thy life within me, O Jesus, King of kings;
Be Thou Thyself the answer to all my questionings.
Live out Thy life within me. In all things have Thy way—
I the transparent medium Thy glory to display.

That's living on the right side of the cross—depending on the life of Jesus.

Thank You, Lord that You are dwelling in me in this wonderful inner union, and that You care for me so much that You've honored me in this way. I praise You that for every need of my heart and every situation in my life there is something about You that can meet my deepest need, and that You are here within me to do so.

How glad I am that, on the authority of Your Word, I am in fact a new person, with Your Son Jesus Christ living in me. How grateful I am for this gift of real life! Because of His life in me I know by faith that I'm clean and righteous—that the real me is fully and forever accepted by You. Thank You for giving me Your beautiful, glorious righteousness, for imparting it to me, making it an actual part of who I am.

I rejoice in the Cross and in the mighty power of the Resurrection, by which You have permanently moved me from the Death side of the Cross and empty tomb to the Life side.

Lord, in simple faith I embrace the righteous, resurrected life of Jesus as my own life. Make me quick to detect when the garbage pail of my indwelling sin takes over, and then to use the lid of truth to stop the flare-up of wrong attitudes, thoughts, and actions.

Thank You that You and I are united in a love relationship in the business of living. I look forward to the increasing confidence and vitality You will build into me as I depend on Your life within me. And, Lord, I ask You to bring glory to Yourself today by making me an influence on the lives of others as Your love and power flow through me.

In Jesus' name…

Your personal gleanings for meditation, prayer, and action:

What Scripture or truth in this chapter do you feel the Lord is especially speaking to you about? What will you do to profit the most from this?

ELEVEN

In His Perfect Love, I'm Truly Free

I REALIZE I'M a beginner at understanding God's love. From time to time I get my feet wet in that vast ocean of the knowledge of God. Now and then I take a plunge and swim a bit, or leisurely float on my back. But all this is very close to shore. There's so much more, both nearby and out there beyond the mind's horizon. Yet even as a beginner I find a delightful blend of feeling not only secure in His love, but also liberated.

Now that's a trick—to experience both security and liberation at the same time. They don't usually go hand in hand. But in this chapter and the next we'll look more closely at both, and at how they come together so beautifully in our experience of God's love.

All through history, leaders of movements great and small have promised freedom to all who would join their cause. Most of these promises have proven false. In 2 Peter 2:19, God warns us about those who lead others astray as they "promise them freedom, while they themselves are slaves of depravity—for a man is a slave to whatever has mastered him" (NIV). Most of these promises of liberty have been issued by those who were enslaved themselves. Furthermore, what they thought was liberty really wasn't.

To understand and experience God's perfect love is the only way to be truly liberated—in fact, to be more than liberated.

OUR STATUE OF LIBERTY

Jesus offers the true promise of freedom. Why did He come to this earth? In Luke 4:18 He gave His reasons: to proclaim release to the captives, to offer recovery of sight to the blind, and to set free the oppressed. He came to bring deliverance and sight and liberty.

And He tells us in John 8:36 that if He, the Son of God, sets us free, then we are free indeed. His freedom is true freedom. And it comes through a personal relationship with Him, through His personal, loving touch on our lives as we draw near to Him.

I like the way the Scottish minister R. Leonard Small portrays Christ's coming:

> Jesus is like the commander of a relieving army, marching into a
> long-besieged garrison town, being welcomed by the starving
> survivors. He is their Liberator, their Savior, the one who sets them
> free from their oppressors.

Jesus Christ, he adds, is "God's own long-awaited answer to the longings of the human heart." We've all longed for freedom, and Christ has made it possible. Satan's master plan was to enslave us to himself and to his goal of keeping us independent of God. We thought this "independence" from God would give us real liberty, but it actually made us slaves to sin and death. But even in our slavery, even in our captivity to our rebellion against His Father God, Jesus loved us. He has freed us from our imprisonment that posed as liberty, so that we can find our true fulfillment.

The Cross is our Statue of Liberty.

And now, even as reborn children of God, when we carefully examine our lives we probably detect further areas of enslavement, which we didn't know were there. We begin to see that we're in bondage to our background, to resentment toward people, to misdirected goals. We're held prisoner by attitudes we can't get rid of, by our own desires, our own emotions, and our own ways of thinking.

But the more we know God and experience His love, the more free we become. The longer we come to His Word and let His Holy Spirit teach us, the more liberation we experience. More and more our personality is freed up to become as beautiful as God designed it to be.

It's the same glad freedom Sidney Lanier wrote about: "I will fly in the greatness of God as the marsh hen flies, in the freedom that fills all the space 'twixt the marsh and the skies."

As another picture of freedom, Malachi 4:2 repeatedly refreshes me: "For you who fear My name the sun of righteousness will rise with healing in its wings; and you will go forth and skip about like calves from the stall" (NASB). I especially like that final promise. Have you ever seen calves leaping about with glad abandon when released from the barn at sunrise? It's with this kind of feeling that we can celebrate our Savior's coming to earth—the long-awaited rising of the Sun of Righteousness. How we can exult that He still sheds forth His healing rays to renew us spiritually and even physically!

This true freedom comes when we give up the false freedom of our fleshly independence and submit to "captivity" under God—captivity to His perfect love. George Matheson sets forth so well what it means to be enslaved by the Lord's matchless love:

> Make me a captive, Lord,
>   And then I shall be free;
> Force me to render up my sword,
>   And I shall conqueror be.
> I sink in life's alarms
>   When by myself I stand;
> Imprison me within Thine arms,
>   And strong shall be my hand.

THE FAVOR THAT FREES

Believing in God's liberating love elevates our hearts, bringing joy in any circumstance. It fortifies us, making us invulnerable to any threat. Do we compare ourselves with others, face or fear disapproval, become discouraged at our weaknesses and sins? Our loving King is not comparing. He delights in each of us; He enjoys us (Psalm 149:4, TLB). He does not condemn, blame, or exclude any of us. His favor is constant. It neither increases when we excel nor lessens when we fail. It shines into our lives as we let it in.

Why then should anxieties keep us awake at night? Why do we ever waste time blaming others, reproaching ourselves, thinking of excuses? These are symptoms of unbelief—of relying on something other than God's grace.

This is what happens: We need favor, and if we do not consciously receive approval from God we automatically resort to seeking it from people. We try to prove to ourselves and to others that we are "somebody," that we are attractive, desirable, competent, trustworthy. But we meet a frown here or a rebuke there, and discomfort sets in. We try worldly remedies. We worry, attempt to change others, try to improve ourselves. We even pray. But any relief we get is temporary because we're dealing with symptoms. The cause—not believing God, not relying on His grace—goes unrecognized.

The remedy? Grace—God's unmerited favor, His unfailing kindness, His undeserved working on our behalf. We confess our sin (symptoms and cause) and let His Word assure us of our forgiveness and adequacy in His Son. The Holy Spirit performs His therapy, dealing with the cause and healing from within. God's grace cures our inner sickness—and frequent doses will minimize recurrences.

"God is so vastly wonderful... that He can meet and overflow the deepest needs of our total nature," including our need to feel "good about ourselves," to feel "okay." People of the world try to feel this way by denying the reality of sin and true guilt before a righteous God. Human "authorities" tell them their guilty feelings are false guilt, and should be ignored. So they ignore them. But that kind of solution, based on falsehood, won't work very long, because there really is true guilt that requires repentance and forgiveness.

Only the Cross frees us to feel good about ourselves in a realistic way. By the Cross we're clean and forgiven, and there's no stain left, and we can live without a guilty conscience (Hebrews 3:14). We can feel alive and strong and competent and adequate to do whatever God wants us to do. How richly He deserves our thanks!

BREAKTHROUGHS

A very practical way of viewing the freedom God gives us is to think of it as a breakthrough. For Warren and me the past year has brought tremendous blessings—and also tremendous pressures and trials for us, our loved ones, and people we minister to. Often we have gone back to 2 Samuel 5:20 (NASB) where David, after winning a great victory, said, "'The Lord has broken through my enemies before me like the breakthrough of waters.' Therefore he named that place Baal-perazim ('the master of breakthrough')".

What a relief and blessing it has been to pray to our Master of Breakthroughs—the One who is able and longing to penetrate and overcome our enemies, our troubles, our distresses, our deep needs. The One who, in majestic and awesome power, rides through the heavens in His eagerness to help us—who is our protecting shield and our triumphant sword, causing our enemies to cringe before us (Deuteronomy 33:26-29). Our God has a long history of releasing His people from all sorts of bondage.

We like to begin by praising God that He is the Master of Breakthroughs, powerful and skilled, motivated by deep and faithful love, and eager to work as He sees fit, whether suddenly or gradually.

Then we pray for whatever breakthroughs are needed to liberate us and others—breakthroughs of love that expels self-centeredness, anger, resentment...of joy that displaces sorrow or depression...of peace that dispels anxiety, turmoil, conflict...of hope that banishes discouragement or despair...of health that overcomes sickness…of His presence that revives and refreshes. We implore Him for breakthroughs against the flesh and its ways, against the world and its lusts, against Satan and his purposes. In other words, we pray for breakthroughs that will bring new freedom of one type or another.

Alone or together, Warren and I do "breakthrough praying" for couples, for individuals, for ourselves, for children and teenagers, for the Lord's servants, for unbelievers. We begin with a few people and needs that are especially on our hearts, perhaps because of a phone call, a letter, a conversation. Then we draw in others, near and far, for similar breakthroughs and blessings. We keep a "short list" for especially needed breakthroughs, and we've seen several notable answers this year. For others we keep on asking.

One night several weeks ago I woke up anxious and concerned. I couldn't get back to sleep so I got up, put on a warm woolen sweater, and settled down in my favorite chair. As I opened my Bible I happened upon 2 Chronicles 7, where God gave special promises to Solomon concerning the temple he had built as God's dwelling place. The Lord reminded me that these promises now belong to each of us as His temple, His own special dwelling: "My eyes shall be open and my ears attentive to the prayer made in this place.… My eyes and My heart will be there perpetually" (verse 16, NKJV). This God of heartfelt and constant attentiveness is the God we pray to for breakthroughs and blessings, both for our own deep needs and for other people. He hears and answers—and though some answers may be long in coming, they'll never be late.

So again and again God's breakthroughs bring freedom in us and in others—freedom from the things that distress us, or freedom of heart in the midst of these things.

WHERE FREEDOM BEGINS

Our experience of the freedom we find in God's love begins in our mind, because our false mental notions are often at the root of our failure to trust the love of God. I like Proverbs 4:23 in the *Good News Bible:* "Be careful how you think; your life is shaped by your thoughts."

Our emotions don't just fall on us out of the blue, but generally arise from how we are thinking. Even when we're facing difficulties that trigger unusually strong and persistent emotions, we can either minimize or maximize our misery simply by the way we think. We have a choice.

Living realistically means living with a full view of the wonderful truths God has given—truths about Himself, about ourselves, about how life runs well, and about victory over sin and Satan. Focusing on the positive realities that flood the pages of Scripture is especially important. Philippians 4:8 says that whatever is true, noble, right, pure, admirable, and worthy of praise, "let your mind dwell on these things" (NASB). This keeps us from the kind of thinking that ensnares and binds us. It prevents us from focusing on things that may not be true, that are disreputable, wrong, impure, repulsive, and worthy of criticism or accusation.

I've often been drawn to Psalm 103:1-5. David begins the passage by tuning his heart to sing God's praise: "Bless the Lord, O my soul, and all that is within me, bless His holy name" (RSV). I'm to let my whole inner being get involved in praising Him. First, my will and my mind. I can choose to focus my mind on the Lord, on His words, and on His promises. And I can let my emotions be touched through a steady stream of positive Philippians 4:8 thoughts—or through a calm inflow and review of a single thought with pauses to quietly absorb the Lord's reality. I often use "Be still and know that I am God" (Psalm 46:10), or, "They that wait upon the Lord shall renew their strength" (Isaiah 40:31, KJV).

David continues in Psalm 103:2, "and forget none of His benefits" (NASB). The list of benefits he then gives should surely help to get our emotions involved in excited gratefulness:

He forgives all my iniquities. I am totally forgiven. I'm all right in God's sight now and forever, through Christ's sacrifice! Not one smudge of guilt left.

He heals all my diseases. By His Spirit, He brings health and strength and vitality to my whole being (Romans 8:11, Phillips).

He rescues me from the destructive pit—be it physical or emotional. "He drew me up from the desolate pit, out of the miry bog" (Psalm 40:2, RSV).

He crowns me with lovingkindness and tender mercies—or as one version says, "encompasses me." I'm surrounded and overshadowed by His mighty love.

He satisfies my desire with good things. This renews my youth, so that I can be strong and overcome, soaring like an eagle.

These things show the kind of God we have—the Source of so many tremendous benefits and the inspiration for our heartfelt praise.

Psalm 126:3 says, "The Lord has done great things for us; we are glad" (NASB). Isn't that simple and powerful? I can revel in the Lord as I recall the great things He has done for us as a family and in other lives; then I can pause quietly and let myself be glad in His Presence.

Gladness is such a refreshing emotion. That is one reason why the Lord is so refreshing as a Person, for far more than anyone else, our King has been anointed with the oil of gladness (Psalm 45:7, KJV).

Focusing on these truths can literally change the way we think, and therefore the way we feel and live. It frees us to trust in the Lord.

THE ART OF INNER VICTORY

Changing the way we think—this takes us back again to truths represented by the acrostic I mentioned in chapter 4—ART—three steps I find so helpful in handling emotional and mental obstacles. It's a process we can work through rather quickly when we need relief from negative thoughts and feelings. It sets us free so we can serve others and do God's will in trustful peace.

First, we *acknowledge* what we're thinking or how we're feeling, pouring out the unwanted attitude to the Lord. For example, when I'm pressing toward a deadline I can simply say, "Lord, I'm filled with fear that I won't be able to meet this deadline on time, and with negative thoughts about how this could affect my future." We don't ignore or repress our emotions. David, for example, did not merely sweep his negative feelings under some inner rug. He freely expressed them before God—then was able to go on to "praise the Lord anyhow."

Sometimes acknowledging includes confessing sin, because we've let ourselves stew for a while in our negative thoughts and emotions. As the saying goes, you can't keep a bird from flying over your head but you can keep it from building a nest in your hair. Negative, unscriptural thoughts and reactions will surely come to us, but we can learn to catch and deal with them quickly. And whenever we don't handle them quickly but let them control us, we can acknowledge and confess this as sin, then move on. We can say, "Forgive me, Lord, for letting these fearful thoughts crowd out my trust in You." (And if I'm behind on my work because I've been negligent, I had better confess that too.)

The second step is to *renounce* the negative attitude or feeling that we've acknowledged and confessed. Back to that deadline, I can choose against my fears: "Lord, I renounce these fearful thoughts and feelings. I'm not going to let them control me or drain away my energy and slow me down. Instead I choose to let Your Spirit control me."

We might also call this *repenting* or *rejecting*. It's an about-face. "Lord, I turn *from* that, *to* You. I don't want to go through my whole day bringing You grief instead of gladness, so I reject these negative thoughts, this negative attitude."

The third step is to *think the truth with thanksgiving*. "Lord, in place of these negative, fearful thoughts, I'm going to think, 'I can do all things through Christ who strengthens me.' Thank You that You are at work in me and that my future is in Your hands, whether or not I'm a bit late in finishing this work."

We think a truth from God's Word, a truth that puts the lid on the garbage pail of thoughts that are fearful, anxious, prideful, or whatever. And we think this truth with thanksgiving, because there's something about thanksgiving that helps us believe. It puts God into the situation and affirms our faith.

I find it helpful to use ART in a variety of situations. When I get worried about how I'll come across in speaking to a group or counseling someone, I acknowledge those feelings and renounce any prideful desires that feed my anxieties. I may do this in prayer, something like this: "Lord, I feel anxious that this won't go well and fearful of what people may think of me. I renounce all desire for glory in people's eyes."

Then comes thinking the truth with thanksgiving. For this particular anxiety, I've learned to use the first verse of Psalm 115: "Not unto us, O Lord, not unto us [I say, "Not unto *me,* O Lord, not unto me"], but to Your name give glory, because of Your mercy and because of Your truth" (NKJV). Then I can go on to thank the Lord, saying something like this: "Thank You, Lord, that according to 1 John 5:14, You hear and answer prayers that are according to Your will. So I can count on You to answer this prayer for Your glory, not mine. And thank You for the release and joy of knowing this will honor You, not me." Then I may as well forget about glory for myself, and so my anxiety evaporates.

R. K. Harrison, in *Psalms for Today,* translates Psalm 115:1 like this: "Do not give us credit, Lord; enhance Your own reputation instead"—another good way to phrase my prayer.

These three steps are the ART of inner freedom—acknowledge, renounce, and think the truth with thanksgiving. How often as we do this God transforms into joy our anxiety, our hostility, our self-condemnation. He gives "the oil of joy for mourning, the garment of praise for the spirit of heaviness" (Isaiah 61:3, NKJV). He enables us, like Paul, to be "sorrowful, yet always rejoicing" (2 Corinthians 6:10).

Often we can be thrust into the need for ART by deadlines, such as getting a meal ready before the guests arrive, or getting packed for a long trip without staying up most of the night, or preparing for an important exam, or being able to make a payment on time. Sometimes I'm slow to recognize my need.

In 1987 I was in the final two weeks of work before my deadline on *Praise, a Door to God's Presence,* a book about worship, praise, and thanksgiving. I kept getting anxious about finishing it on time. Instead of stopping to discern the cause of my anxiety, I ignored it or superficially committed it to the Lord and pressed on. Finally He kept me awake one night and dealt with some roots of this anxiety. These included an area of resentment and a failure to hold the deadline in wide-open hands, intent on His timing whether or not it coincided with mine. Even more basically, I was once again finding my confidence in my performance rather than in God alone. Why do I ever shift back to such a flimsy support when I have such a solid one?

A year after Brian was married, he and his wife, Julie, came to Asia for five weeks, staying at our home in Singapore and also traveling with us to Malaysia and Hong Kong. It was a time uniquely guided and blessed by the Lord, with many vulnerable heart-to-heart conversations, much fun and relaxation, and rich times of fellowship in prayer and in the Word. We had prayed much about the time being one of deepening relationships, and the Lord did far above what we asked. In all these things we rejoiced—even as we shed our share of tears at the pain of separation when the five weeks came to an end.

The day they left I was impressed by 2 Chronicles 20:3, "Jehoshaphat was afraid and turned his attention to seek the Lord." Whatever my distressing emotions might be—at this point it was sorrow at loved ones leaving—here was the solution: to experience what I feel *and* turn my attention to God through honest prayer, praise, and responsiveness to His Word.

Jehoshaphat turned his thoughts to who God was, what He had done in the past, and what He had promised; he acknowledged how powerless he and God's people were in themselves to overcome in a new and very difficult crisis that faced them; he looked expectantly to God to work; he obeyed God's instructions. And he mingled all this with praise, worship, and songs of expectant faith. What an example to follow if we want freedom from our fears!

Perhaps it is through our trials and distressing emotions that God most often says, "Seek ye My face," and wants to hear our reply, "Thy face, Lord, will I seek" (Psalm 27:8, KJV).

FREE FROM GUILT

The most foundational way God liberates us is to free us from guilt and the fear of death. This is the first thing He liberated me from, through causing me to understand John 3:16. For the first time I realized the truths of salvation in an inner, personal way: Jesus had died for *me*, for *my* sins; if I simply believed in Him I would not perish in hell, separated from God forever; instead I would have eternal life. My heart believed, and I bowed my head in prayer, "Thank You! You've given me eternal life." That very moment I was liberated from my sense of guilt and my fear of what might happen after death. The truth set me free.

It's so important to remember and fully grasp where we stand before God as our Judge. I like the way 1 John 2:1 portrays Jesus as our defense lawyer before the Father. Satan the accuser comes charging into the courtroom and says, "Look what this child of Yours did! She should be condemned!" But Jesus rises to our defense and says, "Father, I died for this person and for *all* her sins." Then the Father bangs the gavel and says, "Case dismissed." And notice in this verse that this process happens not when we *confess*, but when we *sin*. Our judicial righteousness is not dependent on our constant confession of sins. Legally, we have been forgiven and accepted forever. Phillips says it so well in Romans 8:33-34: "Who would dare to accuse us, whom God has chosen? The judge himself has declared us free from sin. Who is in a position to condemn? Only Christ, and Christ died for us, Christ rose for us, Christ reigns in power for us, Christ prays for us!"

That's the solution for sin as far as our condemnation is concerned. There's a further solution that relates to family harmony and the sweetness of our relationship with God. As we've seen, we are responsible to get back into fellowship with Him through simple and sincere confession. We're like the little boy who's gone off and played in the mud. When his mother finds him, she doesn't hug him right away. First he must let her hose him off. Then she hugs him and brings him inside for dinner, and everything's all right again. In a similar way, confession and cleansing restore our fellowship with God.

Even when we understand all this, there's one portion of that courtroom scene that so often hits home within us when we sin. It's the accusation made by our enemy Satan. We identify so emotionally. We *feel* accused. We feel we're no good. All we can think is, "I've done it again."

When I find myself in that situation, the sunshine of God's forgiveness is still shining as brightly as ever. But there are a number of ways I can close the blinds and not let it in.

One way is by refusing to admit my sin. The Holy Spirit tells me, "Ruth, that attitude should be confessed." And I think, "Well, it's just human. Most women are like that." Or I say, "I only responded that way because of what *he* did." I justify myself. Sometimes even when we bring our sin before God, we start out confessing it and end up excusing it.

Another way we pull the blinds is by trying to earn forgiveness. We can try to do this either positively or negatively. We try it positively by making promises that we'll really and truly do better from now on. "I'll never do it again!" we tell God. And we think if we go long enough without doing it, we'll earn our way back into His good graces. Or we seek to resolve our guilt by being extra good for a while—trying to balance the scales. Or we try the negative route, thinking that if we suffer long enough for our sin, if we keep berating ourselves long enough, if we feel regretful and terrible long enough, then perhaps we'll finally deserve to be forgiven. We punish ourselves through self-appointed penance. These are worldly ways of dealing with sins, not God's way. They only shut out the warm, free-flowing mercy and forgiveness of God. When I don't accept the truth that I've been forgiven, I'm actually sinning further by not believing God.

The scriptural way to respond is to remember the truth of Romans 8:33-34: The judge Himself has declared us free from sin. When Satan accuses, Jesus points to His blood. So we can approach God boldly, as Hebrews 4:16 says. When Satan whispers, "You can't come before God now! You're not worthy!" we need to remember that we never come before God because we're worthy. We come because God in His perfect love is always ready to forgive.

Romans 4:8 says, "What joy there is for anyone whose sins are no longer counted against him" (TLB). The Lord will not impute sin against us—He will not record it, He will not take it into account. Why not? Because our sin has been paid for by Christ and the account has been closed. When I sin the guilt does not come back on me, because Jesus bore all my guilt on the Cross and I share in His own righteous standing before God—a standing that is secure and permanent.

In His perfect love God frees us from self-condemnation. He shows us how unrealistic it is, because He loves us and accepts us and has forgiven us just as if we'd never done anything wrong.

It's really so simple. First John 1:9 says that if we confess our sins, God is faithful and just to forgive us our sins and also to cleanse us from all unrighteousness. To confess a known sin that the Holy Spirit brings to mind is simply to admit it—to own up to it, specifically and openly. Then God simply forgives it and washes our conscience clean. To get the most benefit from this conscience-cleansing process after we confess, it helps to start praising God that He's forgiven us—that it's just as if it never happened.

Dr. Maurice Wagner—a godly counselor and author—points out three very helpful questions to ask yourself after you confess a sin.

The first question: *Who owns me?* As I admit that God owns me, this gets rid of the basic, underlying root of all sin—taking the controls of our life into our own hands. I may have gotten angry with someone, failing to obey Ephesians 4:31. But I did it basically because I didn't let God be God. I acted as if I owned my own life and had the freedom to react however I wanted, regardless of His instructions.

So I answer this first question by acknowledging, "God, *You* own me, and I again turn over to You the controls of my life."

The second question: *Who forgives me and cleanses me?* The answer again is God. The very One who owns me is also the One who forgives and declares me righteous. If God says I'm clean, then that's a fact. It's true. There's nothing stacked up against us in some celestial account book.

The third question is: *Who restores me to fellowship?* Once more the answer is God. He restores me, His child, just as the prodigal son's father did (Luke 15:11-24). He completely restores, just as if my sin had never happened.

Then I can praise God for all three of these wonderful truths, and enjoy His total forgiveness. I can go on through life on the right side of the Cross and the empty tomb, knowing and feeling that I'm completely clean. What freedom this brings!

Free from Wrong Thought Patterns

In His perfect love God repeatedly frees us from inner thought patterns and emotions that can harm us.

For example, if I'm always thinking, *I can't, I can't,* my unbelief limits the scope of what I can do. Then when God wants me to step out and do something, I'll experience a sense of incompetence. I'll be afraid—and perhaps unwilling—to take that first step of obedience. I won't be prepared to receive, by faith, the strength and competence He's waiting to provide for that opportunity or situation.

Again and again through the years, truths from God's Word have helped dispel false beliefs and thought patterns that would sidetrack me and destroy my peace. But about six or seven years ago, the Lord prodded me to start a more intensive search for any thoughts and emotions He wanted me to deal with in a new way. So I began to pray, "Lord, is there anything in me that hinders my walk with You? Any false thoughts about You or about myself that keep me from fully doing Your will? Any hurts or griefs that I've never faced head-on, pouring out my heart before You and letting You heal and comfort? Any areas where I still operate independently, relying on my own strength and my own ways of handling life? Any false beliefs I've never clearly renounced? I don't want any areas of my life to be walled off to You!"

I began praying through past events from early childhood and how I felt when they happened. I wrote down many things that deeply affected me—that were big to me, though tiny compared to what many people have gone through. For example, one recurring theme, beginning in childhood, was the pain of feeling left out. This surprised me. I had never let these feelings surface fully, yet they had hindered me in hidden ways.

I did lots of talking with Warren about my discoveries, especially when we were on vacation up in the mountains of Malaysia. Then I made several lists, including my false ways of thinking (the big or little half-truths or lies I had learned to tell myself) and the self-centered strategies for living that I had settled on. Later, alone with Warren in a small library in Hong Kong, I prayed over my lists, confessing and renouncing each wrong way of thinking and handling life. These lines from Isaiah 30:15 motivated me: "In repentance and rest you will be delivered, in quietness and trust is your strength."

Here are some of my discoveries: One of the lies I feel when I live in the flesh is: "I've got to achieve in extra-significant ways." Another false belief: "I can handle my own life; I don't need others to rescue me." And here's a "vow" I made when I was very young and then reinforced as I grew up: "I'm going to be strong and self-reliant and independent, able to handle my own problems. Others can be the 'baby,' not me." It's been a help to deal with these things more decisively and deeply. As I shared these discoveries with others, I asked for their prayers that I would respond to the Lord quickly whenever these old patterns tried to reassert themselves, and that I'd be alert to further insights He might want to give.

This process was good but not easy. I shed tears, and I felt the Lord's love and mercy. Again and again, Luke 1:78-79 and Malachi 4:2 refreshed me—prophecies fulfilled in Jesus: "Because of the tender mercy of our God, the Sunrise from on High shall visit us, to shine upon those who sit in darkness... to guide our feet into the way of peace.... For you who fear My name [who honor Me, who stand in awe of Me], the Sun of Righteousness will rise with healing in His wings. And you will go free, leaping with joy like calves let out to pasture" (NASB, NLT).

Perhaps it's time for you as well to do some detective work, seeking to discover what kind of thinking lies behind any problem spots in your life. Ask the Lord to show you.

Again, it's a matter of using truth to keep the garbage can covered. Satan is angry that we've been released from his power into the freedom of Christ's kingdom. So he wants to confuse and discourage us. He wants us to walk around under a dark cloud of self-condemnation, and he has a host of deceitful devices for making that happen. His lies are many. But we have God's revealed truth to expose each of them and protect us.

Such a big part of our growth as Christians is simply coming to the Bible and letting it expose our wrong ideas about God, such as thinking that He's like people we've known, people who've treated us wrongly. We have to see and acknowledge: No, that's not what God is like. So we search the Scriptures, asking Him to open our eyes to see what He really is, so that we can believe the truth about Him. As we encounter special truths about Him in His Word, we discover one or two that really liberate us. So we think about them, and soak in them, and in time they become jewels, beautifully polished by our meditation.

FREE FROM ANXIETY

Perhaps the most common negative or destructive inner pattern I fall into is a fearful anxiety. It's one of the ways I can readily get tripped up. And when it comes, I find that God delivers me as I focus on Him and His Word.

I recall a time years ago when I found myself anxious about possible disfavor with a dear couple we know. I feared that this would hinder a highly valued friendship, as well as a special opportunity to serve the Lord. As I prayed about this, the Lord ministered to me in a new way through Psalm 84:11, "For the Lord God is a sun and shield; *He bestows favor* and honor. No good thing does the Lord withhold from those who walk uprightly" (RSV).

First and foremost, the Lord bestows favor in His own eyes. In view of that, all human approvals fade. But He also bestows favor in people's eyes. As I walk uprightly, He allows no disfavor that would not be good for me, for His glory, and for the advance of the gospel.

Therefore I don't have to be anxious about disfavor or burdened by the need to maintain favor, as though this all depends on me. My part is simply to walk uprightly and trust the Lord, delighting in the favor He has toward me.

Again and again since then, in many situations, the Lord has powerfully reminded me of Psalm 84:11, along with verse 12: "O Lord of hosts, how blessed is the man who trusts in Thee" (NASB). Faith in the truth dispels my anxiety.

HE WILL PREVAIL

Once while we were traveling in India, I had scheduled a morning appointment to meet with a friend and coworker from New Zealand, whom we'll call Rhonda. She had earlier been in one of our extended orientation programs in Singapore, where we taught many things about adapting to Indian culture, from learning to tie a sari correctly to eating spicier and spicier foods in preparation for Indian curries. The training was very personal and concentrated and lengthy, so we got to know one another well. Warren and I really came to love these people.

The night before I was to meet with Rhonda, Warren and I had dinner with a lovely Indian couple. As I talked with the wife in her kitchen, she opened up to me far sooner than I would have expected. Without displaying a critical spirit in any way, she mentioned something that Rhonda was doing that made it hard for Indians to relate closely with her.

What should I do? I thought. I knew my friend was already up to her ears in cultural adjustments and stress. I also knew she desperately wanted an Indian friend, yet she probably wouldn't find one until she recognized which of her Western ways tended to cause offense.

The next morning, as graciously and positively as I could, I talked with Rhonda about it, and she accepted it.

But the following morning I woke up paralyzed with anxiety. What had I done? I was sure I had only added stress to stress. Satan might take advantage of this stress, so discouraging Rhonda that she might just give up. Or she might never again want me to counsel her, or might even reject my friendship.

Usually in a situation like that I would have turned my thoughts to 2 Chronicles 20:15— "The battle is not yours, but God's." So often that verse has helped me overcome anxiety. But now as I opened up the Scriptures I prayed, "Lord, maybe You have a fresh verse for me today."

Later that day I wrote about this (without mentioning names) in a letter to another friend, revealing how the Lord rescued me and met my need:

> Knowing that I could not afford to let this anxiety drain away my vitality, I told the Lord about it and asked Him to deal with it through His Word. He led me to Isaiah 42:13, where I had under-scored the words, "He shall prevail" (NKJV). He's an invincible war-rior, a mighty champion, greater than any outer or inner enemy or any conceivable hindrance. On behalf of myself and the matter about which I'm concerned, He will prevail.
>
> Then across the page I read in verse 4 that "He will not fail nor be discouraged" until He has fulfilled His purposes. This is true in His broad purposes in the world—and in my life and outreach as I look to Him. He will not be discouraged with me, nor will He fail to accomplish what He desires in my life and situation and loved ones.
>
> Verse 3 says, "A bruised reed He will not break, and a dimly burning wick He will not extinguish" (NASB). He will not break and discard a person who is crushed, bruised, discouraged, lacking a sharp "writing point," needing greater effectiveness. Nor will He snuff out or deal harshly with someone who is disheartened or fail-ing in any way. This includes all of us! We all fail to measure up to God's glorious ideal for us. Yet He deeply values us and faithfully continues the work He has begun in us.
>
> "He will not fail nor be discouraged... He *shall* prevail."

I applied this truth to my concerns about Rhonda: "Lord, You will not fail or be discouraged. You will not fail my friend, or our friendship. You will not fail her by allowing her to get too discouraged. You will prevail, enabling her to change and to develop good friendships with Indian women. Thank You ahead of time!" And my anxiety melted away. Once again I experienced the reality of Jesus' words in John 8:31-32: "If you continue in My word you will know the truth, and the truth will make you free" (RSV).

Many times since then God has used these brief, potent statements of truth from Isaiah 42 to rescue me from anxiety. Even as I review them now, He reassures my heart.

The man who wrote Psalm 94:19 experienced the same thing: "When my anxious thoughts multiply within me, Thy consolations delight my soul" (NASB).

DO NOT FRET

A close cousin to anxiety is fretfulness. Psalms 36 and 37 have repeatedly helped me not to fret or be troubled but to focus on our delightful and reliable God. Let's take another good look at these chapters.

Psalm 37:1 tells me not to fret because of evildoers. I apply this to not fretting about evil in the world that I can do nothing about. I also see it as a caution against worrying about the evil in godly people, whether their wrongdoing hits the headlines or affects me directly. How easily I sometimes fret at small bits of wrongdoing (or seeming wrongdoing) that hurt me in some way. In Psalm 37:3-5, God tells me what I'm to do instead of fretting at evil. I'm to trust in Him and see to it that I myself do good rather than evil—and this includes choosing against my evil inner responses to evil! Instead of fretting, I'm to dwell securely in the rich possessions God has provided in Christ, commit my way to the Lord, and trust Him to act. I'm to be still before Him and wait patiently for Him.

I'm also to delight myself in the Lord. I find this to be one of the basic keys to inner release.

Early one morning in Hong Kong I started fretting inside because of something Warren did. (Or was it something he didn't do? The issue was so small

I can't remember.) Later as I reviewed Psalm 37 in my quiet time, my eyes fell on Psalm 36:5-6 in the preceding column: *"Your* love, O Lord, reaches to the heavens, Your faithfulness to the skies. Your righteousness is like the mighty mountains, Your justice like the great deep" (NIV).

Whose love reaches to the skies? Mine doesn't; Warren's doesn't. We love each other dearly, but only the Lord's love reaches to the skies. Only He never does wrong. Only He is always fair. What a God to delight in—the one perfect partner and friend! Even the most delightful human relationship can never provide perfect love or utter reliability. Only one relationship has the potential of being perfect, with imperfections only on my part.

One message I get from these two psalms is, "Ruth, why choose to fret? Why not choose delight rather than fretfulness?" The quality of my life moment by moment does not rest on what people do or fail to do. It rests on my choice of focus. As I choose to delight in the Lord, He gives me the desires of my heart, including the power to obey the other soul-releasing commands in Psalm 37.

FREE FROM BURDENS TOO GREAT

So much to do, so many bright opportunities, so many deadlines, so many demands, so many unfinished items on my to-do list, so many folders of letters to answer.

So what's new?

At times I find myself living under these pressures instead of on top of them. Why? Because I get sidetracked from God's solution—a heart focused on Him in faith and praise.

Often my excessive inner stress, my feeling of being overwhelmed by too much to do, is connected with the feeling that it all depends on me. The feeling that if I don't work every waking moment, too many essential things won't get done. But if I remember the truth that it does not all depend on me, I can put my burden on the Lord's shoulder and let Him bear the pressure.

Or our inner response may be anger: It all depends on me because Joan isn't doing her share, or because John expects too much. So we add to our life the stress of inner arguments or outbursts of anger. Dr. Wagner said we should envision ourselves in a tug of war with the other person. Then we should decisively put the rope into God's hand and let Him do the tugging. And if we find the rope in our hands again, we can again put it back into God's hand. This self-dependence also applies to angry outbursts with our children. On what are we depending—God's power or our "forcefulness"?

In His perfect and mighty love God liberates us from burdens that are too heavy for us and from inner responses that sap our energies.

It's amazing how the Lord releases us when we respond to the truth in Psalm 68:19-20: "Blessed be the Lord...who daily bears the burden of our life; God is for us a God of victories" (Moffatt). So I tell Him, "Lord, here's this big burden: Too many things to do, too much to cope with." Then I let Him take the burden. And I ask Him for wisdom to say no to things that would be too much. (Lorne Sanny, former president of The Navigators, says that many of us need a "don't" list more than a "do" list.)

Psalm 127 begins, "Unless the Lord builds the house, they labor in vain who build it; unless the Lord guards the city, the watchman stays awake in vain" (NKJV).

As I came across this negative warning, several positive realities confronted me: *The Lord builds and the Lord guards.* He does these things as I depend on Him, and so my labor is not in vain. He makes it significant and enduring— whether or not I get everything done that I think needs doing. As Warren often says, "It takes faith to leave the unfinished unfinished."

The fact that God works does not imply that we should be passive. We are to actively cooperate, both in changing our own life patterns and in reaching out to touch other lives. We're to build positively and to guard against evil and danger, but always with one great truth echoing in our hearts: The Lord builds and the Lord guards.

This rescues us from that compulsive, incessant labor—that treacherous undertow of anxiety because we subtly feel it all depends on us. "He gives to His beloved even in his sleep" (127:2). Always God is *the* Giver, *the* Builder, *the* Protector, working in us, through us, for us.

Whether or not I feel the reality of His working at any given moment, I'm to proceed by faith, choosing to trust Him to work in me and along with me. Then I'm to assume my responsibility to do His will: "His will—nothing more, nothing less, nothing else."

His part and ours—where does one end, the other begin? We cannot tell, for they inseparably interact. In response to His working we choose to work and to rely on Him, and then He works in new ways. As Paul said, "I exert all my strength in reliance upon the power of Him who is mightily at work within me" (Colossians 1:29, Weymouth). Or as the *New Century Version* puts it, "I work and struggle, using Christ's great strength that works so powerfully in me." Paul worked hard, but with a restful, inner dependence on God's working in and through him.

And Jesus said, "I have finished the work You gave me." That's our one responsibility—to do only what He wants, to fit in with what He is doing. As Warren often says, even if we took a pill and could stay awake twenty-four hours a day, we'd still probably not get everything done we'd like to do—or even everything we feel we should do.

It's in my shoulders that I most easily experience stress and tension, so I am often blessed by Isaiah 9:6— "The government will rest upon His shoulders" (NASB). I apply this to the government of my life, as I submit to the Lord's yoke and rely on Him. I find it most helpful to envision Him not so much beside me bearing the main weight of the yoke, but in me, with His powerful shoulders strengthening and relaxing mine. His shoulders uphold the government of worlds—how adequate they are to reinforce mine and protect them from chafing and excess tension.

The end of Isaiah 40 says, "Those who wait on the Lord shall renew their strength" (NKJV). We can look back at earlier verses in that chapter and see that God is the Strong One, the Everlasting Strong One. He has strength and energy that will never fail. There's never any energy crisis or power shortage with Him. He is the I Am, the self-existent One, lacking nothing. As we let this One give us inner strength we have all the energy we need to cope with life. In that special way He relieves us from the heaviness of burdens that have become too great, just as we've seen in Psalm 68:19—"Blessed be the Lord, our saving God, who daily bears the burden of our life" (Moffatt).

FROM REFRIGERATOR TO ROCK

A couple of years ago I had a dream—a long dream about a huge refrigerator I had somehow acquired. I was outdoors in an unfamiliar area, and I felt amazed at how I was managing to move the refrigerator from place to place. It just seemed to be there with me all the time, wherever I went. But soon my amazement dissolved into frustration. Somehow, somewhere, I had to find a safe place to store this valuable but exceedingly troublesome piece of equipment. Place after place fell through, until I woke up feeling troubled. Burdened. Overwhelmed. Just like I often get to feeling about everything that begs to be done.

I finally decided I'd better get up and spend some time with the Lord. I pondered awhile, still feeling the dream. Then the Lord reminded me, "This burden can be Mine, not yours." So I prayed something like this: "Lord, this is Your refrigerator. So I choose to leave it with You; I choose to trust You with it, to let You do the carrying." What a relief to be free of that burden!

Again and again I go back to Psalm 61:2 in the good old *King James Version*: "When my heart is overwhelmed, lead me to the rock that is higher than I." I have a choice. I can ignore this safe, high Rock and go on feeling overwhelmed. Or I can let the Lord lift me up and set my feet on the Rock, where I'm safe and can see things from His point of view. I don't have to do any rock climbing! He's eager to give me a lift, and He does so as soon as I let Him. At the speed of thought, at the speed of choice, He lifts me up. Or you might say, He simply welcomes me into a fresh experience of Him as my Refuge. Into His freedom, gladness, and light. Into the secret place of His presence where I'm safe from the storm, sheltered from its turbulence. Into His everlasting arms: "Jesus, Lover of my soul, let me to Thy bosom fly, while the nearer waters roll, while the tempest still is nigh."

LEAVE IT ALL QUIETLY TO GOD

When I depend on the flesh instead of the Spirit, my personal assortment of false beliefs and strategies create needless stress within me. I find that God's powerful Word, coupled with prayer, relaxes my heart and drains away my inner tensions. An excellent verse when I feel tense and pressured is Psalm 62:1-2 in the Moffatt translation: "Leave it all quietly to God, my soul; my rescue comes from Him alone. Rock, rescue, refuge, He is all to me. Never shall I be overthrown." This verse leads me to pray:

> Dear Lord, I quietly leave in Your hand
> each concern that could cause me stress today:
>> The things You want me to do
>>> and the things You want me to leave unfinished
>>> or even unstarted.
>> The relationships You want me to have
>>> and the ones You want to withhold or take away.
>> The joys You will bring my way,
>>> and the trials You will allow or send.
>> The ways You want me to succeed
>>> and the ways You may let me fail, or seem to fail.
>> The opportunities You want me to accept
>>> and the ones You want me to pass up.

The doors You want to open

    and the ones You want to close.

The ways I would like to glorify You

    and the ways You may use others instead of me.

The times You want me to meet people's needs actively,

    and the times You want me just to listen,

        or to stand aside and "merely" pray.

The deadlines You want me to meet

    and the ones You may want me to miss.

The results of my labors—

    great or small, noticed or hidden.

The ways I will bless or disappoint other people,

    and the ways they will bless or disappoint me.

The human approvals that You will give,

    and the disapprovals that will prod me to rest

        in Your gracious evaluation.

I leave it all quietly to You, my God,

and depend on You to work in me and in those I love:

        to nurture and protect,

        to tear down and to build up

        to wound and to heal

        to reprove and to guide—

    as it seems best to You, my wise and loving Father.

I step out of Your shoes and leave Your responsibilities to You.

I let my life drop back behind You, to follow at the pace You prescribe.

Help me sense inner tensions quickly and then "leave it all quietly

    to You."

I am Your servant. I'm available to You to fulfill Your purposes,

    and Yours alone, in Your way and time.

Amen.

Free from Wrong Behavior

In God's perfect and patient love He also delivers us from self-defeating behavior patterns. When things go wrong, how do we react? Some of us tend to withdraw into silence. I'm a good withdrawer. Others of us would never withdraw; we're quick to speak up or act in an unwise way. And some of us alternate between those two reactions, sometimes withdrawing, and sometimes acting or speaking unwisely and in haste.

God delivers us from both these wrong reactions, for in His Word He has given us behavior patterns for how to cope with life's difficulties in appropriate, godly ways. In our family relationships, for example, He's spelled out gracious, pleasing behavior patterns that really work.

He's also given us some wonderful promises that can calm us down, or cause us not to take matters into our own hands either by our silent treatment or by our lashing out. One of my favorites is Psalm 37:5-6— "Commit your way to the Lord; trust also in Him, and He will do it" (NASB). The *New English Bible* says, "and he will act." Isn't that wonderful? If I just tell the Lord about the problem and commit it to Him and say, "Lord, I'm believing You to work," He will act. He's promised to. It's such a relief!

I came across this poem that says it well:

> With thoughtless and impatient hands
> We tangle up the plans the Lord has wrought.
> And when we cry in pain He says,
> "Be quiet, dear, while I untie the knot."

How often our actions or reactions tangle things up, making them worse rather than better. But God is so loving that He graciously works with us to untangle the knots, free us from our self-defeating behavior patterns, and lead us into more constructive ways of living.

FREE TO LOVE

Only God's perfect love can deliver us from our inability to love others. How often have you been frustrated because you were unable to love family members or friends as perfectly as you wanted? Occasionally something comes out of you that is just the opposite of how you really feel. You know you're supposed to love them, yet in little ways here and there you find yourself hurting them instead. But as we more and more embrace and rest in God's love for us, the experience of that love empowers us to more freely channel it to others.

On the other hand, if I let hostility toward another person block the outflow of love from my life, the inner flow of God's love is also hindered. The feeling against the other person plugs or clogs my whole life. Keeping short accounts with others as well as with God is essential.

The Lord has given Warren and me a delightful relationship, and I am so grateful that for about ninety-nine percent of the time Warren channels to me the delightful love and graciousness of God. Sometimes instead of enjoying this love in a God-centered way, acknowledging its Source, I let Warren become my main prop and stay. I depend on him *instead* of God, rather than depending on God first and Warren second. This spells trouble, for it means I'm out of touch with my indwelling Source of a gentle and quiet spirit. Sooner or later I end up feeling for some reason that Warren is being unfair or unloving. And more often than not, as we talk over the situation, I discover that I myself have done something to trigger his response—a further fruit of my misplaced dependence.

How encouraging it is that even in self-induced trials the Lord gently knocks at the door of my heart! Even my failures give me fresh opportunities to respond to our all-sufficient God! Warren and I find that as we open ourselves to Him with renewed dependence, He meets our inner needs. Then He works with us in restoring sweetness to our human love.

FREE FROM FEAR

In God's intensely personal love for us He delivers us from all kinds of fears.

When Brian and Doreen were in elementary school, we memorized Psalm 34 together. One day I asked what had helped them most from the chapter. One of them replied, "I just feel more free to cry to Him anytime to deliver me from my fears and troubles when anything goes wrong." What a challenge this is! I can bring the Lord joy rather than grief by daily, hourly coming to Him for freedom from fearful reactions!

Another of the main ways I grieve Him is by fearing human disapproval, especially from people near to me. "The fear of man brings a snare [it draws me into anxieties, hurt feelings, defensiveness], but he who trusts in the Lord is safe" (Proverbs 29:25, RSV). So one of the big things I've asked of God is a more constant, unwavering trust in Him—that I will be immediately aware when I slip into old ways and will quickly return to attitudes of trust and love that make Him glad.

Another fear we often experience is fear of failure. I sometimes detect an undercurrent of distress regarding the things I have failed to do or to be. Accompanying this comes the feeling that I can never do enough to make up for various lacks and failures throughout my past. Just bringing this subterranean struggle to light has helped much, especially as I also meditate on God's grace and let it shine into my heart.

The Lord has also shown me that one way my flesh takes over is through the subtle but strong fear that for *rewards* I need to balance the scales. If I have done fifty-one percent good and forty-nine percent "bad," the scales concept leaves me with two percent. Rather bleak, for I do want to experience not just His warm welcome (which is fully assured) but also His hearty "Well done." The Lord reminded me: "Not so, this two percent conclusion. If you have done forty-nine percent bad (unloving, unbelieving, or whatever) Jesus has canceled all of that, never to be entered into My account book at all, for any purpose. Never to be remembered! That leaves fifty-one percent for My 'Well done.'" That is grace—both the cancellation and the reward for what He enables me to do!

FREEDOM'S LIGHT

Many of our fears are not unlike the fear of darkness we may have experienced as a child. But "God is light" (1 John 1:5).

Psalm 36:7-9 speaks of security, satisfaction, and delights, then says, "For with You is the fountain of life; and *in Your light we see light*" (NKJV).

The gospel of John connects life and light, revealing Jesus as both the life and the light. He is the light of life, "and *the life was the light* of men." Our Lord is the one Source of light—of spiritual light, emotional light, direction, enlightenment, freedom from the perils of darkness. He is clear, constant, reassuring, inspiring, healing light. And He provides us light because He Himself is our life.

Once a year our Hindu neighbors in Singapore would celebrate a festival of lights, lining their driveway, fence, and gate with small bowls of oil with wicks. How beautiful when lit! But this light is temporary and dependent on their efforts. In contrast we have eternal and internal light, by the infusion of Christ's life, so that we *"are* light in the Lord"! (Ephesians 5:8).

So I don't have to make my own light. I simply have to focus on the Lord with a trusting, obedient heart. I only have to turn from expecting consistent or adequate light from lesser sources. And isn't expecting or demanding light from human sources often the cause of our dark hours? How foolish, for though all around us may be dark, we "have the light of life"—the source of true security, satisfaction, and delight.

And God directs His light specifically to me. How refreshing to me is the truth in Micah 7:8, "The Lord is a light for me" (NASB). He's a sun, infinitely more glorious than any sun or star in the universe. He has risen in the lives of us who fear His name, ending the night and bringing brightness and warmth. He has risen with "healing in His wings"—spiritual, emotional, and often physical healing. We never experience a moment of the utter darkness that enshrouds the world. And even in dark situations or struggles or pressures, He floods our hearts with light as we let Him do so.

In His intensely personal love, God is a light for me. What a joy to say, "Thank You, Lord! Right now, in this situation, You are a light *for me,* You are a refuge *for me!"* Amazing grace, to be enjoyed in the freedom of His love!

How I thank You, Lord, for the perfect freedom You both promise and give in Your love. You are my Liberator, my Savior; You marched into my besieged life to set me free forever from sin and the fear of death.

And You are my Lord and Master. Show me any areas of my life where You want me to turn the controls over to You more fully. I know that the more control I place in Your hands, the more truly free I will become. "Make me a captive, Lord, and then I shall be free."

Thank You for the breakthroughs You have already provided in my life, and also for those You will accomplish in the future as I bring my needs to You in prayer.

Lord, I give You my mind. Show me any damaging thoughts and attitudes You want to free me from. Build into my mind the positive thoughts that reflect reality—true thoughts about who You really are and who I really am.

Help me to practice regularly the art of inner victory, acknowledging and renouncing my negative thought patterns, and then displacing them by thinking of truth. Lead me to passages in Your Word that will be filled with personal meaning for me. Then may they become beautifully polished jewels as I meditate on them and let Your Holy Spirit reveal their truth more clearly and more deeply.

Thank You for Your perfect love that gives me freedom from guilt, from anger, from anxiety, from all manner of fears. Freedom from wrong patterns of thought and action. Freedom from excessive stress and from burdens too great for me. And freedom from my inability to love as You desire.

Help me day by day, hour by hour, to rise up and soar in the freedom of Your love.

In Jesus' name…

Your personal gleanings for meditation, prayer, and action:

What Scripture or truth in this chapter do you feel the Lord is especially speaking to you about? What will you do to profit the most from this?

TWELVE

IN HIS PERFECT LOVE, I AM SECURE

WE FEEL SECURE when we're convinced that someone important to us views us with love and approval—especially if we're convinced that this someone is sincere, has good judgment, and won't make an about-face tomorrow. This gives us a stable identity, a stable sense that we are acceptable persons. Just as we use a mirror to see that we look all right physically, so we also use mirrors to find out if we're all right as persons. Emotionally, spiritually, and psychologically we need a mirror in which to see what we're like.

The mirror people most often depend on is the mirror of other people's responses. When they receive smiles and compliments and encouragement from others, they feel great. But often they don't receive these things. Instead they encounter negative responses ranging anywhere from frowns to tragic abuse. Then they wonder, or subconsciously feel, "What's wrong with me?"

Some try to ignore what others think about them. They turn inward, seeking to find some mirror within themselves—some abilities they've developed, some ways they are as good as (or better than) other people. They don't realize that if they want a true understanding of themselves, one that is accurate and stable, they must build it only on what God tells them about who they are.

Each of us who believes in Jesus has come into real, living contact with the one true mirror, the mirror of God's love. This mirror always reflects genuine acceptance and a totally accurate picture of who we are. It shows us wonderful, uplifting truths about how acceptable we are in Christ and how much God values the unique person He has created each of us to be. It also shows us humbling truths about our limitations, needs, and flaws as human beings. It doesn't gloss over our sins and failures, yet it never condemns us for them. The more personally we embrace this picture, the more it gives us a profound sense of being accepted and secure in spite of being far from perfect.

God wants us to see ourselves this way—loved, accepted, and secure—because in truth this is what we are in Christ. These are facts, and God wants us to know they're true of us because of Jesus.

It's so good to go back often to Romans 8:38-39 and reflect on our strong, stable, permanent acceptance and security in Christ:

> I am convinced that nothing can ever separate us from His love.
> Death can't, and life can't. The angels can't, and the demons can't.
> Our fears for today, our worries about tomorrow, and even the powers of hell can't keep God's love away. Whether we are high above the sky or in the deepest ocean, nothing in all creation will ever be able to separate us from the love of God that is revealed in Christ Jesus our Lord. (NLT)

God puts the means of our security all around us. In Psalm 5:11, David speaks of taking refuge in the Lord and exulting in Him; then he says to God in verse 12, "For You, O Lord, will bless the righteous; *with favor You will surround him* as with a shield" (NKJV). Psalm 32:10 tells us, "He who trusts in the Lord, *lovingkindness shall surround him*" (NASB). To think that we're surrounded by permanent favor and perfect love! What security, and what wonderful and delightful surroundings! So what if our earthly surroundings change and aren't always what we'd prefer—in God we always have the very best of all possible surroundings, and we have them permanently. Doesn't this give you a strong, stable sense of security?

With such security in such a God, how safe it is to pray at any time, "Lord, do in my life what will honor You, even at my expense." God is trustworthy to do only what we will be forever grateful for, though at times we might choose otherwise if He consulted us. As we honor and obey Him, we will never be cheated or shortchanged. It helps me to remember Job, who eventually received twice as much in earthly blessings as he had lost, plus the surpassing privilege of knowing God better.

HOME

The place many of us associate most with security is simply *home*—and, more importantly, the relationships that form there. Earlier I told the story of my mother's move out of her home in Minneapolis—out of the house that had been such an earthly anchoring place for all of our family. Five years later, in the late spring of 1985, Mother was hospitalized for a few days. She was eighty-nine years old and her body was frail, yet her love and prayers continued to provide strength for me and others, as they always had.

My brother, Jake Barnett, realized Mother was no longer able to stay alone during the day. Always ultra-generous, he graciously offered to fly me home from Asia to stay with her for the coming month, if by chance I would be free. At almost any other time I could have changed my plans and seized this opportunity. But at that particular time a long-standing commitment for us to minister in Japan ruled out my going. Instead, my sister, Mary, stopped working as her husband Gene's assistant and stayed home to give Mother the special loving care she needed.

During that time I opened my heart afresh to the Lord, telling Him that He had my full permission to fulfill Mother's longings and take her Home, though it would be so costly for me and others. Of course He didn't need my permission, nor had I been unwilling before; but I felt a need to consciously release her.

In July I was staying at the Christian Guest House in Bangkok, Thailand. Warren had just left for a week in Burma when the news came that Mother had passed away. How I longed to fly back to the U.S. and be with the family. Yet that was not really an option, nor did I feel it was the Lord's will.

How I missed having Warren there to listen, to encourage, to weep with me, and to offer me a warm shoulder to cry on. But the Lord used my aloneness for good. I'm sure I turned to Him more fully than I would have if Warren or other family members had been near.

A passage that comforted me again and again as I grieved over my deep loss was Psalm 91:1. When reviewing this verse I like to insert the Hebrew names of God and what they mean:

> He who dwells in the shelter of Elyon
> (the Most High, Possessor of heaven and earth)
> will rest in the shadow of Shaddai
> (the Almighty, the all-sufficient God who is enough).

He who dwells…will rest…. When I choose the right dwelling for my heart—the right home—I experience deep inner rest and security. How this undergirded me even in the midst of my sorrowing. And what a comfort it was to know that Mother was now dwelling and delighting in the Lord in a perfect, unending way. Her longings had come true. She was Home!

I wrote to our children the same day I received the news. Here's one of the letters:

Dear Brian and Julie,

How I would love to talk with you directly today. But since that is not feasible I'll visit by letter. About three hours ago I received word that Grandma had gone to be with the Lord. Much has gone through my heart and mind since then. I gave some thought to flying home for the funeral, not because anyone there needs my comfort but just to be with loved ones and experience with them the end of an era. Strange how, though for years I have

seen Grandma only occasionally, yet it has been extremely important to me—comforting, strengthening—to know she was there
on the other side of the earth loving, caring, praying, continuing to
be a sweet fragrance of the Lord, and being the focal point, the
essence, of home to me.

When Grandpa died, I felt exposed from behind—as though a
strong backing, a source from which I had come, was gone. Now I
feel that home, with all its unique connotations from birth on, is
gone. I felt this in another way when Mother moved from 2519
Upton. Then my feelings focused on a *place* called home, now they
focus on the *essence* of home.

Not that I am at all homeless. I have a happy home with Dad in
Singapore; and the home of each of you children is ultra special in the
tender, fresh, forward-looking way of new generations. But the home
from which I came, in which I was nurtured by loving parents and
which has always symbolized open arms of welcome and support which
began before I was born—that home is no more. So I shed my tears.

And even as I weep, I shift my focus to a home that will always
be, a home in which I was welcomed before the foundation of the
world and where I will dwell forever. A place to which the Father is
one by one calling His children Home; a place where Grandma and
Grandpa and your Daddy are now, still loving and caring.

But more importantly, a home that is a Person. Even as Mother
in her person had become home in my heart, yet far more actually,
"Lord, Thou hast been our dwelling place in all generations. Before
the mountains were brought forth, or ever Thou hadst formed the
earth and the world, even from everlasting to everlasting Thou art
God." Here is the focal point for the wanderer and rest for the
weary. The home Mother kept was uniquely a place where I could
rest, feeling utterly accepted and unjudged, feeling totally safe in our
relationship, able to relax in a way reminiscent of childhood. My

home in God Himself offers all of that but more fully, more perfectly. So in a new way I choose to pack my remaining bags heartwise and move into this Home in a fuller way.

And how exciting that Grandma has made her final move! From weakness of body, from the imperfections and limitations of even a good earthly home with Uncle Gene and Aunt Mary, into joy unmingled with grief and untinged with disappointment.

One of the poems that comforted me when your daddy died now returns to mind:

> I am leaving, I am leaving for the country of my King!
> Let not words of grief be spoken,
> Let not loving hearts be broken,
> Rather let the joybells ring,
> For earth's wintry life is changing into everlasting spring.

...More soon.

Oceans of love,

Mom

On the day of the funeral, I wrote to Gene and Mary from Bangkok:

...It crystallized yesterday how much I'd love to see Mother's face once more, and I felt a deep sense of grief at not being able to come home to be with her after her stay in the hospital. After struggling with this for a time, I offered the "missed chance to see her" back to the Lord as a love gift.

As I was thinking about this, I decided to have my own formal funeral in my heart with the Lord—went through the whole service, mentally preached the funeral sermon; reviewed much of 1 Corinthians 15, which speaks of death being swallowed up by victory; sang the songs (including the "Hallelujah Chorus," "It Will Be Worth It All," and "Living for Jesus," a song we sang a lot when

Daddy and Mother were in the pastorate); went through a eulogy honoring her and the Lord; prayed; went past the casket and touched her dear face; met and hugged and visited briefly with various loved ones; went to the gravesite and remembered with tearful joy, "It is sown a perishable body, it is raised in glory; it is sown in weakness, it is raised in power."

It was a most helpful time....

God and His love are our secure dwelling place to enter in times of grief or pressure or disappointment, and in all seasons and moments of need in our lives. It's the place where we can discover who we really are as persons, for our true sense of identity and security comes from the accurate self-identity that only God provides.

OUR LEGITIMATE NEED

It's been said that every problem we face, either within our personalities or in our relationships, can somehow be traced to a false sense of identity or a lack of inner sureness about who we are. In my life, at least, this tends to be true. I display a negative response that I know is not from the Holy Spirit, and I ask, "Lord, why did I respond that way?" Then I discern that I've stopped finding my confidence as a person in His unchanging and perfect love. Instead I've gone back to relying on someone else's approval. I have two mirrors to choose from, and I've chosen the wrong one—the mirror of what some human being thinks of me. Repeatedly I find that my unpleasant emotions are symptoms of looking to someone other than God for assurance of what I'm like. This is especially true of my angry feelings, my feelings of unhealthy guilt, and my anxieties or fears.

Some of us put up a strong front; we press through life with confidence and perhaps gritted teeth. Yet deep down inside there's a shaky little "me" who, in one area of life or another, is fearful, uncertain, hesitant, a bit jittery. Each of us has a deep longing to feel more complete as a person, to have a sense of identity that's more stable and strong—to know with certainty that *I'm all right.*

Not long after we were born we started on our quest for evidence that we were acceptable persons. We sought first of all to gain from our parents some impression of what we were like. To the degree that they met our emotional needs we felt all right as persons. We were very self-oriented; in our little subconscious mind we related everything to how it reflected on us. (I wonder: Are we more mature than that now?)

Of course God's plan is that a young child should get his identity from his parents. They are God's representatives. A little child with good parents can see in them a deep love that affirms his sense of being accepted and approved. The child draws from them a feeling that he belongs and has value. From their discipline he gains a sense of security. And he develops a sense of competence as they teach him how do things and praise him when he does them well, without expecting his performance to match that of an adult. As a child grows, he or she searches the responses of other people (siblings, friends, grandparents, schoolmates, teachers), hoping to find approval and affirmation.

But the parents are like a rocket's booster stage. They're to put their child in orbit around God, then gradually drop off. God's plan as children grow older is that they find their identity in Him and in His love, the only source of a truly mature sense of identity.

Whatever our age, our basic needs are the same: We require the confidence, inner sureness, and security that only perfect love can give. We need an acceptable image of ourselves—a sense of worth, of belonging, and of competence. There's nothing wrong with needing and wanting what we might call ego support—but there is something wrong with seeking it apart from God.

In Christ "all things hold together" and only in Him are we complete, whole, held-together persons (Colossians 1:17, 2:10). We often try many other ways to feel complete, but something essential is still missing. God created us to have *Him* filling us up within. And until we let Him fill us we experience an emptiness inside, and we feel scattered, fragmented, divided. Only the

Lord—nothing else and nobody else—can make us full and complete. Only in Christ can we see ourselves as persons who lack nothing, who are integrated and adequate and acceptable.

Romans 10:3-4 applies to how we can see ourselves as being "all right." This passage describes people who seek to establish their own righteousness, while God's righteousness comes only through faith in Christ. The word *righteousness* in the New Testament basically means a position of acceptance and approval. That's what a good sense of identity is—realizing I'm accepted and approved. So this full passage could be loosely paraphrased, "Since they were ignorant of the sense of identity God gives, they tried to establish their own identity without submitting to the identity that's from God. But to everyone who believes, Christ is the end of seeking identity through self-effort, through trying to live up to some set of rules and expectations."

APPEARANCE, PERFORMANCE, STATUS

Perhaps you can recall moments or days or even months of life when you truly felt all right about yourself because you were so conscious of God's perfect love. You knew you belonged to Him. You were upheld by His approval.

But there have also been times when you and I have reverted to that needless quest of trying to find our inner support in the responses of people. We can tell when that's the case because we get upset and disturbed inside. We lose our peace because someone disapproves of us, or we imagine they do, or we fear they will. We become angry (whether or not we show it), or we scold and punish ourselves for not doing better, or we experience anxiety and fear. A variety of subconscious reactions surface within us. We don't want them, but they rise up because we've failed in our efforts to protect ourselves from disapproval and to shore up our feeling of being all right.

We look to others for approval and identity support in three basic ways—through our appearance, our performance, and our status.

First let's consider appearance—how good we look. A little girl learns early that just by being a pretty little brunette she can get lots of smiles. If her needs aren't met on a deeper level as she grows older, she may develop an inordinate desire to look good. Meanwhile the rest of us who aren't so well-endowed still try this route quite often. We cultivate an image we want to project—casual, or sophisticated, or beautifully made up with our hair styled perfectly, or conservative, or even sloppy, depending on the people whose approval we care about most.

I'm not saying it's wrong to look good. The children of the King should appear as attractive as they can. I believe it's part of our testimony for the Lord. But to the degree that we find our inner support in our appearance, we become spiritually vulnerable and emotionally unstable.

Does it bother us when we can't afford some of the clothes that are "in"? Or when someone hints that we've gained a few pounds or gray hairs or wrinkles, and this doesn't fit with the image we're trying to project? How long does such a remark disturb us? Or if someone compliments our appearance, how long afterward do we keep replaying their words in our mind? It's fine to be pleased with compliments and to give them; the Bible gives many examples of encouraging others and commending them for how well they're doing. And being human, we're bound to be bothered at times by disapproval. But how quickly do we get back to the firm foundation of what God thinks about us?

Then there's performance—how well we do. We want to be a success in something. It's not wrong to work hard and perform well, but *why* do we want to succeed? Do we want to be known as a skillful teacher or manager or salesperson or workman or entrepreneur? Or as a successful parent? ("You should see how their children turned out!") Do we want others to see us as an effective communicator, a proven leader, an expert organizer? Even as a faithful Christian? Is it because we're trying to gain people's approval, instead of resting in God's love and approval for our inner support? Do we seek to do our best in order to build a reputation—or in order to please and honor God?

We want to be known as competent, so we drive ourselves to succeed. We anxiously strive to protect ourselves so that others won't know that we've failed, or that we're likely to fail. This quest to gain human approval and avoid dis-approval often shows up in little ways. Have you ever been disturbed when someone came into your house and it wasn't as clean or orderly as you like it to be? Or when someone got a glimpse inside that messy garage or workshop or closet or desk drawer where everything gets tossed? How long do you let such things bother you?

There's also status—how important we are. Are we a bit too pleased when others call attention to our promotions or possessions or achievements—even our effectiveness in serving the Lord, or our golden opportunities—anything that makes us appear more important than others? In God's eyes worldly status has no value. Yes, He has His Davids and Esthers—kings and queens—yet He esteems just as highly His servants like Dorcas the seamstress and Peter the fisherman and Lazarus the beggar.

Appearance, performance, status. How do you rate on the matter of wrongly pursuing these things to bolster your sense of being somebody? As I've prayed about this and examined my heart, I've found that in one form or another I've been guilty of all three. I've felt extra good when someone noticed I had lost five pounds, extra bad when the scales showed I had gained them back again. I've felt extremely anxious when my children went through problems which, if not overcome, would throw questions on my performance as a mother. I've struggled when I felt we were near the bottom of the ladder in terms of how well our ministry was going.

FROM GRASPING TO RECEIVING

We seek security apart from God in other ways as well—even going to the refrigerator and compulsively grabbing something between meals. Eating more than we should is often a love substitute in a way, an attempt to meet inner emotional needs. We've failed on a human level to find our inner support, so now we're trying to minimize the pain and feel better about ourselves through eating. In the same way we revert to other ways of indulging the lust of the flesh, yielding to shameful desires and to thoughts we know we shouldn't entertain or cultivate, but still do.

Another wrong search for security is in our closest relationships. Most of our conflicts with other people arise because deep inside we're upset that they're not meeting our needs. We're longing for love, for a perfect love. The longing springs from a legitimate need. But when we grasp for love from people, we end up disappointed. Our spouse cannot meet our need. Our children cannot. Our friend—even our best friend—cannot. Only in friendship with God can we connect with the love we need.

No matter how mature we are as Christians, to the end of our days we're members of one body and will profit when other people show that they love us. But deep and tragic problems come when we focus our reliance on those loves instead of saying, "Thank You, Lord, for this special expression of Your love through my friend. And thank You that Your love is the best love of all."

There's nothing wrong with taking pleasure in what God has provided. He "gives us richly all things to enjoy" (1 Timothy 6:17, NKJV), including relationships. But if we rely on His gifts to feel all right as a person, we may feel secure momentarily, but it can't last. Our heart ends up being dissatisfied, disoriented, and worse. We grasp for human love that's more ideal than people are able to give. The more we let God's love satisfy our quest for ideal love, the more our grasping for love can yield to giving.

Whoever or whatever supports us inside is our god. That's one of the functions of a god. So ask yourself: Who or what do I depend on for my inner support? Who is on my throne of my life? Is it myself? Is it something or someone else—anything or anyone other than God?

Who or what am I trusting? Is it my ability to look good? My ability to perform? Or the status I can muster through the person I marry, or my family's prominence, or my education, or my personal success, or whatever?

All this is part of the world's pride system in which people strive to be something in other people's eyes. It can take the form of obvious pride or an inverted pride cloaked with false humility. Either way, self is on the throne and the garbage pail is uncovered. This whole pattern of finding my inner support on the visible level is what worldliness is all about.

Pride tells us, "Do it on your own. Find some earthly way to feel important, to feel superior, to feel acceptable and approved." God tells us that this pride of life is a basic symptom of worldliness (1 John 2:16). Therefore God instructs us, "Do not love the world, nor the things in the world." Why? Because "if anyone loves the world, the love of the Father is not in him" (2:15, NASB). Or as the *New English Bible* says, the person who has these symptoms "is a stranger to the Father's love." Whenever I experience these symptoms, it's because I'm not letting the love of God shine in and support me inside. I'm not responding to His deep longings for me to dwell in His love and lordship and find my security there.

CRACKED MIRRORS

Any sense of identity we develop on the human level alone, outside of Christ, is temporary. It will eventually fail us. Those deceptive mirrors have a way of cracking.

And even if they don't crack, are they reliable? It's like trying to see what we're like in a crazy mirror house, where all the mirrors give us a distorted view of ourselves. Some human mirrors make us feel we're the center of the universe; others make us feel we're ugly or no good or never able to do anything right. Human approval is variable; it's not sure to be the same day after day, hour after hour. Building our sense of identity on human responses is like building on sand, which easily erodes when the winds blow and the rain descends. It cannot give us the foundation we need both today and all our lives. In one way or another, sooner or later, human approval fails to meet our needs.

The stories of these failures are many. The desolate wife who lost her husband after building her identity around him and their marriage. The athlete living in the past because middle age has stripped him of his competitive skills. The man paralyzed by lack of purpose in life because he gave his all to his business until he was sidelined by a heart attack. The desperate woman who found her identity in being youthful and attractive, but who can no longer hide the wrinkles.

Decades ago a letter from a wise friend included this observation about God: "I'm learning He loves me for what I am, not for what I or others may wish I were." Yes, God's perfect, permanent, and intensely personal love offers us our only deep stability, our only lasting stability. He's the one and only Source of an accurate image of who we are. He wants us to accept the gifts He offers: ideal and unchanging love, total forgiveness, strength and encouragement when we need it, and exciting purposes for living. As we accept what He offers, He solidifies our confidence and our realization that we are truly new persons, children of the King, important and loved and secure.

A solid self-concept is God's unique and individually designed gift to each of His children. When we look in the mirror of His love, in the mirror of His Word, we see the unchanging truth about who we really are. Only on this basis can we truly be strong and confident and secure, regardless of what happens. Even when we forget who God says we are and get discouraged or even despair, the mirror of God's love is always available. We can run to that mirror and discover anew, and in ever deeper ways, the unchanging truth about ourselves.

In addition to His Word, God uses trials to rescue us from the world's pride system. He uses problems and troubles to collapse our flimsy, fleshly identity supports and prod us to let His love hold us up inside. Trials show us how vulnerable we are, how easily disturbed by things that threaten our sense of identity. This pressures us to find our firm identity in God alone. Each trial is an opportunity to let His warm love assure us that we are safe, protected, and cared for—that we are His personal concern, supported by His perfect love and power.

Obstacle to Faith

Faith is so important in seeing ourselves as God sees us in all the situations of life. God says so much about believing and trusting Him, and this is clearly one of the basic things He's looking for in our lives. But Jesus asked in John 5:44, "How can you believe, who receive honor from one another, and do not seek the honor that comes from the only God?" (NKJV). Seeking approval and praise anywhere but from God is an obstacle to faith. Have you ever tried to trust Him more and can't? Have you felt you'd like to have more faith but it just doesn't seem to come? You claim this or that promise, but can't really believe it? You read what God says about Himself and about you, but you can't seem to lay hold on it with a steady faith?

How can you believe if you're reverting to the worldly system of trying to gain honor from other people? There's nothing wrong with seeking honor, as long as we seek the honor and praise that comes from God alone. And we do this by living for His glory in people's eyes, not for our own.

I once saw a cartoon showing two ladies playing golf. It was time for one of them to tee off, but she was petrified because two birds in a nearby tree were watching. Her friend admonished her, "Fran, hit that ball! Those birds don't care how you do!" Sometimes there are too many birds in our trees, and it immobilizes us to really do anything meaningful in God's sight—and to believe God for anything meaningful.

Faith cannot come until we turn from man's approval to God's. Faith is believing, and believing is basically receiving. But our pride hates to be a receiver. Our pride hates to admit, "I am nothing in myself. I was never created to be somebody in myself. But I am a complete person—all right forever as a person—because of Christ and His death for my sins and my union with Him." Our pride loathes the idea of patiently learning inner confidence through a persistent relationship with God, on His terms.

Pride robs us of the heart-rest and security that comes from humbly walking with God. Andrew Murray, a well-known author in the 1800s, wrote:

Humility is perfect quietness of heart. It is never to be irritated or anxious or disappointed. It is to expect nothing and to wonder at nothing that is done to me. It is to be at rest when no one praises me, and when I am blamed and despised. It is to have a blessed home in the Lord where I can enter and be at rest, when all around and above is a sea of trouble.

God cuts through our pride by revealing in His Word humbling truths about ourselves as well as uplifting truths. He tells us that we are tiny specks in a vast cosmos; that we fall short of His glorious ideal for us; that we are inadequate in ourselves; that we are poor and needy. Accepting these humbling truths prepares the soil of our life to receive the positive truths we've been considering. And trials—including our own failures—can help us embrace the truths that humble us as well as those that lift us up.

SECURE ENOUGH TO DO GOD'S WILL

In one of Daniel's visions, the Lord's angel said to him, "The people that do know their God shall be strong, and do exploits" (Daniel 11:32, KJV). You and I like to put the cart before the horse. Without continually enriching our knowledge of God, we try to appear strong and act strong. "How are you?" people ask. "Great!" we answer, though inside we're feeling like deprived persons, or we're about to fall apart.

And we want to do "exploits." We don't necessarily expect to make headlines, but in the perception of a few people who are important to us, we want to be seen as performing well.

But God tells us that knowing Him must come first, for it is the basis for strength and for performance that pleases Him. As we know Him better, we become strong with a deep inner strength that is not a mere front, and that won't disappear when the bottom seems to drop out of life. We become free and secure enough to do the true exploits He has called us to do—His exciting will for our lives, which will always be good and well-pleasing and perfect.

Perhaps the best test of our security is whether or not we're content and diligent in doing God's will, whatever that is for us. What security we find in God's love as we simply do His will for this moment, this day! My sister and I used to sing, "Sweet will of God, still fold me closer till I am wholly lost in Thee." This kind of praying sets us up for knowing Him better and enjoying the delights of living close to Him.

One year the Lord gave us a record six-week stretch at home in Singapore with no trips to take and no training programs to oversee. During that time the Lord took me to Micah 6:8, which describes the refreshing simplicity of what God asks of us: "He has shown you, O man, what is good; and what does the Lord require of you but to do justly, to love mercy, and to walk humbly with your God?" (NKJV). Here are some thoughts the Lord brought to mind.

To do justly—I'm not to spend my efforts monitoring others, trying to assure that they do justly toward me, or complaining that "the justice due me escapes the notice of my God" (Isaiah 40:27, NASB). These verses made me aware that I was inwardly complaining that certain things did not seem fair. This meant I was stepping into God's department. He is the one true Judge, who alone is always right in His assessments and who asks me to trust Him. My department is to be sure I personally am being just and fair to others. The Lord provides more-than-sufficient resources for me to "do justly," but not for the strain of trying to make sure life is fair to me.

To love mercy—Instead of giving me what I deserve, God is patiently considerate. He feels with my weaknesses; He is always ready to forgive; and He delights to do good to me although I do not deserve the least of His mercies. So I'm to delight in His immense mercy and channel it on to others. If I fail to be merciful to others, I block God's mercy toward me: "Blessed are the merciful, for they shall receive mercy" (Matthew 5:7, NASB).

Perhaps you've heard the story about a woman who complained to a portrait photographer that the picture he had taken didn't to her justice. He thought a bit, then replied, "Madam, what you need isn't justice but mercy." Wonderfully, God gives both justice and mercy with no snide remarks. He wants us to do the same.

And to walk humbly with your God—What a blessing it is to bow before God in worship for His infinite greatness, His holiness, and His sufficiency, and to acknowledge with humility my vast need for Him. As I affirm the truth about God and myself, I can walk humbly with Him and enjoy His merciful presence as He revives my spirit (Isaiah 57:15).

What simple things God requires, yet what enrichment comes when I faithfully attend to them! How foolish to ever take on the burden of trying to make sure I am treated with the justice and mercy I think I deserve! Why complicate my life and drain away my energies when God Himself is looking out for my best interests as I simply do His will? Why cheat myself?

The Lord capped this off by reminding me of the attitude He wants me to have whenever I am treated unjustly: "If when you do what is right and suffer for it you patiently endure it, this finds favor with God" (1 Peter 2:20, NASB). Unfair treatment provides an opportunity to rejoice God's heart and enjoy His favor and security in a special way.

Doing God's will includes both what I do and how I do it. It means doing what He wants in His way, at His pace for me. At times when I've battled fatigue and exhaustion, I've often gone back to Isaiah 32:15— "In returning and rest shall you be saved; in quietness and in confidence shall be your strength." This would remind me of Psalm 23:2 together with Isaiah 8:6— "He leads me beside the still waters…the waters of Shiloh that flow gently." On the corner of the table where I used to sit and write, I pasted a quote that says, "Let your life drop back behind God, to follow at the rate He prescribes." How often I need to drop back from intensities that reflect the modern drive to achieve, to a quiet perseverance in simply doing God's will. I need to remind myself that at times it's okay to back off and do less, to actually sit in my rocking chair and revel in God's handiwork, in nourishing memories, and in the Lord Himself.

A TEST OF OUR SECURITY

Are we really secure in God's love because we truly understand our identity in Christ? If so, that security will especially work itself out in how we relate to others.

Sometimes we feel insecure because of fears we have for our loved ones. Isn't it hard to see them suffer, whether physically or in other ways! Doreen, our daughter, has suffered from chronic fatigue syndrome for more than five years—extremely difficult for one who bears the responsibility for running a home and raising three children, and difficult as well for her dear husband, Gary. How often my heart wants to cry out to God to heal her *right now!* Then He reminds me that He knows best how to do the beautiful things He wants to do in her life and in the lives of her husband and children—and in our lives. It's great to know that God never wastes His people's experiences.

Besides, God doesn't need me to counsel Him, to advise Him. Who but He knows what is best for us at all times? And I'm not smart enough to figure out His specific reasons for what He's doing or His methods of working. So time and again, I step back from trying to put God into my timetable—from handing Him a clock or a calendar. Instead, I pray, "Lord when You have done all You want to do in this person's life through this affliction, then I ask You to bring complete recovery." Often Psalm 140:12 strengthens my faith: "I know that the Lord will maintain the cause of the afflicted."

Trusting in God's ways and wisdom can keep us from becoming hovering parents. It can help us step back from constantly trying to protect and guide our grown children in ways that actually undermine their security and their dependence on the best Parent of all.

There's also another and more prevalent way that our security in God's love affects our relationships with others. Often we "help" people—including our children—in strange ways. In our eagerness to see them grow we constantly channel their attention to their faults and shortcomings.

Perhaps most of us do build up the people we're close to in some of the big ways. We tell our children we love them, show them physical warmth, and perhaps even let them see our pride in their achievements. We kiss our partners goodbye in the morning and care for their practical needs. We listen to our friends and demonstrate concern for their welfare.

But how often do we verbalize specific ways in which we like them as persons? Many of us seldom do. Sometimes our silence, our failure to express direct praise or appreciation, conveys a general negative attitude. And our day-by-day comments can easily run toward the negative, directly or by implication—even in the presence of others. "She's never on time." "He has no self-discipline." "How many times do I have to tell you that?" "My wife is always too sensitive." "You're being selfish and unkind." Through a continual undercurrent of negativism and criticism (perhaps almost unnoticed by us) we cut down the very people we most want to build up. We wash away the foundations of their self-acceptance. Even a ready flow of suggestions and advice, though gently given, can carry an undertow of negative implications, casting doubt on the other person's intelligence and creativity.

The Lord calls us to focus primarily on what is desirable and uplifting in other people (Philippians 4:8). If you have strong tendencies to harp on negatives you may find the following somewhat structured approach helpful. Namely, practice sharing three positive observations before letting one negative comment or correction pass through your lips. Even though you may not stick to an exact three-to-one proportion, having a specific goal can heighten your alertness to feed in positive observations.

This doesn't mean that we should dish out overdoses of sugary praise. One especially useful way to comment on things we appreciate is to tell how they make us feel. "I feel so grateful when you go out of your way like that to help." "I felt great when I saw you showing an interest in my friends." "I really enjoy conversing with you—I find your thoughts stimulating." Sharing feelings in this way leads the other person to healthy conclusions about his or her worth; it also fosters greater emotional closeness. Often our corrections themselves can be made by verbalizing feelings. "I feel so afraid that something terrible has happened to you when you come home so late without phoning." "I feel insecure in our relationship when you shut me out by your silence." "I feel utterly frustrated when I find the bathroom left in such a mess. It seems like too much for me to cope with." This is better than the "You're a terrible person, won't you ever change?" approach. It helps the other person identify with us rather than resist us or get discouraged.

The suggestion of three positives for one negative does not imply a quick rehearsal of several positives so that we can immediately zero in on the negative business at hand. Such a practice can make a person shrink at positive comments. "Oh, no—what's coming next?"

Rather it means a continual *attitude* of observing and mentioning positives. It means focusing primarily on the things that are true and just and pure and lovely and of good report in others (again, Philippians 4:8). Then when a correction or suggestion is appropriate, it falls on soil kept soft by an inflow of support and encouragement.

Maybe some of us object to this idea because we feel it will encourage pride. We often see ourselves as guardians of the humility of others. But it is not pride for a person to acknowledge with gratefulness the positive qualities and abilities that a wise Creator has given him. In fact, realistically seeing our God-given strengths and successes as well as our weaknesses and failures can help us break out of the pride system. It frees us from the need to constantly try to prove we are superior to others. It can also free us from the vague, chilling fear that we are predominantly a bundle of inferior, unacceptable qualities—a fear that lessens for a moment when we divert our minds to how sinful and immature someone else is.

Could this be the reason many of us keep sending negatives toward those we love? To succeed in changing this pattern, might we need to let God parent us in His gracious, loving way? He wants to set us free from our underlying, deep-down negative feelings about ourselves. He's a master at telling us positive, even glorious truths about who we are. The more we let these in, the more we'll be able to build up others rather than tear them down.

LOVING OURSELVES

Let's explore this a bit more. Our tendency to focus on the negatives in others is often the offensive odor that comes from painful, perhaps undetected abscesses within us—our feelings of insecurity, inferiority, and self-hate. We need to put others down because we're down on ourselves. The toxins from our emotional infections spread throughout our own personalities and into our attitudes toward others as well. How can we help others develop a healthy view of themselves if we see ourselves in an unhealthy, basically negative way—perhaps masked by a prideful spirit?

Jesus said that the second greatest commandment is "You shall love your neighbor as yourself" (Matthew 22:39). He did not mean the kind of self-love Paul warned about in 2 Timothy 3:1-4— "In the last days perilous times will come: For men will be lovers of themselves...lovers of pleasure rather than lovers of God" (NKJV). Instead he meant the healthy, inbuilt love that nourishes and cherishes our bodies, feeding and caring for them (Ephesians 5:28-29). We're to extend this inbuilt, caring kind of love to include others. The more we know and love God and experience His love for us, the more we're able to do this. Could this be one of many reasons why the first and greatest commandment (to love God with our whole being) precedes the second?

There's one ideal, always available cure for a negative view of ourselves and our corresponding negativism toward others: to learn in a new way how secure we are in the love of God. What an example His positive, uplifting attitude toward us is! He repeatedly seeks to strengthen our hearts by warmly describing who we are as new persons in Christ. His love and grace shine through on page after page of Scripture, and He fortifies us deep inside as we expose ourselves to these truths. This prepares us to face the loving rebuke and correction He also brings through the Word.

One good place to expose our hearts to God's positive feelings and attitudes toward us is the book of Ephesians, especially the first three chapters. I've been immeasurably blessed by reading these chapters in several versions, copying the verses or phrases that show God's view of me, and of every other child in His family. Each of us is accepted fully and loved intensely...is freed from all guilt and blame...is valued and delighted in as God's treasure...is inconceivably rich...is endued with unlimited power...is exalted in Christ to a position of high honor...is called to an exciting purpose and gifted in specific ways to fulfill it.

Couple this with the wonderful uniqueness with which God has endowed each of us naturally. This gives us a solid basis for holding our heads high in humble, grateful self-acceptance. This provides a basis for cultivating positive relationships with other people. It enables us to receive one another as Christ has received us and to love others as He loves us.

So we can launch a twofold attack on our negativism. We can tune in day by day to God's positive evaluations of us, and we can follow His example of frequently expressing admiration and appreciation to those around us.

The more God's perfect love deepens our security, the more we can be His channels for deepening the security of other people.

I rejoice, Lord God, in the mirror of Your love, where I can see so accurately who I truly am. Thank You for the security that comes through Your Word, where You reveal the real truth about me, truth that is both humbling and uplifting. Thank You for surrounding me, now and forever, with Your favor and lovingkindness. Your perfect and intensely personal love is my only real home, my dwelling place, my shelter and shield, and my eternal resting place.

Lord, day by day give me a deeper and richer understanding of Your truth about me, a growing awareness of how You view me. May Your truth keep me from pursuing my sense of identity and security in the wrong ways, by looking in the wrong mirrors. You know how my prideful flesh wants to depend on myself and other people to meet my inner needs for a secure identity, rather than looking to You. But, Lord, I acknowledge that You and You alone are the answer to those needs. How I praise You that You are available to meet them so lavishly and generously with Your own fullness! I have no reason ever to turn elsewhere!

Thank You also that this security You provide frees me to relate to other people (especially my loved ones) in a loving, upbuilding way. It gives me a firm foundation for fully doing what pleases You. You are my God, and I ask You to be in control of my activities and pursuits, of my commitments, of my relationships. I want to be Your child in Your place doing Your will. And in whatever place and circumstances You see fit, I'm willing to wait until eternity for the rewards You promise. In faith and hope I look to You.

In Jesus' name…

Your personal gleanings for meditation, prayer, and action:

What Scripture or truth in this chapter do you feel the Lord is especially speaking to you about? What will you do to profit the most from this?

In His Perfect Love, I Am Significant

AT THIS POINT in my life I can't help noticing how fast the seasons speed by. Recently even the weeks seem to elapse with incredible speed, gone almost as soon as they begin. This brings me back to a poem—Ralph Spaulding Cushman's "I Want the Faith"—that has deeply touched my life for years. The first stanza reads,

> I want the faith that envies not
> The passing of the days;
> That sees all times and ways
> More endless than the stars;
> That looks at life,
> Not as a little day of heat and strife,
> But one eternal revel of delight
> With God, the Friend, Adventurer, and Light.

I especially like the view in those last two lines. My life, too, can be "one eternal revel of delight" as I deeply and intimately experience God as my Friend, my Adventurer, my Light. The passing of earthly days won't matter, because in faith I look forward to the eternity of this experience.

Only this eternal perspective can lend true significance to my brief existence on this earth.

OUR INFINITY OF MEANING

Years ago in Singapore I was having my quiet time in a little fan-cooled Chinese coffee shop not far from our home, and my heart was stirred by David's prayer in Psalm 39:4— "Lord, make me to know my end, and what is the extent of my days. Let me know how transient I am" (NASB). The thought came to mind that with the Lord a thousand years are like a day (2 Peter 3:8, NIV). I calculated that to Him our normal human lifespan of eighty years is therefore about the same as two hours!

Following that ratio, if I have ten years left on earth, they'll be the same to God as about fifteen minutes. If I have twenty years left, that's about half an hour. How transient I am! How fleeting my life is—a mere breath, a shadow, a vapor, or as J. B. Phillips puts it, "a puff of smoke visible for a little while and then dissolving into thin air" (James 4:14). As David concluded in Psalm 39:5, "My lifetime is as nothing in Thy sight."

How humbling—and instructive. If I had two hours to live, would I frantically try to fill those hours with ultra-significant activities to help me feel I'd made a great impact? Or would I quietly love the Lord and people, and simply do His will for this moment?

The opposite holds true as well: 2 Peter 3:8 also says, "With the Lord a day is like a thousand years" (NIV). So two hours of my time here is like eighty years to the Lord. God is not caught in time's limitations as we are. He can compress an infinity of meaning into a brief span. Think of the cosmic significance He condensed into the brief three to four years of Jesus' ministry, and then into His six hours on the Cross. In all this, Jesus' goal was never to look or feel "successful," but simply to do His Father's will, seeking only "the honor that comes from the only God" (John 5:44, NKJV).

Likewise for us God can compress meaning into our moments and hours, our months and seasons, making them immensely significant in our personal growth and in our influence on others. How deeply or obviously or broadly He uses us is not ours to choose; it falls under the jurisdiction of our loving Father. Is He not free to do what He wishes with that which is His own (Matthew 20:15)?

One night when I was unable to sleep—perhaps because I had recently been reminded that one of our books was not selling well—I got up and paged through A. W. Tozer's *Renewed Day by Day.* The title of one daily reading especially caught my attention: "God Is Not Dependent on Our Human Success." After quoting 1 Peter 5:6—"Humble yourselves therefore under the mighty hand of God"—Tozer wrote:

> Why is it that the professed Christian church seems to have learned
> so little from our Lord's plain teaching and example concerning
> human failure and success? We are still seeing as men see and judging
> after the manner of man's judgment.... The Christian should turn
> away from all this. No man is worthy to succeed until he is willing to
> fail... until he is willing that the honor of succeeding should go to
> another if God so wills. God may allow His servant to succeed when
> He has disciplined him to a point where he does not need to succeed
> to be happy... when he has learned that success does not make him
> dearer to God or more valuable in the total scheme of things.

Did I feel I needed to succeed either to be happy or to be valued by God? Was I willing instead to fail?

In my two hours on the stage of earthly life, what does it matter if I am a prominent Daniel or a despised shepherd, a Queen Esther or a widow putting two mites into the treasury? Will earthly success or failure in people's eyes (including my own) affect in the least my eternal rewards? No. His "Well done!" will rest simply on my doing His will, by His power, and leaving to Him the specific ways He wants to glorify Himself through my life.

The man who wrote Psalm 84 chose an attitude of holy indifference to earthly status and holy delight in God: "For a day in Your courts is better than a thousand anywhere else. I would rather merely stand at the threshold in the house of my God than dwell at ease in the tents of worldly men" (84:10, several versions combined).

Again and again, thoughts similar to these have brought joy and rest to my heart. In His bountiful, all-wise love, God fills my fleeting days and simple tasks with significance—and along the way I keep experiencing His presence as Friend, Adventurer, and Light.

OUR ADVENTURER

As our Adventurer, God in love gives us exciting purposes for living, better than any we can conjure up for ourselves. In His perfect love I'm freed from purposelessness and the fear of insignificance.

This is one of the big problems of modern living: Why am I here? People look and look, but fail to find a purpose big enough to really challenge them and keep them from being disappointed and frustrated with life. They try something new that promises purpose, then it fizzles out and they feel bored and purposeless again. God created us first of all for a loving, intimate relationship with Him, so we'll always be empty until we find that. Our chief reason for being is to glorify God and enjoy Him forever. But we cannot find that enjoyment until we begin to know Him better and to grasp His love more fully.

A popular song decades ago was titled, "You're Nobody Till Somebody Loves You." We rise far above being "nobodies" as we experience God's love. We are *somebody* in Christ.

Once more, reflect on the wonder of it, and let the truth soak in again to your heart: *The supreme Ruler of the universe desires a loving, intimate, life-long and eternity-long relationship with—me!*

One of my favorite Christmas songs has these lines:

> Long lay the world in sin and error pining
> till He appeared and the soul felt its worth.

To know that we are worth more than we can know to Someone we admire more than we can tell—if anything can bring the true "Christmas feeling" year round, this can.

Yet we cannot experience the unshakable sense of worth He gives if we are trying to feel worthy in ourselves—trying to accumulate evidence that we are good or right or significant on the human level.

When Jesus came to earth, some people already realized their failure and unworthiness apart from Him. They were ready to receive His forgiveness and the feeling of worth His love alone could give. Others needed to have their false self-esteem and "goodness" shattered first.

And the paradox of His coming is this: It revealed the vastness both of our sin and of our worth to God!

His presence, like sunshine, exposes "dirt" that is unnoticed in dimmer light. The closer we live to Him the more we realize the offensiveness of sin in our flesh compared to His unblemished righteousness. Yet if we have given ourselves to Him, we are totally acquitted and justified, possessing inestimable value to God.

Why then do we try to cover today's evidence that we are sinners, justifying our specific sins? "I'm not as bad as *she* is." "It's just my temperament." "It runs in my family." "It's John's fault." "Besides, I'm tired." Miserable attempts, aren't they? We feel so alone in them.

The Lord isn't interested in helping us maintain a sense of worth independent of Him, and He cleanses confessed sin, not excuses. So He arranges circumstances—and even uses our failures—to break through our resistance until we honestly acknowledge our specific sin.

The moment we accept the shattering of our independent self-esteem, for the first or thousandth time, a greater truth can take over inside—the truth that we belong to the Most High God and that He delights in us. As a father treasures his child and a bridegroom his bride, so God values us. He has placed us in a high, unshakable position, and there He increasingly works in us both to will and to do of His good pleasure.

All through life we need to be aware of our sin and weaknesses to humble us, and of our significance and worth in Christ to lift us up. To maintain this dual awareness we have God's help—through His Word and prayer, through His Spirit, and sometimes through other people.

MY BIG PART IN GOD'S BIG PURPOSES

My earthly life can have significance because God Himself has big purposes for all that happens in the world.

God tells us in 1 Peter 2:9 that we're a special chosen race and a people claimed by God as His own possession, His special treasure here on earth. And the reason for it, He goes on to say, is so that we can show forth the excellencies and perfections of Him who has called us out of darkness into His wonderful light. In all we do, in all our joys and trials, in daily drudgery and daily delights, we have a part in this grand purpose of showing forth His excellencies by our life and by our lips. Therefore we're significant not only as persons, but also as servants of the Lord.

God has two primary purposes in this world around which I think all His other purposes revolve. First of all He is at work here and now to call out from this fallen world "a people for His name" (Acts 15:14)—a people for Himself who will believe in Him and let Him be their Savior and Lord.

Second, He plans "to bring many sons [and daughters!] to glory" (Hebrews 2:10). This does not mean simply transporting us physically up to heaven. It means that He will change us into glorious people, conformed to Christ's image. We'll be part of His vast family of sons and daughters who all reflect without fault or blemish the glorious excellencies of Christ.

Won't it be wonderful to live in a family like that forever? No more garbage pail. No more rough edges to be rubbed off. No more things to gripe about. No more disappointments, no more abuse, no more anything that's harmful.

God is looking forward to that even more than we are, and His plan for now is to put disciples of Christ everywhere, disciples who will follow Him ever more closely and honor Him ever more fully.

This is His purpose, and we have a part. What tremendous significance He bestows on us!

POOLS AND STREAMS

God also gives me the significance of simply channeling His perfect love to others. I treasure the picture Amy Carmichael paints:

> All our love flows from His heart of love. We are like little pools on the rocks when the great sea washes over them and floods them until they overflow! That is what the love of God does for us. We have no love in ourselves, and our pools would soon be empty if it were not for that great, glorious, exhaustless sea of love. My chief prayer is that your pools may be kept full to overflowing.

We don't have the kind of love others need. Our love is too puny, too fluctuating. But if we let God's perfect love saturate our inner being, so that we begin to understand His attitude toward us and the value He places upon us, it profoundly alters our attitude toward others. With heightened spiritual sensitivity we realize: "Just as I am beloved by God and uniquely valuable to God— so is she, and so is he." God's love toward us is intensely personal, but it is not exclusive. Out of the fountain of His love within us He gives a flow of consistent love, unlimited and unfailing love, which He uses to meet the needs of others.

In Romans 15:7, God tells us to receive one another as Christ received us. When we deeply understand that Christ has received us with wide-open arms and no reservations, just as we are, we're able to receive one another in the same way.

Colossians 3:12 is a beautiful verse, describing us as God's chosen ones, "holy and beloved." And as His chosen and holy and beloved ones, we're told to "put on" a heart of love for others—"a heart of compassion, kindness, humility, gentleness and patience" (NASB). Ask yourself, "Which of these five qualities do I most need these days?"

It's so easy for me to see something in others that I don't like or don't agree with, and then get critical in my inner attitude toward them—and sometimes in my outer attitudes, words, or actions. It's so easy for me to pick out some character fault and magnify it as if that's the whole person, forgetting that I have just as large an assortment of flaws myself.

The following lines from a longer poem (author unknown) help me see other believers as God does:

> Oh that when Christians meet and part
> These words were carved on every heart:
> *They're dear to God.*
>
> However willful and unwise
> We'll look at them with loving eyes.
> *They're dear to God.*
>
> When we're tempted to give pain for pain,
> These thoughts should then our words restrain:
> *They're dear to God.*

In eternity we'll be together with these believers in a delight we can't imagine, where we'll be perfect and will never offend them, and they'll be perfect and will never offend us. In our eternity to come, Jesus will be the oldest brother in a "vast family"—all of whom will bear the family likeness, resembling their tremendously desirable, incredibly loving Elder Brother. What belongingness forever—and with what a company! As David Morken used to say, "We belong to Him and to one another for eternity."

And even now we can love them with Jesus' love just as they are, walking the path of obedience to the One who said, "Love one another as I have loved you."

God's love for us is a supernatural love. We can't learn to know it unless the Holy Spirit teaches us through the Scriptures. Likewise the love He asks us to expend for others is a supernatural love. It's His love flowing through us. It's not something we're supposed to stir up ourselves—"He irritates me to no end, but I'm going to love him if it kills me." Only by channeling *His* love can we love in the way 1 Corinthians 13 describes—love that is patient and kind. Love that is not jealous or boastful, proud or rude, selfish or irritable. Love that keeps no record of wrongs done to it. Love that is not happy with evil but rejoices whenever the truth wins out. Love that patiently accepts all things, never loses faith, and always hopes and perseveres in every circumstance. This is the kind of love God has for us and wants us to have for others. Its source is God, not us.

The way God channels His love through us is not like water in a pipe but water in a stream, where it permeates and saturates the stream-bed, and then there's an overflow. God wants us to let His love fill us and amaze us, and then we'll more fully channel that love to others. We'll love them just as they are, in the same way He loves us just as we are.

He loves us just as we are, while He also longs for us to become more than we are. So we can love others just as they are, while we also pray that they (along with us) will become more than they are. One of our biggest prayers for one another and for ourselves should be, "Lord, may he or she (and I) love You as You deserve, and therefore love others as You desire."

Even if those we love this way do not love us back, we still have in God a source of love that constantly replenishes our depletion, for we're one with Him in a permanent union.

INVESTING MY LIFE

God, in His beautiful love, also gives us the priceless significance and privilege of being His witnesses. "You will be My witnesses," He says in Acts 1:8.

We're witnesses of Him both to unbelievers and to believers, and we witness by both our life and our words. I believe we're all called to witness both ways to both groups. We're to help win unbelievers to Christ and help believers grow closer to the Lord.

We have to let people know about Christ. In whatever way God gives us the ability, we are to speak for Him. Some of us have a special gift of evangelism and will lead more to the Lord than others will. But all of us can share what Jesus means to us. All of us can simply share the good news about Jesus by our words as well as by our lives.

As we are His faithful witnesses, our God of love also gives us the significance of investing our lives in others.

In 1949, Dawson Trotman, the founder of the Navigators, came to our campus at Northwestern and spoke in chapel. He spoke about being diligent in studying the Bible and in memorizing God's Word. I had memorized quite a few Scriptures, but had forgotten most of them and really felt guilty about this. Dawson helped me get over that guilt. But the most challenging thing he explained to us was that reaching the world for Christ can best be done through one-on-one disciplemaking.

He gave a comparison. He asked us to suppose we had a friend who was very gifted in personal evangelism and who, on average, personally won someone to Christ every month. We, of course, would consider that quite remarkable. After a year our friend would be responsible for twelve new converts. In ten years' time the total would be 120. Even more remarkable!

Then Dawson asked a question that bothered me greatly: "How many people whom you've won to the Lord are still walking with Christ today because you nurtured them? You didn't just take them to church, but you discipled them, so that they're faithfully following the Lord now." I was smitten. I had led a number of people to the Lord, but I couldn't think of a single one who was walking with God.

To help us understand the need not just to reproduce but also to multiply, Dawson continued his comparison. I mentally followed his lead. As he suggested,

I pictured myself praying, "Lord, give me one spiritual baby. Lead me to one prepared heart that I can win to You." Then I pictured what God would do and what I would do. First, God answers my prayer. Then I spend a year discipling this new Christian, meeting regularly with her to help her feed on God's Word and pray and memorize Scripture and spend daily time with God. I point her to the Lord and His Word to find help for needs and problems. I teach her how to share the gospel and how to give her testimony.

By the end of a year, she hasn't learned everything there is to know about the Christian life, but she's probably more mature than some people who've attended church for many years.

After a year of ministry, I've "multiplied" myself, from one disciple to a total of two. Not much compared to the twelve converts produced by our friend, but at least a start.

At the end of that year I tell this new disciple, "Why don't you look to the Lord to give you a hungry spiritual baby you can start nurturing? You can teach her everything I've taught you." Meanwhile I pray for someone else I can disciple as well. God answers our prayers, and each of us spends the second year nurturing a new believer. At the end of those two years there are now four growing disciples, compared to 24 converts for our friend. Still a big difference.

But the multiplication continues. During the third year, we four disciples again focus our ministry on discipling one new person each. So by the end of that year there are eight—compared to 36 converts as a result of our friend's ministry.

The process goes on. After four years, our total is 16, while our friend has 48 converts. After five years, our total is 32, compared to his 60. In six years, the numbers are almost even: 64, compared to 72.

Now the multiplication becomes dramatic. In the seventh year, the disciples grow to 128, to 256 in the eighth year, 512 in the ninth, and finally 1,024 in the tenth year. Compared to a ten-year total of 120 converts through our friend's ministry, that's more than an eight-to-one ratio. By the fourteenth year, the ratio swells to almost a hundred to one.

You may protest, "But I don't think the process would work that well." No, it wouldn't. But those numbers do show the potential. It never works out that perfectly, but then no other evangelism method does either.

All this greatly excited me. I planned on going to the mission field, but what work should I do there? The process Dawson explained—simply giving myself to one-to-one ministry—appeared to be the most strategic ministry I could have anywhere. And it was *something I could do!* In fact, it seemed to me that we women really have the edge in this, since nurturing comes more naturally to us.

Even before I left for Asia, to be married to Dean and to serve the Lord in Taiwan, I began to pray for one Chinese woman to train. I knew Dean and I would probably have children, and that I'd also be busy learning the language and adjusting to the culture. I wouldn't have as much time as I'd like for ministry outside the family, but I could certainly commit myself to training one woman.

When I reached Taiwan and discussed this with Dean, he said he knew just the woman. She was Chinese and in her forties. That really stirred up doubts within me. I was only twenty-four. Even in America the difference in our ages would pose difficulties. But in the Chinese culture where age is so much more important, why would this woman listen to me?

Dean encouraged me. "She's so eager. She's the one," he said. So I got together with her, ministered to her—and she grew and began to multiply. It was so rewarding to see God use her to both win and train others. She continued to minister one-to-one for years. We still hear from her. She's in her late eighties and still walking with the Lord.

It really pays to ask God for *one.* And when He gives that one, and you're faithful to disciple him or her, who knows what God will do from there on.

AN APPROVED WORKMAN

So God, in His matchless love, gives me significant work to give myself to. And He also offers me the significance of being a good workman, not a mediocre one. In 2 Timothy 2:15, Paul says, "Be diligent to present yourself *approved to God as a workman* who does not need to be ashamed, handling accurately the word of truth" (NASB).

As I reflected on those words, I thought, "Oh, does this mean I'm not yet approved? Am I a disapproved person?" No, from other Scriptures we know that as believers we're all approved as persons. If we know Christ, we're all on the right side of the Cross and the empty tomb. So we're new persons in the core of our being. God accepts us because we're righteous with Jesus' righteousness.

But to be approved as a workman is something else. It takes hard work. To help us, God tells us in the next chapter (2 Timothy 3) that He has provided us with His inspired Scriptures. Day by day we can let them teach us, correct our errors, guide us, and train us to live upright lives. Verse 17 says, "Using the Scriptures, the person who serves God will be capable, having all that is needed for every good work" (NCV). The Scriptures equip us to help others know and understand and use them. So if we want to become (and remain) approved as workmen, we must work diligently to learn God's revealed truth so that we will "handle it correctly" (NIV).

Work as significant as this takes preparation. To prepare ourselves, we first of all present our bodies as a living sacrifice (Romans 12:1), a process that involves more than we imagine at first.

After I became a widow I came across these words that bothered me:

> But simply to drop all our dreams and ambitions and preferences
> and to have no mind about it at all, but be willing for God to shift
> us anywhere on life's checkerboard, or bury us anywhere in life's
> garden, counting not our lives dear and loving them not unto death,
> gladly yielding ourselves for God to please Himself with, anywhere
> and anyway He chooses—that is rarely done. (Author unknown)

How this challenged me! And confused me a bit. Drop *all* my dreams and ambitions and preferences? What about the dreams and plans that I believe are from God? How could I drop those?

God reminded me, "Ruth, I'm not asking you to drop them into a vacuum. I'm asking you to drop them into My hands, My loving hands. Even if they're what I've told you to do, I don't want you to *grasp* them."

I found myself eager to do that which is "rarely done." I wanted to bring God that pleasure. So I answered, "Okay, Lord, I just drop them into Your hands."

In an earlier chapter we considered the poem that began, "I would be simply used." What joy there is in choosing to simply fit into the Lord's plans! What release comes when we tell Him, "Lord, I'm here to do Your will, whether or not it fits into my dreams and preferences—or into the values of our day."

MY CORE ROLES

We don't accomplish our work as approved workmen in our own strength. Neither do we accomplish it by simply drifting along through life, reacting to whatever presses in on us. Instead we need to sort through our priorities and put first things first.

We must keep our priorities straight because God has given each of us certain core roles. He has assigned us certain basic responsibilities appropriate for the privileged position He called us to in our relationships with others, especially in the family. In eternity I don't want to stand before the Lord and say, "I did this and I did that," and have Him answer, "But you didn't do what I specifically wanted and told you to do as a woman, as a wife, and as a mother."

These core roles, these central, basic responsibilities, are not identical for men and for women. As I go through the Bible, it seems to me that God gives man the basic responsibility to provide for his family. It's man whom God instructed to till the soil and produce its fruit. That doesn't mean a wife should never earn money or doesn't at times have to do so. But God has delegated the family's provider role primarily to the husband and father.

God has also given him the basic role of leading the home, but not in a domineering or harsh way. He's not to be a military sergeant who says "Jump!" and his wife and children answer "How high?" He's to be a leader like Christ, and Christ is a leader who loves so much that He died for those in His care. God specifically instructs the husband to love with a sacrificial love—the kind of love Christ showed at great cost to Himself. I personally feel the Lord has given the husband the most difficult role!

Over the years I've repeatedly gone back to certain Scriptures that help me as a woman set my priorities and keep them clear—such as Matthew 22:37-38, Proverbs 31:10-31, Ephesians 5:22-33, and Titus 2:3-4. These Scriptures help me base my priorities and my choices on what God says, not on what my preferences or my culture may be saying. My intention in sharing my conclusions is not to force them on you or anyone else. And I choose not to judge women who differ with me in this area. I encourage you to come to the Scriptures with an open heart and let the Lord guide you.

Here are my basic conclusions. My first priority is God—loving Him, cultivating my relationship with Him, and obeying His commands. My second priority (and my primary ministry) is my husband. This is a spiritual ministry. I'm serving the living God when I love and take care of Warren and honor the leadership I believe the Lord has assigned him. My third priority is my children—especially as they were growing up. Priority number four— closely linked with the previous two priorities—is to be diligent in running my household well. I consider number five to be attending to my personal needs such as exercise, adequate sleep, eating well, taking time to relax, grooming, and maintaining friendships. In no way are these things optional, for they keep me fit for all the rest.

This one-to-five order does not mean I do all I possibly could do in number one before I go on to number two, or in number one through four before I go on to number five. Life isn't that cut-and-dried. I have to exercise wisdom in juggling them all. When one of them escalates for a week or so (as when someone is sick), then later I seek to give extra attention to the others.

Beyond these basic priorities I'm to fit in other activities and opportunities as time permits and as the Lord leads. Warren plays an important role in His leading. Most of our decisions are mutual, but I value a statement I heard years ago: "God gave us a lot of leading when He gave us a husband."

This last, catch-all priority includes many important things—ministering side by side with Warren (this is also part of priority two), using my spiritual gifts, ministering to other women, helping my husband bring in the family finances when that is wise or necessary, helping the poor, hobbies, leisure activities—on and on. After Brian and Doreen were grown and gone (and to a lesser degree when they were in high school) I found it possible to fit in more of these above-and-beyond activities. But even when they were small, I felt that reaching out to help others was part of raising them well; it demonstrated Christlikeness and prevented an "us four, no more" mentality.

Even at my age I still have to work on keeping my priorities straight. I don't have the children around now; but sometimes, if I'm not careful, I can put my husband on the back burner. And Warren's such a kind and forbearing man that he might let me do it, at least for a while.

None of us will fulfill these core responsibilities perfectly. I haven't, and still don't. But with God's strength and guidance we're to do them with all our heart. If one gets somewhat neglected for a time, then we give it extra attention for a while. And always we're to remember that the first priority for both man and woman is relating to God. Each of us is first of all His child, His loved one. And relating to Him empowers us for all of our human priorities.

PRIVATE LESSONS

As we encounter and experience the significance God gives to our lives, it doesn't mean things become easier. God knows that we need the "private lessons" of trials to adequately prepare us now for greater significance in this life, as well as in eternity.

When I was struggling with Dean's cancer, I came across this poem by Martha Snell Nicholson that helped me then, and many times since then.

> Does your bitter load of grief,
>> Tears, and pain,
>> Seem too hard for you to bear?
>> Don't complain;
>> You are only being made
>> Fit to reign.
>
> Fit to reign with Christ our Lord;
>> Destiny
>> Far beyond imagining!
>> How could He
>> Ever use as potentates
>> you and me?
>
> Surely we are all unfit,
>> All untaught,
>> And of wise and kingly lore
>> Knowing naught.
>> All the gold of Ophir could
>> Not have bought
>
> Private lessons from a King!
>> Precious pain,
>> Used of God to teach His child
>> How to reign,
>> Taught by very God Himself—
>> And we complain!

How that touches me. Most of the time we don't suffer quite as much as the poem says, but things that are extremely difficult for one person might not be so hard for another, and vice versa. Our sufferings have their own mysterious measure.

There's another reason for the increased difficulties we'll encounter along the pathway of significance. The more we tap into the significance God gives and begin living it out, the more strategic a target we become to the enemy. We get more involved in spiritual warfare, in battles large and small.

Years ago Dean and I read that Satan especially likes to attack *after a victory* for Christ or *before a venture* for Christ. During times like these we need to pray against Satan's attacks—and especially against his small, subtle assaults. For example, he likes to ride in on the crest of a small trial, making it mushroom—as when a little misunderstanding or a perceived unfairness draws us into self-centered and self-protective thinking, perhaps for hours or even longer.

On our own we do not have what it takes to fulfill God's grand purposes for our lives and to overcome the trials and enemy attacks that go with them. That's why we need to remember that one of God's names is *El Shaddai*. This name tells us that He's the mighty, all-powerful God, the "breasted one"—mighty to nourish, satisfy, and supply. He is all-sufficient, all-bountiful—the source of blessing, of fullness, and of fruitfulness. He's able to fulfill His plans and purposes for using our lives, even as He did for Abraham in giving him Isaac at the age of one hundred (the situation in which He first revealed this name).

So we must be as Abraham was, not staggering or wavering in unbelief because we don't naturally have what it takes to fulfill God's purposes. Then we can know the most gratifying significance of a fruitful life.

"I am El Shaddai: Be fruitful and multiply" (Genesis 35:11). To each of us He says, "Be fruitful in the way I have planned for you—trust Me to make this possible." From Him our fruit comes; He is everything we need to take root, to sprout and blossom, to be fragrant and fruitful for Him (Hosea 14:5-8). Psalm 92 says that those planted in the house of the Lord will flourish, continuing to yield fruit even in old age. They will still remain vital and green, displaying to others what God is.

This was true in the Old Testament. And how much more it's true in the New, for through His grace Christ has linked us in a new way with the Father and given us His Spirit to fill and empower us.

OUR HAPPY CERTAINTY

God, in His gracious and wise love, helps us focus on our eternal significance by teaching us how to hope.

I've been deeply impressed with the amount of emphasis the Lord puts on hope—on the glad, assured confidence He wants us to have regarding the future. This includes our earthly future, for the Lord gives us hope for this life (Jeremiah 29:11). But far more, hope is the happy certainty that Jesus Christ will be revealed in all His glory, that we will see our Most Loved One face to face, and that we will be gloriously changed to be all He has in mind for us to be. According to J. B. Phillips, Christ's return will be "splendor unimaginable" and "a breath-taking wonder" (2 Thessalonians 1:9-10).

What a hope! No wonder we are to exult in it with happy uncertainty, with tremendous joy that words cannot express, even in the midst of trials and troubles (Romans 5:2, 1 Peter 1:6-8, Phillips).

This hope is a sure and steadfast anchor for our souls. It motivates us to live pure lives, keeping our wedding garments spotless. Hope is not a luxury that we can take or leave, for it is one of the three basics of our inner life: faith, hope, and love.

I'm praying that in a new way my life will be characterized by glad, exultant hope. And the Lord has spelled out my part in His answer to this prayer. Through the power of the Holy Spirit I am to simply believe (Romans 15:13). I am to fix my mind on truths that produce hope, just as Jeremiah did in Lamentations 3:21-24: I'm to recall God's unfailing love and mercy, His great faithfulness and goodness, and then reaffirm that He is my portion, my share in life, now and forever. On this solid base, I am to fix the full weight of my hopes on the grace that will be mine when Jesus Christ reveals Himself (1 Peter 1:13, Phillips).

What a delightful prescription the Word gives for hope: focusing on the God of hope and the total, glorious, mind-expanding future we will enjoy with Him, and with one another, forever and ever!

And according to God's design, the joy we find in our hope is inseparable from the joy we display in our tribulations. Helen Morken used to say, "God allows trials to bring the scum to the top in our lives, and we stir it right back in." God wants us to cooperate with Him in skimming off the scum. But we miss this opportunity when, by our wrong responses to trials, we stir the impurities back into the gold. But God is faithful. He'll lead us into another trial to bring up the same scum! He has glorious purposes He's going to accomplish one way or another.

So we can rejoice not only in our hope, but also in our tribulations, because trials produce in us perseverance and character and hope. And as a result, the love of God is shed abroad in us and through us in new ways (Romans 5:3-5).

The word *rejoice* can also be translated *exult*. What a triumphant word! For me, it often takes a while to get into that mode when a trial comes. In fact, at times it takes a magnificent work of God in my heart to get me there. But it's our privilege to exult in our trials. With every adversity we can glory in the marvelous fact that we're on the way to becoming glorious beings for all eternity, and that our present trial is preparing us for that. Paul wrote, "If we endure, we will also reign with Him" (2 Timothy 2:12, NIV).

A BETTER WELCOME

"One by one," Helen Morken used to say, "God is calling His children home." And as He calls us home when we die or when Christ returns, it will be glorious for us all—breathtaking, unimaginable splendor. And each of us will hear and know His personal greeting, "Welcome, My beloved child."

But not all of us will hear His "Well done, good and faithful servant."

The splendid, breathtaking wonder for all, and His warm welcome for all—but His "Well done" only for some.

I deeply desire to hear both greetings—don't you?

When we stand before Him, He won't ask how successful we were in other people's eyes, or even in our own eyes. He won't ask how high we climbed on any earthly ladder.

After Dean and I had been in Taiwan about a year and a half, in the midst of learning the language and adjusting to the culture and starting a family, we had done quite a bit of ministry. But the ministry wasn't flourishing the way we wanted it to. From time to time we would go up to Taipei, the capital, and visit other missionaries who seemed to be more fruitful. We began comparing ourselves with them.

After Dean and I returned from one of those trips, I remember riding home from the train station in a pedicab (a bicycle-drawn rickshaw). As we rode along I said, "You know, the nice thing about being on the lowest rung of the ladder is that we can't go any lower." But later we found there was a lower rung. And still later we discovered that, from God's point of view, there wasn't even a ladder.

The ladders we picture in our minds and the ways we compare ourselves with others—these are not valid in God's eyes. Our knowledge is too limited, too time-bound, too flawed, to judge either ourselves or others. Only God knows enough to compare us with others, and He does not choose to do so.

And remember Jesus' verdict on earthly status or honor: Many who are first here will be last there, and the last will be first.

In 1 Corinthians 15, where Paul discusses our eternal future, he reminds us that one star differs from another in glory. All stars are glorious, but their glories differ. Then he says, "So will it be with the resurrection of the dead" (15:42, NIV). In other words, that is what it will be like when the dead rise. We will all be glorious. But I believe that the degree to which we respond to God in this life will affect something highly important in the next life. Might it be how glorious we will be? Or how much capacity we'll have to delight in God forever?

There will be rewards, but different rewards for different believers. There will be rewards for having developed a close relationship with Him, if indeed we have done so. Rewards for having let Him build character into our lives, if we've let Him. Rewards for how much we have obeyed Him, so that the fragrance of Christ was expressed in us. Rewards for how much we responded joyfully to troubles and problems, so that our trials became a platform on which He could reveal Himself to us and to others—a stage on which He could show how powerful and loving and wonderful He is. He'll reward us for having been faithful in our core roles, if we have been faithful. Many rewards—many ifs!

He won't reward us for how prominent we were in serving Him, or how much people noticed or applauded us. He won't reward us for how well we thought we were doing. He'll reward us only for how faithful we were in doing just what He wanted us to do.

It's that simple. We have One Person to please, and one assignment: to please Him.

That is what He asks.

And if we do what He asks, He'll reward us for keeping our priorities straight and persisting in doing His will. And He'll say, "Well done, good and faithful servant." How I want to hear that!

This One we serve is the only One worth serving. And serving Him means significance now by faith, and significance later by sight—eternal treasures laid up in our eternal Home by our God of perfect love and wisdom.

Dear Lord, exalted high above all, I worship You as the glorious Master of all creation—and as my Master. You are the God of perfect love who has included me in Your glorious eternal purposes. Thank You, Lord, for the gift of significance—that in

You I can live a life of adventure and fruitfulness. Thank You for the part I can share in Your exciting plans and purposes.

I praise You for calling me out of this fallen world to be a part of Your family, of Your chosen, royal, and holy people. Thank You for revealing Your plans for bringing us to glory, for transforming us into the image of Your Son Jesus. Thank You that I belong both to You and to Your loved ones forever!

Enable me to be a permanent dropout from the world's race to be important in people's eyes. I leave to You the specific ways You want to glorify Yourself through my life. May I be ready each day to have You use me, or not to be used at all. Help me focus day by day on the wonder of my significance in Your sight, as Your loved one and as Your servant.

Keep refining me as a channel of Your supernatural love, so the flow to those around me will grow fuller and sweeter.

Help me to clearly understand my core roles, and to receive from You the daily strength to be faithful in them. I pray especially for Your grace in my role as _____. Work in me that which is pleasing in your sight.

And Lord, I want to invest my life in the lives of others. Give me someone I can nurture and disciple in the faith — someone with a prepared heart, who will hunger to know You more and more, and who will in turn nurture and disciple others.

I drop into Your loving hands all my dreams and ambitions and preferences. They are Yours to fulfill, or not to fulfill, according to Your own perfect wisdom. I trust You, Lord.

My loving Lord and Master, I want to hear Your "Well done" on the day I stand before You. So I beseech You to help me be wise and faithful today and all the remaining days of my brief life here on earth.

I praise You, for You alone are worthy of my service.
Amen—so shall it be.

Your personal gleanings for meditation, prayer, and action:
What Scripture or truth in this chapter do you feel the Lord is especially speaking to you about? What will you do to profit the most from this?

FOURTEEN

In His Perfect Love, I Am Honored

"YOU ARE PRECIOUS in my eyes," God says to us, *"and honored,* and I love you."

Me? Honored in *God's* eyes? He's the Most High God, exalted above all. *He* is honored, and we stand in awe of Him. So how can He say that I am honored?

In the Moffatt translation, Isaiah 43:4 reads, "So precious are you to Me, so honored, so beloved." *So* honored? That's what I am to Him? It doesn't make sense; it's darkness to my intellect. But it's true. And it warms my heart! You and I have been brought to the place of highest privilege. God Himself honors and favors us.

GREATER THAN GOD'S HEROES

In Matthew 11:11, Jesus said, "I tell you the truth: Among those born of women there has not risen anyone greater than John the Baptist." John the Baptist—living in the wilderness, dressed in coarse clothing and eating grasshoppers and wild honey—was as great as any person ever born. That includes Abraham, Moses, David, Daniel, and all the great heroes of the Old Testament, plus all the other great people who had lived in history up to that time.

Then Jesus added that even the least person in the kingdom of heaven is greater than John. You and I, born into the kingdom of God, transferred from the power of darkness into the kingdom of light, are greater than the great forerunner of Jesus—John the Baptist—and we're therefore greater than all the other great people of God who came before him.

The Lord further explains this in the book of Ephesians. In 1:20 we read that God raised Jesus from the dead and seated Him at His own right hand in the heavenly places, far above all rule and authority and power and dominion. Then in 2:6 God tells us that He raised us up *with* Christ, and seated us with Him in those same heavenly realms. We are with Him in a realm far above any nation or empire on earth, past or present, with a status of indescribable honor.

This refers not to location, but to position, for we are already seated with Christ in the heavenly realm even while we're living here on earth. It's similar to the fact that an earthly king is "enthroned" as a monarch whether he's actually sitting on the throne or riding forth to battle or golfing with a friend. He has the *position* of kingship regardless of his location. And you and I, wherever we are, share the honored position of being seated with Christ. We share His authority over Satan and his helpers, and His dominion over all things. By His grace we can reign in our actual daily lives now, as more than conquerors in all the situations that come our way (Romans 5:17; 8:35-37).

What incredible honor is ours because we've been transferred to the right side of the Cross and the empty tomb. We're chosen, royal, and holy; we're God's very own possession and members of His household (1 Peter 2:9, Ephesians 2:19).

In His infinite love, God has given us honor that is not just for time, but also for all the eternal ages to come. In 1 Peter 1:6-7, He tells us that He sends trials to prove that our faith is genuine, so that our faith will bring us "much praise and glory and honor when Jesus Christ is revealed to the whole world" (NLT). Our Lord will praise and honor us when He returns! We'll know the privilege of reigning with Him and sharing His eternal honor and glory as we live forever in His presence. Ours is a destiny far beyond anything we can now imagine. In *The Weight of Glory* C. S. Lewis says we will be "everlasting splendors," so glorious that if we saw such beings now, we would be strongly tempted to worship them. And Romans 8:19 says, "The whole creation is on tiptoe to see the wonderful sight of the sons of God coming into their own" (Phillips).

An Honor to Pursue

The honor God gives us is also an honor to pursue. In 1 Samuel 2:30, God says, "Those who honor Me, I will honor." In a unique way, if we honor Him on earth He will honor us in heaven. And He'll honor us on earth in ways far more significant in His eyes than winning a gold medal in the Olympics, or becoming a Nobel Prize winner, or being graduated summa cum laude from Harvard or Yale, or any other earthly honor.

I'm really challenged by that. As I mentioned before, I've often told the Lord, "Not to me, O Lord, not to me, but to Your name be the glory." I don't want honors from others on earth when the glory rightly belongs to God. "Don't give me glory here," I tell God; "take it Yourself." But I certainly do want to receive the honor that comes from Him, just as He tells us to seek the glory that comes from the one and only God (John 5:44). That's the one glory worth seeking.

And we seek glory from God by living to bring Him glory and honor. Not that any of us honors Him all the time. We so easily slip into the pride of life—the desire to impress people. But in His perfect love He trains and leads and enables us to honor Him more consistently.

With such honor from the high King of heaven, what should be our attitude toward receiving earthly honor from people?

Earlier I wrote about a barrier that had risen between us and a couple we knew well. We had uncovered no reason for the barrier, no offense that we needed to seek forgiveness for, so the problem may have been three-quarters in my imagination. But something was amiss, and this troubled me. I was very subjective about it. I longed for favor and honor in this couple's sight. I didn't want the friendship disrupted.

That's when the Lord took me back to Psalm 84:11 (by now you know this is one of my special life verses)— "He bestows favor and honor. No good thing does the Lord withhold from those who walk uprightly" (RSV). I saw anew that God's own favor and honor would always be more than enough for me. I realized also that earthly favor and honor comes from God, and that He bestows or withholds them according to His wonderful though sometimes mysterious purposes. If Joseph, back in Genesis, had been given favor and honor in his brothers' eyes, he would never have been sold as a slave and sent to Egypt. And as a result he would never have been used by God to preserve Israel during those seven devastating years of famine. If all people had honored Jesus while He lived on earth, He would never have become the sacrifice for our sins, reconciling us to God. We would have no gospel.

So the Lord bestows favor and honor in people's eyes, or at times withholds it. The favor-and-honor department is His, not mine. My department— the place where I'm to focus my energies—is the walk-uprightly department. So I decided to step out of God's department and trust Him to handle it. I prayed, "Lord, forgive me for stepping into something that is Your responsibility, not mine. Forgive me for not trusting You to handle it. Now I commit this friendship to You. When and if it's a good thing, I ask You to restore our relationship with this couple."

Over time things changed, and the barrier we had sensed was no longer there. But the experience of dealing with it helped me realize in a new way that the honor I get from God Himself gives me significance, so I don't have to worry about losing honor from others on earth. When it suits His purposes He gives us earthly favor and honor in ways great and small.

FAVORED AND HONORED — OR DEPRIVED?

The Lord has delighted my heart as I've meditated on what *grace* means: favor, unmerited yet real. We often dwell on its being unmerited, on our unworthiness, and fail to glory in the fact that it is *favor*. We stand in a permanent position of approval with the King of kings. His grace has superabounded to us, with more added to that, and we don't have to earn it.

"Look how the Eternal marks me out for favor!" (Psalm 4:3, Moffatt). Our King, altogether desirable, distinguished above ten thousand, favors and values us—and honors us!

Think of it. We were beggars, misfits from heaven's viewpoint. Yet He paid an unprecedented price to have us as His very own. He desired us, sought us, won us for Himself. He lifted us to share His Son's position at His right hand, the place of supreme honor, a place infinitely superior to any conceivable earthly status (Ephesians 1:21, 2:6, Phillips).

Again and again the Lord keeps reminding us in the Scriptures of how special we are to Him. In 1 Thessalonians 1:4, Paul says, "Knowing, brethren beloved by God, *His choice of you...* " (NASB). Repeatedly in his letters to the Thessalonians Paul mentions that we have been "chosen," "called," "destined." God obviously wants us to keep clearly in mind our high privilege and honor as His loved and chosen ones.

What a motivation to have high rather than low thoughts, attitudes, and actions. Colossians 3:1-2 puts it this way: "If then you have been raised up with Christ, keep seeking the things above, where Christ is, seated at the right hand of God. Set your mind on the things above, not on the things that are on earth" (NASB).

Yet I wonder if we really look upon ourselves as highly privileged individuals? As raised-up ones with Christ? As highly favored by the high King of heaven, who is predisposed to look upon us with favor at all times because we're united to His Son? As highly honored?

Do people looking at our lives get a sense that we're overwhelmed by God's favor, that we live in the light of the high privileges we have in Christ?

This is our identity, our true standing—so why do we so often live like deprived persons, like beggars?

Perhaps it's because of something that happened in our past, something beyond our control. But it did happen. And as we think about it we feel like losers.

A godly Christian counselor tells about a man who had experienced a terrible background because his father was schizophrenic and abusive. Now, as a Christian, he sought help because he didn't want to hurt his little son who had just been born into the world. He so regretted having missed out on a godly father's example to follow.

The counselor led him to Colossians 2:10— "in Him you have been made complete" (NASB). After the man read it and pondered a bit, he exclaimed, "That means I haven't missed a thing!"

If we belong to Christ, we are not deprived persons in any way. We aren't missing anything. It's true that we're poor and needy, because that's the way we're meant to be—just like a Mercedes right out of the factory is poor and needy in the sense that it needs gasoline. It won't run on its own. Likewise we have needs waiting to be met, but we've been taken into the King's household and given access to the supply of all the resources we'll ever need.

We are not deprived persons, and God doesn't want us to live as though we were.

Sometimes it's not our past but our present that causes us to feel deprived. Life's demands and uncertainties seem too enormous to cope with. So we live shaky, faltering, overwhelmed lives under the burden of our circumstances. We're tense, anxious, discouraged, never dreaming that we're so highly privileged.

But God has glorified us. He has lifted us to a heavenly dignity and state of being (Romans 8:30, Amplified). He gives us a dignity beyond what we can imagine, an elevated position that can't be surpassed.

I feel honored to be married to Warren because he's a man of God, a man of strength and tenderness and more. But marriage to him is nothing like the honor of having the Lord as my life partner, knowing that at any moment I can come boldly before His presence and be received with gladness and warmth. And knowing that this honor, this high privilege, will continue to the end of my days here on earth, and forever.

In God's eyes, we're precious, honored, loved. There can be no greater honor!

Yours, O Lord, is the kingdom and the power and the glory. I praise and extol You as the King of heaven—the King eternal, immortal, invisible, the only God, exalted as head over all. You alone are worthy of all honor.

Therefore my heart is overwhelmed with gratefulness that You bestow honor on me, honor that is eternal and unchanging.

Thank You for giving me a share in the death of Your Son Jesus Christ, so that I've been released from the shame and dominion of sin. Thank You for giving me a share in Christ's resurrection, so that I've been raised up with Him to new life. And thank You for giving me a share in Christ's ascension to Your right hand in heaven, so that I may experience and partake of His honor and authority and dominion, both now and in all the ages to come.

How grateful I am that earthly honor fades into insignificance in the light of the honor that comes from You—that I no longer need to seek honor from people because I already have the greatest of all honors. I'm so glad I can trust You to take care of the favor-and-honor department of my earthly life, with perfect love and wisdom.

I love You, Lord, for turning Your eyes and Your heart to me. And I exult in the astounding truth that in Your eyes I am precious, and honored, and beloved... and that this will never change.

In Jesus' name...

Your personal gleanings for meditation, prayer, and action:

What Scripture or truth in this chapter do you feel the Lord is especially speaking to you about? What will you do to profit the most from this?

FIFTEEN

In His Perfect Love, I Am Satisfied

C. S. LEWIS ONCE defined history as "the long terrible story of man trying to find happiness apart from God." For so many people, that's their personal history as well.

God tells us that apart from Him and His perfect love there is no true happiness.

He also tells us that when we finally discover true happiness in Him, it will continue and deepen only as we cultivate a deeper relationship with Him.

And He tenderly yet firmly assures us as that we'll be able to experience this happiness day by day, hour by hour, if (and only if) we learn to depend on Him more constantly.

I've found that when I don't consciously depend on the Lord and His love, it's easy to become self-protective rather than happily vulnerable and expendable. I've adapted some lines by Alexander McClaren into the following prayer of commitment—a prayer that motivates me to delight in the Lord and respond to Him more quickly in every type of circumstance, large or small. Would you like to pray these words with me?

O God my strength, if I fix my happiness on anything less sta-
ble than the heavens, less sufficient than You, sooner or later

> *I will lose it. If my life entwines around any earthly prop, some time or other my prop will be plucked up, my poor vine will be torn, and its sap will bleed out of it. Therefore I choose to entwine the tendrils of my life around You.*

I like to add, "My wonderful God, help me to do this more and more."

The secret of a satisfied heart is not the pursuit of satisfaction or happiness. Satisfaction and happiness are by-products. The secret of a satisfied heart is the pursuit of God. Discovering God and His love not just in our minds but also in our actual experience—this is the basis of true joy in life. It is also the basis of true growth in Christlikeness which, in turn, brings us still greater joy.

Repeatedly Warren and I enjoy the simple way the *New Century Version* states this truth in Psalm 16:2,5— "You are my Lord. Every good thing I have comes from you.... The Lord is all I need. He takes care of me. My share in life has been pleasant; my part has been beautiful."

Our God of intensely personal, overflowing love has given us Himself as our share in life. He is the source of all good things, the all-sufficient God who is enough. He satisfies us with a beautiful part in life, a pleasant share.

Yet with reflection you and I may discern areas in our lives where we lack satisfaction and character growth. If that's true for you, I urge you to take time to think about this. Write down these areas, then bring the list before God. Tell Him that you keep having trouble with this temptation or in that relationship, or with this or that responsibility or circumstance. Then pray, "Now, Lord, show me the cure," and await His answer. Bring your request to Him time after time. Spend time in His Word, time enough for Him to both examine your heart and express His love. Gradually find in the Scriptures a "handle" for each need or problem that concerns you—a specific passage, verse, or phrase that brings you the release, the motivation, the comfort or instruction that You need. Then use that handle again and again to think the truth with thanksgiving.

In our God of perfect love, you'll find the cure you need.

I praise You, Lord, that You are so vastly wonderful, so utterly and completely delightful, that You can meet and overflow the deepest needs of my total nature, mysterious and deep as that nature is.

Thank You for giving me a beautiful and pleasant share in life—abundant life—life in all its fullness! I rejoice that in Your perfect love I can live in freedom and security, with a deep sense of significance and honor. I can live with confidence that You are at work in my life to make me more like Christ. And I praise You that You will not drop the work You have begun.

Do you remember what Moses prayed in Psalm 90:14? "Satisfy us early with Your steadfast love, that we may rejoice and be glad all our days." *All* our days, he said. In both good times and hard times, an undercurrent of rejoicing can be ours, rejoicing that arises from a heart satisfied with God's unchanging love.

What more could we really ask of life than such deep satisfaction with God, and along with that, a contentment with what life brings?

Remember Tozer's words, "The man who has God as his treasure has all things in one, and he has it purely, legitimately, and forever."

Because this is true, the psalmist wisely instructs us, "Make the Eternal your delight, and He will give you all your heart's desire. Leave all to Him, rely on Him, and He will see to it" (Psalm 37:4-5, Moffatt).

As you delight in Him and manifest His fragrant love to others, you begin now the joyous pleasure that will be the bread and wine of heaven, when God has gathered His entire family home.

And keep in mind the great and unique advantage you now have in your relationship with God: It's an *internal* relationship. It's not bounded by the spatial distance that limits all other relationships, allowing them to get only so close. Your relationship with God can become more ardent, more intimate, more intensely joyful than any other, for He is dwelling in you to flood your heart with His love and fullness.

Eternal Lord, You are my truest delight! It is wonderful to know You. I'm glad I've got You—and I'm even more glad that You've got me! "My Beloved is mine, and I am His.... His desire is toward me." Day by day may my roots go down deeper into the soil of Your marvelous love.

Thank You for the amazing truth that my soul is a vast reservoir from which You can receive eternal pleasure. I praise You that I am a part of Your eternal longings coming true.

How I want my heart to be more consistently captivated and satisfied by You, Lord, on both my good days and my difficult days, in moments of peace and pleasure as well as moments of pain. I ask You to work in my heart so that this will be so. Satisfy me early, satisfy me soon, satisfy me daily with Your steadfast love.

We don't usually go to the expense and work of adding on to our house until we begin to feel a bit crowded. Likewise, for most of us, we don't desire greater spiritual maturity or deeper intimacy with God until we're genuinely uncomfortable and dissatisfied with where we are.

You and I both have some growing to do. Each of us has areas of immaturity in our lives, areas that we don't have to stay in. We can come out of them and move on!

Are there areas of life in which you're holding God at arm's length, so that He cannot demonstrate His personal love and desire for you? Is there any area in which your heart may be closed to His love? Have you been afraid to open it further?

Are you afraid of anything He might ask you to do? I urge you to pinpoint your fear, write it down in your own words, and present it to Him in prayer. Ask for His answer to this fear, then listen for His answer in His Word. Ask Him to work in you both to will and to do of His good pleasure—to make you willing to be willing. Keep on asking until He does it.

Jim Elliot once wrote, "That which is lifelong can only be surrendered in a lifetime." I would not discredit the moment when you first said to the Lord, "I will," when you first told Him, "Lord, You can run my life." But to what new surrender is He calling you today?

My Lord and my God, today I affirm before You that, by Your grace, the knowledge of You and Your love will be my life's major pursuit. This is the purpose of my heart, for You are worthy.

I exult in the knowledge that You created me to be indwelt and controlled by You, and I thank You for showing me that my life cannot run well any other way. You are my Master, for my good! You want me to obey You so that it may be well with me!

I'm amazed and thrilled that Someone as wonderful as You could want my total love. Take my love, dear Lord. Do what You must to open my heart so I can give You more and more of it.

You will always be the biggest factor in my environment, the deepest joy of my heart. I rest in the truth that the future holds You, and You hold the future.

A reader can easily feel overwhelmed by the teaching in a book this large. You've read so much that you may feel sort of numb, unable to do anything about any of it.

So a final word: I encourage you to go back over your gleanings at the end of each chapter, and perhaps to other things you have marked in the text. Find a few major things that really caught your attention and spoke to you. Begin to pray about these day by day. Reflect on them, and ask the Lord which one He wants you to focus and work on. Ask Him to make it operative in your life. Let it be more than a momentary blessing; let it make a permanent difference.

Look especially at the Scriptures that touch on this matter. Pore over these truths from His Word that have really meant something personally to you. Soak in them. Go back to them often. Memorize them, think about their meaning, and let the Holy Spirit grip you deep inside with that truth— with that message from your God of love. Let Him flood your heart with God's love.

Lord of love, I worship You as the One who is majestic yet tender and filled with boundless love. I praise and adore You as the One who will never fail me or disillusion me. And so, as the years go by, my heart can keep rising up to You in adoration that is ever growing, ever more delightful.

I pray that day by day I'll discover more fully how perfect Your love is, and that hour by hour I'll rest in Your intensely personal, overflowing, never ending love for me.

You are my first love, my best love, my perfect love. You are my highest goal, my chief delight for time and eternity.

To You be the glory forever and ever. Amen.

INDEX OF QUOTATIONS AND SOURCES